A Vineyard in Napa

A Vineyard in Napa

Doug Shafer

with Andy Demsky
Foreword by Danny Meyer

UNIVERSITY OF CALIFORNIA PRESS

Berkeley Los Angeles London

University of California Press, one of the most
distinguished university presses in the United States,
enriches lives around the world by advancing scholarship
in the humanities, social sciences, and natural sciences.
Its activities are supported by the UC Press Foundation
and by philanthropic contributions from individuals and
institutions. For more information, visit www.ucpress
.edu.

University of California Press
Berkeley and Los Angeles, California

University of California Press, Ltd.
London, England

Library of Congress Cataloging-in-Publication Data

Shafer, Doug.
  A vineyard in Napa / Doug Shafer with Andy Demsky;
foreword by Danny Meyer.
    p. cm.
  Includes index.
  ISBN 978-0-520-27236-1 (hardcover : alk. paper)
  1. Wine and wine making—California—Napa
Valley—Anecdotes.   2. Wineries—California—Napa
Valley—Anecdotes.   I. Demsky, Andrew, 1965–
II. Title.
  TP557.S53 2012
  641.2'20979419—dc23

                                              2012015843

Manufactured in the United States of America

21   20   19   18   17   16   15   14   13   12
10   9   8   7   6   5   4   3   2   1

The paper used in this publication meets the minimum
requirements of ANSI/NISO Z39.48-1992 (R 2002)
(*Permanence of Paper*).

Book cover photo: Russ Widstrand

CONTENTS

FOREWORD

A Vineyard in Napa is at first blush a tale of one man's choice to impose manifest destiny on his family. But the story of John Shafer and his family wouldn't be nearly so interesting if that's all it was. For practically *anyone* can convince his wife and kids to pick up sticks and move west. And how unusual is it, really, to tackle a midlife crisis by giving up the comfort of a secure and successful corporate career to plant new roots—indeed, vines—on an unknown hillside positioned fifty miles north of San Francisco?

But this is a far richer tale than "Midwest midlife mogul moves westward." With the hindsight of forty years, it is clear to me that this is one of those very rare instances where one man's initial vision has been executed so *brilliantly, consistently,* and *fully* that it demands being studied, understood, and documented. Along with his remarkable team, led chiefly by his son, Doug—one of the sharpest, gentlest, most persistent, and genuine human beings you will ever meet—and his colossally gifted and sensitive winemaker, Elias Fernandez, John Shafer has transformed his midlife dream into one of the greatest California wine stories ever written.

I don't think I know anyone who doesn't feel great affection for Shafer Vineyards. And while all those fans may think they adore Shafer for its unfailingly excellent (and I'd say category-defining) Merlot, its bone-rattling Red Shoulder Ranch Chardonnay, its powerful Relentless Syrah, its eminently satisfying Cabernet Sauvignon, and its elegant and peerless Hillside Select Cabernet Sauvignon, there are perhaps some other—less understood—reasons that Shafer has so quietly and humbly attained its towering stature in the world of wine.

Indeed, there is the fate that brought John Shafer to Napa Valley's Stags Leap District—an area little known to wine lovers when he bought his land in 1972 but now recognized as *the* Napa Valley source for grapes that express stunningly soft and silky elegance. That good fortune alone might have been enough to create a winning winery. But somehow Shafer stands tall even among the pack of the district's other elite producers.

In my judgment, the glory of Shafer's first forty years has all to do with the family's culture and philosophy of how to do business. Up and down the Shafer organization are people of integrity who are fully consumed with pursuing the journey of excellence—always with humility and always in a way that leaves something good in its wake for each of the winery's stakeholders.

First and foremost, the Shafer team acts like a loving family toward *one another*, exuding respect and trust between grape growers, winemakers, and those who work in administration. I imagine it must be a lot of fun to come to work at Shafer Vineyards. That has to have created the crucial foundation upon which these folks are able to distinguish themselves in every other way. Comfortable and confident at home, the Shafer team never misses one opportunity to go the extra mile for their customers—taking a caring and active interest in the lives and fortunes of those with whom they do business. You don't just love the wine. You fall in love with the people behind the wine!

In these pages you'll read a lot about how the Shafer wines came to be—and it is a fascinating tale. John is always generous in according credit to the people who have grown his grapes and made the wines, but in his usual modest way, he rarely takes the credit *he* deserves for creating a winery with a conscience—one that deeply cares for people, understands its responsibility as a steward of the environment, and plays a distinguished leadership role in caring for its community with *generosity* and *grace*—two terms that appropriately describe every wine I've ever savored bearing the Shafer label.

Forty years is a long and significant amount of time to hang in there for any business (my industry is notorious for gobbling up and spitting out new restaurants in short increments—like *months*). But somehow I suspect the Shafer story is just beginning. Doing something so well in a way that makes so many people feel so good takes a farsighted and principled discipline. But for John Shafer, his family, and his team, that path is the only natural way to do business. And that is why Shafer has created an institution that, like its wines, will endure and endure.

Danny Meyer
New York City, 2011

ACKNOWLEDGMENTS

Thanks to Annette, the love of my life, who is my best friend, partner, and sounding board and who loves and supports me as we share this exciting adventure called life.

To my children, Katie, Kevin, Stephen, Tate, and Remington, your love and support sustain me and have made all of this worthwhile.

Thanks of course go to my dad, John Shafer, who has been a world-class companion on this journey—a parent, mentor, and friend. And to my mom, Bett, who had such a profound effect on my life and on the early years of this winery and whose spirit I feel here every day.

This project has involved much more than simply sitting down and outlining what I remember of the past forty years. It's involved lengthy interviews, discussions, conversations, philosophical meanderings, and editing sessions between me and my collaborator, Andy Demsky, as well as interviews with Dad; Elias Fernandez, our winemaker; David Ilsley, our director of vineyard operations; and Mary Kay Schatz, our director of marketing and administration (which actually means she's the ringmaster who runs this three-ring circus). I'd like to offer enormous gratitude to: Danny Meyer, for his friendship and the beautiful foreword he wrote for this book; Heather John, who took time out of a packed professional and personal schedule to pore over early draft material and offer equal measures of encouragement and insight; Megan Kostecka, who assisted Andy with research; Katy Howard, who helped us edit early drafts; Nancy Bialek, director of the Stags Leap District Association, for preserving an invaluable archive of papers related to the formation of the district; and to my daughter, Katie, for showing a seventy-five-page Shafer history we self-published in 2004 to literary agent Kelly Sonnack at Andrea Brown Literary Agency, who saw the possibilities of this project. Kelly worked relentlessly playing matchmaker between us and our publisher, University of California Press. Many thanks also to our editor, Blake Edgar, for his support of this project.

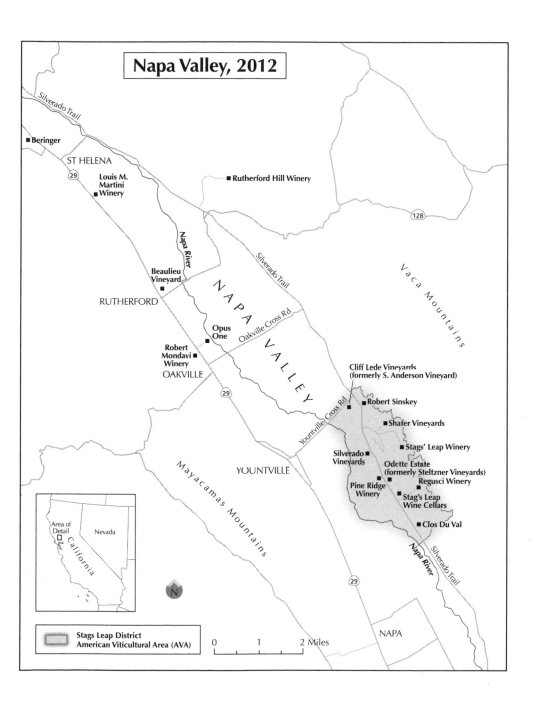

Napa Valley, 2012

■ Beringer

Silverado Trail

ST HELENA

(29)

Louis M. Martini Winery ■

■ **Rutherford Hill Winery**

(128)

Napa River

Silverado Trail

Beaulieu Vineyard ■

N A P A

V a c a

RUTHERFORD

V A L L E Y

M o u n t a i n s

Oakville Cross Rd

Opus One ■

Robert Mondavi Winery ■

OAKVILLE

(29)

Cliff Lede Vineyards (formerly S. Anderson Vineyard)

Yountville Cross Rd

■ **Robert Sinskey**

■ **Shafer Vineyards**

■ **Stags' Leap Winery**

Silverado Vineyards ■

YOUNTVILLE

Odette Estate (formerly Steltzner Vineyards)

Regusci Winery

Pine Ridge Winery ■

Stag's Leap Wine Cellars

M a y a c a m a s   M o u n t a i n s

■ **Clos Du Val**

Napa River

Silverado Trail

Area of Detail

California

Nevada

(29)

N

NAPA

Stags Leap District American Viticultural Area (AVA)

0   1   2 Miles

Prologue

What you have here is pretty simple: one person's story covering forty years in the life of a Napa Valley winery. Within these pages you won't find an attempt to offer the definitive scientific and socioeconomic overview of the phylloxera epidemic of the late 1980s and early 1990s. Nor is there an ambitious endeavor to, say, map out the entire history of technology in winemaking or recount the biographies of all the Valley's major players. Those books have been written by others. What you will find here is more personal: a narrative of what it was like for us at Shafer and our neighbors, sweating through setbacks in the cellar, learning how to grow the best-quality grapes, coping with economic recessions, understanding changes in public tastes, reacting to various insect infestations, and rolling with our own evolution as a wine region.

My hope is that the story in these pages will give a unique behind-the-scenes look at what it has been like to live through the four decades in Napa Valley during which this region was transformed from a rural backwater to one of the finest winemaking regions in the world.

Without a doubt there are other vintners, grape growers, and local characters who could write their own books about these decades, and I hope they do. But for the moment very few of those who could tell you what it's been like on the inside—buying the grapes, trying out the new techniques, abandoning old ones, selling the wines, making the mistakes, enjoying the occasional successes—have taken the time to do this. And with each passing year, those who played important roles here in the 1960s, 1970s, and 1980s move out of the picture. Wineries have changed hands and changed names. Those that were prominent in one era have faded into the background in others. Sadly, a lot of great names have been taken from our midst: Mondavi, Martini, Tchelistcheff, Davies, Fay, to name just a few you may recognize. I would love it if this book could help shed further light on why those names earned such respect and admiration from fellow vintners.

Beyond the loss of dear friends and colleagues, though, I don't regret the changes that have come with the passing decades, since many have been necessary and even exciting. For a thing to survive it must evolve, and that's a dynamic at the heart of both the Napa Valley story and our own story. Shafer Vineyards started in the late 1970s as a glorified hobby (or so I thought) of my dad's. Then it transformed into an actual family business, which for a time involved the combined efforts of my dad, mom, sister, two or three employees, and myself. Even with that concerted push it seemed as if the winery had the strong potential to flounder, even to fail—as others around us were failing—and as a young, inexperienced winemaker it was going to be squarely my fault. After all, what is a winery that makes lousy wine?

Fortunately, through a lot of scrambling, long hours, and some luck, the winery kept not failing through the 1980s, and by the early 1990s it looked as if this thing was actually going to fly.

In 2003, I was at the winery early one morning reveling in the romance of vintner life—reviewing columns of sales numbers, going over the terrifying amount of money Elias Fernandez, our longtime winemaker, was proposing we spend on barrels and bottles, looking at résumés for a new front-office position, and trying to play catch-up with too many emails.

At some point I turned to the latest stack of wine-related publications on my desk and, while paging through *The Wine Advocate*, came across a piece by influential wine critic Robert Parker in which he was praising a Napa Valley wine producer as being "one of the world's greatest wineries."

It took a moment for it to sink in that he was writing about us. The first thing I thought of was the time in the mid-1980s when Parker had warned his readers in pretty strong terms that our 1982 Reserve Cabernet, a wine I had a hand in producing, was so underwhelming it should be "avoided." Fortunately, though, with a lot of hard work the wines had gained richness and complexity. Parker's opinion, along with that of others, of what we produced had changed over time and the reviews had improved. But "one of the world's greatest"?

I realize that this might not sound like a big deal—one sentence from one writer. But it stuck with me. Was there something I was missing?

The write-up in *The Wine Advocate* came around the time *Wine & Spirits* magazine had named our hillside vineyard as one of the top twenty in the world and Elias had been named Winemaker of the Year by *Food & Wine* magazine (not to mention being honored at the White House for being a Hispanic role model).

Everyone at the winery was grateful for these accolades, but they were hard for me to absorb, because they seemed so entirely disconnected from daily life. When I'm in Napa Valley, I'm not on vacation, luxuriating in a multiday lovefest of eating, wine tasting, and spa treatments. This is where I live and work. Likely as not, when I'm here I'm reviewing our property taxes or buying a new irrigation pump for one of the ponds, wrestling with day-to-day struggles.

Beyond that, praise of this kind makes me uneasy. It can lull a vintner into a dangerous sense of grandiosity. I've seen wineries settle in comfortably on these kinds of laurels and essentially go on autopilot. They soon realize that their finest days are behind them.

Looking at Parker's words that morning, though, I realized I was sensing something that hadn't occurred to me before: I was too close to see our winery the way others did. The Shafer Vineyards that I still carried around in my head—the uncertain family enterprise that might or might not make it, the Little Engine That Could—was out of date. And I *was* missing something important. Being so caught up in the minutiae of running a business, I was missing out on the fact that somewhere along the line I'd become very fortunate—fortunate that in spite of all the odds and the tremendous obstacles, the winery had become successful; fortunate that my drive to work in the morning takes me up the Silverado Trail past some of the most inspiring vineyards to be found; fortunate that I enjoy a life surrounded by a great family and by smart, funny, good people who love vineyards and wine as much as I do. More than anything, I'm very lucky to have spent the past decades working alongside my dad, John Shafer, who took a big gamble on this vineyard in the early 1970s, knowing next to nothing about a) growing grapes, b) making wine, or c) running a family business.

A quick word about family businesses: imagine taking all of the ups and downs of familial life and mashing them together with the whitewater wallops and splashes of running a small company. I've seen places where it has turned ugly and unpleasant, bringing out the worst in everyone involved. Fortunately, our story is not one of a family business spinning out of control. From day one Dad maintained that family and business were separate. He set a tone that valued hard work, authenticity, creativity, forgiveness for mistakes, collaboration, and high standards. If the story of Shafer Vineyards is one of success, it's owed in large part to my dad and the core values he championed.

It wasn't until I sat down to work on this book that it struck me how deeply intertwined our story is with the history of Napa Valley. Again, being so focused on keeping all the plates spinning here, I've only recently been struck by the realization that forty years have flown by, and we've woven our way into this tapestry. From our arrival here in January 1973 through the next four decades we were in the middle of the mix—doing business and forging friendships with some people you know of, others who have not yet claimed a spot in the history books. We've lived through the Valley's highs and lows (and there have been a lot of both). We've seen the changes, been a part of them, and in one or two cases have even sparked them. Sometimes the story has been a drama, sometimes more like a comedy. However you label them, these have been some of the four most tumultuous decades ever seen here. It's been a wild, thrilling, and sometimes heartbreaking ride.

For some here in the Valley, their stories started back in Mexico, Germany, Italy, France, Argentina, or other exotic places. Ours began in Chicago.

ONE

John Shafer

Up until 1973—when he was forty-eight years old—very little indicated that John Shafer was a future Napa Valley vintner. If you know where to look in his life story, you'll find some key moments of foreshadowing here and there, but it's all pretty subtle. Even now it's startling to realize how it all could have gone in such a different direction, and the story of our hillside vineyards could easily have belonged to someone else.

Dad was born in 1924 and spent most of his childhood in a small northern suburb of Chicago called Glencoe, to this day a secluded enclave of arts and affluence. His mother, Adeline, hailed from Peru, Indiana, where she was a schoolmate of music legend Cole Porter. My dad's father, Frederick Shafer, was born in 1886 in Booneville, Indiana, into a family of strict Methodists. They didn't have a lot of money, but he was an exceptionally hard worker and mechanically inclined, traits that got him into Purdue University, where he earned an engineering degree. My dad still remembers his father, a lifelong teetotaler and upright citizen, heading into the gray dawn in a felt hat and three-piece suit to attend to business at Imperial Brass Manufacturing, the Chicago brass foundry where he had worked his way up to the office of president.

My dad was born in a time of economic boom. Small investors across the country were pouring money into Wall Street. Credit was easy.

Wealth was within reach for a whole new generation. It was an era in which the phrase "safe as banks" was coined.

Then came the sickening free fall in 1929 from which the nation did not truly recover for a decade or more. Banks closed. Credit dried up. Despondent moneymen ended it all by leaping from their office windows. The national unemployment rate hit a catastrophic 25 percent.

The Depression formed my dad, as it did many of his generation. Yes, his family enjoyed a level of financial stability, but poverty and uncertainty were everywhere. Dad remembers people coming to their door begging for food. Even if the Shafer family had a bit of money, it wasn't something they spent ostentatiously. On the contrary, Frederick was well known for only buying things on sale.

Throughout his life, Dad, the Depression-era kid, has distrusted the booms and planned for the inevitable busts and has always been a fan of understatement, character over pizzazz, the solid long-term idea over short-range sizzle, qualities I would see play out later as he launched and then managed our winery.

As a teenager Dad attended New Trier High School, which was a fertile environment for a young mind. The alumni include a who's who of American public life, such as actors Charlton Heston and Ann-Margret, former Secretary of Defense Donald Rumsfeld, writer Scott Turow, chef Charlie Trotter, and Chicago mayor Rahm Emanuel, to name a handful.[1] Dad remembers a boy named Roy Fitzgerald in the class behind his, a solitary, quiet kid who hardly anyone knew. When this kid grew up, Hollywood renamed him Rock Hudson and down the road he and Dad would have their own connection to Napa Valley (we'll get to that).

During a summer in high school, Dad worked in the foundry of his father's brass works. In those torturously hot, backbreaking, dangerous working conditions he befriended men of all backgrounds from Chicago's great melting pot—immigrant Poles, Latinos, and African Americans, whose grandparents had experienced both slavery and emancipation. In

---

1. "Famous Alumni," *Chicago Sun-Times*, May 23, 2007.

the heat and noise he learned a lifetime's worth about people whose lives were filled with struggles far different from his own.

After graduating from New Trier, Dad entered Cornell University in September 1942 and, at the urging of his father, signed on to major in engineering, a career that they both saw as a source of solid, steady income.

Over Christmas break that year, as a college freshman, Dad volunteered for service in World War II, enlisting in the Army Air Corps. His call to duty came in April 1943. Part of his flight training took place at Davis–Monthan Army Air Corps Base in Tucson, Arizona. While there, he met Bett Small, whose father owned the *Tucson Citizen*, the local newspaper.

She had attended the University of Arizona and had gotten a job with American Airlines in the early days of air travel. Dad and Bett went out together as often as possible and quickly developed a special affection for each other. Her house happened to lie on the flight path of the air base and when Dad was landing at night, coming in low over her rooftop, he'd flick the plane's lights on and off.

Dad received his wings in June 1944 and turned down an offer to become a flight instructor, choosing combat instead. His crew went to southern England, where they became a replacement crew flying B-24 bombers in the 445th Bomb Group with the 8th Air Force. Once there, he discovered that film star Jimmy Stewart was wing commander, in charge of a number of bomber groups. Dad remembers how surreal it was to hear that unmistakable voice from Hollywood in his headphones, conveying commands as they flew over the dark English Channel on missions to Germany.

At the age of twenty, Dad was the oldest of his flight crew. All the other crew members—the radio operators and gunners—were draftees with just six weeks of training under their belts; many were fresh out of high school. Here he was in a similar position as in the brass factory: thrown in with guys of every background and disposition—this time under even more dangerous and stressful circumstances. Dad not only

John Shafer, 1945, with the
B-24 bomber he piloted while
stationed in England.

had to do the job right, but also had to protect the lives of these men, kids really, who looked to him for leadership.

I think a person finds his or her moral center under these conditions. In short order he was faced with the issue of doing what was right versus doing what was expected. During a practice flight exercise with the squadron in the skies over England, one of his crewmen got violently sick, and Dad made a judgment call—he pulled out of formation and returned to the air base to get his crew member emergency medical attention. His superiors soundly dressed him down for this, but Dad held firm. It was an exercise, not the real thing, and his first duty was to the well-being of his crew.

After the war he returned to his engineering degree program at Cornell and before his senior year married Bett. And I'm glad he did because, among other things, she became my mom. She was smart, opinionated, straightforward, and classically beautiful (in my completely unbiased opinion).

After graduation Dad and Mom moved to Cleveland, where Dad was hired as a college trainee in a machine tool company, Warner and Swasey. Within about a year it became clear to him that his heart wasn't in it, and he began to review his options.

Some fortunate family connections helped him on a new path. My mom's grandfather, William Coates Foresman, and her grand-uncle, Hugh A. Foresman, had been founding partners in 1896 of the Scott Foresman publishing company in Chicago, which specialized in educational materials (most people know them as the publisher of the "Dick and Jane" basic readers). My mom's family still owned a one-third stake in the privately held company, but no family members actually worked there any longer. After some inquiries Dad was offered an entry-level sales job with the publisher where, in spite of his connections, he'd again have to earn his wings.

His initial territory was northern Ohio, but within a couple of years and after he wore out a lot of shoe leather, his sales territory moved to the Chicago suburbs of Cook County, where he sold and promoted schoolbooks and teaching materials.

While selling and marketing weren't in his background, he took to these things readily, absorbing all he could of their key concepts. Dad came to understand that there is no good substitute for meeting with your customers face-to-face. Besides, he was, and is, a gregarious guy—he loves meeting people and has an easy, gracious way with those to whom he's just been introduced. He traveled extensively, meeting with hundreds of teachers, principals, and school staff members. The company was an educational innovator, producing newsletters for teachers all across the country that focused not on Scott Foresman products, but on the latest trends and techniques in education. The concept behind this was to act as a real resource for teachers with the hope that, long-term, educators would be more likely to turn to Scott Foresman when it came time to purchase classroom materials. A favorite maxim of the company's president was "a good book seldom mentioned is soon forgotten"—a motto that Dad would adapt years later, substituting the word "wine" for "book." Indeed, much of what he learned in this period would reverberate decades down the line when he transferred a lot of his marketing smarts regarding selling textbooks to the art of selling Cabernet Sauvignon.

In the summer months when schools were closed, Dad had extra time on his hands, which always drives him a little batty. One year before he and Mom had kids, he decided he wanted to work outdoors, get his hands dirty, and feel the wind in his hair. So he drove out to western Illinois and stopped at a farm. When the farmer came out, Dad said that he wanted to work. He told the guy, "You don't even have to pay me." The farmer probably thought he had a kook in his driveway, but eventually saw that my dad was sincere. For the next five or six weeks the city boy from Chicago built up some calluses tossing bales of hay onto the back of a truck.

(I think a lot of people at some time in their lives must develop a craving to get outside and get dirt under their fingernails. Many summers later a successful attorney from San Francisco asked Dad if he could do the very same thing at the winery.)

In spite of Dad occasionally disappearing into farmland, things were going well on the home front. My parent's first baby was my sister Libby. Two years later my brother Bill came into the picture. I was born in 1955, and finally our youngest brother, Brad, joined us in 1960. By this time we lived on Oak Street in Hinsdale, Illinois, in a three-story Victorian with a big screened-in porch and a sloping green lawn.

We enjoyed a noisy, rambunctious life with snowball fights in winter and coasting our bikes down the lawn in spring and summer. My memories are filled with water fights, sleepovers, ping-pong on the front porch,

Shafer family home on Oak Street in Hinsdale, Illinois.

catching fireflies, and watching Dad and his friends practice chip shots and knock back gin and tonics on the lawn. There were always one or two black labs in the mix.

During the school year, we benefited from Dad's career, which bridged education and salesmanship. In the bedroom I shared with my brothers, Dad created a system of sliding blackboards. In the evenings, we would "play school" with him. With chalk in hand he would make up fast-action math and word games that were such fun we had no idea he was teaching us key concepts and ideas.

By the early 1970s, after two decades of applying himself full-bore at Scott Foresman, Dad had worked his way to the office of Vice President of Long-Range Planning. He took the "long range" part of the title seriously and advocated that the company invest in experimental educational tools, such as video and other technology that were barely out of the starting gate. His proposals were apparently viewed as a bit radical and became mired in subcommittees, meetings with consultants, endless cost-benefit analyses, and countless other tools the corporate world uses to kill ideas. Working in that top-floor office, which sounded impressive, had turned as gray and uninspiring as the old machine tool job in Cleveland.

Around this time Dad read a newspaper story that struck a chord. It said that if you were going to embark on a second career you needed to start by the age of fifty. The wheels started turning.

Soon afterward he read an intriguing investors' report from Bank of America called "Outlook for the California Wine Industry." The document laid out a compelling case for the future of wine in the Golden State in just twelve pages, beginning with its opening paragraph, "The strongest growth in wine markets ever recorded will occur during the next ten years. Annual U.S. consumption will approach 400 million gallons by 1980..."[2] (The actual consumption in 1980 was, in fact, even higher than predicted at 480 million gallons.)[3]

The report cited a number of factors that would contribute to this unprecedented rise. One was the anticipated growth in disposable income and the fact that 40 million new young adults, who favored wine, would reach drinking age during the 1970s. They weren't calling us the baby boomers yet, but our numbers were already reverberating throughout the business world.

A change of fortune was already being felt in Napa Valley, where in the five years from 1964 to 1969 the value of the annual grape harvest had soared from $2.9 million to $8 million.[4] Other areas of the state were doing well too, as my dad would learn.

2. Bank of America, Economics Department, *Outlook for the California Wine Industry*, 1970, p. 1.

3. Wine Institute, *Wine Consumption in the U.S.*, accessed August 1, 2011, www.winein stitute.org/resources/statistics/article86.

4. Aldo Delfino, Agricultural Commissioner, *1964 Napa County Agricultural Crop Report*, Napa County Department of Agriculture, Napa, CA, 1965, and *1969 Napa County Agricultural Crop Report*, Napa County Department of Agriculture, Napa, CA, 1970, accessed June 28, 2011, www.countyofnapa.org/AgCommissioner/CropReport.

Several dots connected for him, including that itch to work outside. Mind you, his agricultural background until then had only included tossing hay bales and growing flowers in our backyard. The other element that ate at him was the idea of being his own boss. No matter how hard he worked or cut his own path at Scott Foresman, he was still there as the result of family connections, and it seemed that every long-range proposal he put on the table was getting torpedoed. A move into the wine business would be a venture purely of his own creation. It would sink or swim based on his ideas, drive, and resourcefulness.

At some point in 1970 Dad started reading everything he could find on winemaking and grape growing. In early 1972 he flew to California and scouted vineyard property in Edna Valley, Monterey, and Santa Maria. At one point he was chatting with an old-timer who owned a roadside winery outside of Gilroy. When the man learned that Dad was interested in the wine business, he said, "Well if you're interested in wine, what're you doing here? There's nothing happening here. You need to be up in Napa."

Dad eventually did make his way north to Napa Valley, where he worked with real estate agent Jim Warren (whose stepfather, it turned out, was the Supreme Court Justice Earl Warren). They toured quite a number of sites Dad found unpromising. Most were located in the center of the Valley with deep fertile soils, drawing lots of moisture from the nearby Napa River. Dad's goal was to find a dry, rugged hillside, having read that grapes from terraced hillsides were favored for centuries throughout the Mediterranean world. A saying that dates back to the Roman Empire, *"Bacchus amat colles,"* which translates as "Bacchus loves the hills," illustrates the idea that the Romans believed their god of wine had a special affinity for wine sourced from hillside vines.

Finally, Jim mentioned a remote site in an area known locally as Stags Leap. He warned Dad that it had been on the market for three years and a number of knowledgeable winery owners had already seen it and turned it down.

It seemed foolish not to at least lay eyes on the site, so they drove out, and Dad has often recounted being awed by the beauty of the hillsides and the huge rock outcropping beyond called the Stags Leap Palisades, which soars some two thousand feet. Even so, he understood Jim's warning. Once you got past the scenic magnificence, this was not an obvious gem to the eye of a Napa vintner of that era. Besides a rundown house and outbuildings, it was a rambling 209-acre site, with steep, boulder- and rock-choked hillsides on the eastern and northern flanks. A full three-quarters of the property was unplantable, thanks to the steepness of much of the terrain. The 30-acre vineyard established on the flatter, western portion sported a hodgepodge of red and white grape varieties, interspersed with walnut trees, and last planted in 1922.

But rather than view those steep, wild hillsides as a detriment, Dad was thrilled. The site was almost a photograph of what he had been searching for, chiefly, those south- and west-facing hillsides composed of thin layers of volcanic soil, ensuring that grapevines would struggle for survival, holding out the promise for producing rich, opulent, concentrated fruit.[5]

Dad returned to Chicago having completed his research and a year's worth of property hikes—he had all the data he needed—but ultimately it took something gut-based to push him to the very edge of the decision. He put together a business plan, in which he projected his costs and profit, and drove it over to his accountant's office.

The accountant sat at his desk and reviewed Dad's figures. Then he took off his glasses, shrugged, and said that frankly it was impossible to

---

5. Our hillside vineyards have a soil depth of eighteen to twenty-two inches before hitting weathered bedrock. Both the steep slope and the permeable soils offer quick drainage, meaning that grapevines are never awash in moisture or nutrients. A variety of factors also creates a beneficial mix of long hours of sunlight—thanks to southern and western slope exposures—and overall cooler temperatures due to the site's location in the southern end of the Valley, which places it in the path of late-day marine breezes from the northernmost portion of San Francisco Bay, located just eighteen miles to the south.

gauge if Dad could make a success of running a winery. "Anyone can put together numbers that make a great-looking projection," he said.

It wasn't what Dad had hoped to hear, but he appreciated the frankness. As Dad headed for the door, however, the accountant stepped out of his role as financial analyst, and he said rather wistfully, "You know, John, you only go around once."

Years later Dad told me that's what did it: the featherweight of those words finally tipped the scales. Dad knew he wanted—needed—to make the leap into this new life in Napa Valley. He didn't want to live in Chicago for the rest of his life, drinking gin and tonics and playing golf while wondering what if—*what if* he'd purchased that hillside? *What if* our family had pursued the dream of making wine?

Not long after, one night in November 1972, Dad stunned us all by announcing that we were moving to a place we'd never heard of called Napa Valley.

TWO

January 1973

There must be a million American stories that begin with a family packing themselves into a station wagon.

I can still remember my dad at the wheel of our wood-paneled Country Squire flying west on I-80. He was trim and handsome, his hair thinning a bit on top. My younger brother Brad, twelve, was in the backseat with our dog, Dingo. I was riding shotgun, a lanky, basketball-obsessed seventeen-year-old who wore glasses. On that gray, frigid day in January we'd packed into our car and started driving toward California.

The sense of adventure is hard to overstate. The only home I'd known was our three-story Victorian in genteel Hinsdale. This was going to be the longest trip I'd ever taken by car.

As the skyline of Chicago receded in our rearview mirror and the vast American heartland spread out before us, it was like finding ourselves in a huge novel on page one.

Like any good road story, within hours we ran into trouble, which began as drifting, popcorn-sized snowflakes. A charming flurry turned into a white pummeling and then a violent blur. Long stretches of interstate were hit hard with snowstorms, and we inched along, hoping not to slide off into a snowbank, praying not to smash into the back of a stalled truck. Each evening, as the trip continued, we stopped at a different white-blobbed, featureless motel and snuck Dingo in with us for the night. (My mom, who was probably smarter than all of us, was flying out and would meet us in San Francisco. My older siblings, Bill and Libby, were in college and missed all of this.)

Each day we crawled closer to that 200 acres of vineyard in a place called Napa Valley. As he drove, Dad's mind was on grape prices, vine cultivation, the future of the wine industry, and a thousand other things.

My seventeen-year-old brain was absorbed with—what else?—my social life. In Chicago I'd gone to Hinsdale High, a big school, where I'd been a pretty small fish, although I'd gained a little late-game cachet as the kid who was moving to California, which my friends and I envisioned as a sunny partyland, where it was going to be Malibu and beaches and bikini time. I had high teenage hopes for life in the Golden State.

As such, this complete uprooting of our family and our lives didn't seem traumatic or unwelcome. If anything, it felt very much a part of the ethos of the times. Just as my dad's early life was molded by the Depression, mine was shaped by the change going on all around us. By 1973 America had been to the moon, schools were still working on racial integration, and teenagers were listening to acid-inspired rock. Meanwhile, there was still a whole generation of grandparents who had been born in the 1880s and 1890s. (My great-grandfather Coates Foresman had only passed away a couple years prior to all this.) When *their* parents had traveled west, it had been *Little House on the Prairie*-style in ox-drawn wagons and later by steam locomotive. They had played banjoes and split rails.

One generation was slowly and uneasily handing the reins to another. Former president Harry Truman had just passed away in Kansas City, Missouri, in the week after Christmas, following a long illness. A few weeks later, former president Lyndon Johnson died unexpectedly of a heart attack. President Nixon had just won reelection and was sworn in for his second term on January 20; he was all smiles despite a news story that was just showing up in newspapers about the "bugging trial," which was later dubbed "Watergate."

As 1973 began, the United States had stepped up a bombing campaign in North Vietnam, but by January 20 a peace pact was signed, and it looked like the POWs would start coming home within weeks.

On the way to California we passed movie theaters showing *The God-father* and *The French Connection*. When my mom flew to California she'd be one of the first airline passengers to pass through the newly mandated security systems designed to stop hijacking. (New Trier High alum Charlton Heston was starring in a now-forgotten but timely movie called *Skyjacked*.)

Looking back, I believe we were caught up in another element of that time: the "back to the land" movement. The hippie version of that was to join a commune, surround yourself with goats and naked toddlers, learn the dulcimer, and grow some pot. Others were starting the organic farm movement and creating food co-ops.

According to one study, in the 1970s more than one million people in Canada and the United States engaged in this reverse migration from the city to small rural farms.[1]

The Napa Valley version of that movement brought Jack and Jamie Davies from Los Angeles to Napa Valley to start Schramsberg. It brought the Brounsteins of Diamond Creek, the Trefethens, the Duckhorns, and Gary and Nancy Andrus of Pine Ridge. Jim Barrett came from Los Angeles to breathe life into Chateau Montelena, Joe Phelps was lured away from his construction business in Colorado, and Warren Winiarski left a professorship in Chicago to launch Stag's Leap Wine Cellars. Men and women from diverse walks of life were drawn to this place in the late 1960s and early 1970s and committed everything they had to pull Napa Valley out of its long doldrums.

---

1. Jeffrey C. Jacob, "The North American Back-to-the-Land Movement," *Community Development Journal* 31, no. 3 (July 1996): 241–49.

THREE

A Wine Country Emerges from a Wilderness

This wave of newcomers in the late 1960s and early 1970s—full of new ideas and enthusiasm—was simply the latest in a series of migrations to Napa Valley over the past 150 years, each one just as bursting with energy and ambition as the one before.

Napa Valley's first vintage date was 1841 or 1842, when pioneer George Yount (namesake of Yountville) made the Valley's inaugural wine from a small vineyard he'd planted not far from the river. Yount, whose original Scandinavian name was Jyunt, hailed from North Carolina by way of Missouri. He was a veteran of the War of 1812, a Freemason, and a frontiersman who knew how to trap and scout and live pretty well off not much in the wilderness. Native Americans, probably members of the Wappo tribe, stomped Yount's grapes and fermented that first Napa Valley wine in ox-hide bags strung up between trees.[1] Those who tried it said it was tasty, but then again they were probably pairing it with squirrel.

When Yount arrived, this area was a region of Mexico called Alta California. The first Mexican presence had come in 1823.[2] The Valley was

1. Charles L. Sullivan, *Napa Wine: A History from Mission Days to the Present*, 2nd ed. (San Francisco, CA: Wine Appreciation Guild, 2008), 19.
2. Lin Weber, *Old Napa Valley: The History to 1900* (St. Helena, CA: Wine Ventures Publishing, 1998), 17.

divided up into large swaths of land that historians call the Mexican land grants. Where our winery sits today was once part of Rancho Yajome. Other land grants at that time included Rancho Caymus (which belonged to Yount), Rancho Tulocay, Rancho La Jota, Rancho Las Putas, and the peculiarly named Rancho Carne Humana (translates as "human meat"). In 1846, after the Bear Flag Revolt (which gave us an animal for the state flag but had little political or military impact) and some more serious action by U.S. armed forces in the southern part of the state, Napa Valley became U.S. territory along with the rest of California.

In the decades that followed, pioneer vintners such as Charles Krug followed Yount's lead and established one vineyard after another, and a wine country began to emerge from a wilderness.

The first person to actually construct a commercial winery was a British immigrant named John M. Patchett, whose winery was located approximately where today you'll find the intersection of First and Monroe Streets in Napa,[3] several blocks down from the West Coast offices of *Wine Spectator.*

Like the sites established by Yount, Krug, and Patchett, all the first vineyards were planted, sensibly, on the Valley floor. The land was flat and easy to work, plus the Napa River and its various tributaries offered reliable sources of water.

The first hillside vineyard was planted by a German immigrant named Jacob Schram in the 1860s. Though vines had been planted on hillsides in the Mediterranean world for centuries, it was a first here. And it took some doing. Schram had to clear dense forest on Diamond Mountain near Calistoga in order to establish his vines, which he dry-farmed—meaning that he didn't attempt to irrigate them.

Over time, Schram's vineyard earned a reputation for producing outstanding wines, and by 1880 Charles Krug, the Beringer brothers, and many others were following suit, situating vineyards on steep sites,

---

3. Charles L. Sullivan, *Napa Wine: A History from Mission Days to the Present*, 2nd ed. (San Francisco, CA: Wine Appreciation Guild, 2008), 25.

including Howell Mountain (Krug) and Spring Mountain (the Beringers). In his book *The Silverado Squatters*, celebrated author Robert Louis Stevenson writes of visiting Schram and enjoying both the man's company and his wines. While he referred to the wine of this region as "bottled poetry," he also clearly saw it as a grand experiment, comparing it to prospecting for gold and silver in terms of its uncertain future.[4]

The wine boom started about the time of Stevenson's visit here, as San Francisco's new crop of gold and silver millionaires looked for promising places to invest their fortunes and perhaps to take on the trappings of aristocracy. Not for the last time Napa Valley found itself awash in wealthy investors, new landowners, and would-be winemakers. In 1880 there were forty-nine wineries. Within six years that number more than tripled to 175, according to historian William F. Heintz.[5]

The old Mexican land grants, which had been populated mostly by cattle, were cut into parcels and sold as quickly as buyers could snap them up.

Just to the south of present-day Shafer was the property of Horace B. Chase, a wealthy Chicago merchant who built a castle-like manor house, which he called Stag's Leap. Terrill Grigsby and family bought vineyard land throughout the Valley and built a beautiful stone winery, just south of Chase's property, called Occidental, still in use today at Regusci Winery.

Terrill Grigsby was a leading light in that viticultural heyday and something of American royalty. His father was a nephew of General William Henry Harrison and had fought with him in the War of 1812. Harrison later became the ninth U.S. president.

Along with his social standing, Grigsby was also known to have a temper. He once went ballistic on a man he suspected of shorting him

---

4. Robert Louis Stevenson, *The Silverado Squatters* (London: Chattus and Windus, 1893), accessed June 20, 2011, http://sunsite.berkeley.edu/Literature/Stevenson/Silver adoSquatters.

5. William F. Heintz, *California's Napa Valley: One Hundred Sixty Years of Wine Making* (San Francisco, CA: Scottwall Associates, 1999), 121.

on a load of grapes, thrashing him into near-lifelessness with a shovel. Grigsby beat a murder charge only because the man happened to live.[6]

While numerous colorful stories and key records survive from this period, no one today knows the origins of the name Stag's Leap. According to a story that's been handed down for generations, a band of hunters long ago were closing in on a stag that eluded them by leaping from one crag on the palisades to the next.

It's plausible that both the myth and the name were dreamed up by Chase and/or his wife, Minnie. The area was, and still is, home to a lot of deer (as we would later discover), and the term "leap" shows up in various place-names often associated with steep, rocky cliffs, such as Huntsman's Leap and Byard's Leap in England, the Priest's Leap in Ireland, Ivy's Leap in southern Australia, and so on.

Another possibility is that it was tied to a neighbor a mile or so down the Silverado Trail from the Chase manor named William K. Staggs. In at least once instance, the local newspaper in the 1890s referred to this area as "Staggs Leap."[7] As late as 1973, the *Napa Register* referred to the property next door to us as "Staggs Leap Ranch."[8]

(About one-third of the original 75 acres owned by Staggs is now our Borderline Vineyard, a source of Cabernet Sauvignon for us, located along Silverado Trail.)

What this means is that the name could be the result of clever word-play, working in both the stag's myth and the Staggs' neighbor. Pioneers had a sense of humor, after all, when they weren't whacking each other with shovels.

By the early 1890s, a national economic downturn was hurting the wine industry in a big way, but the darker player was a near-microscopic,

6. William F. Heintz, Stag's Leap Wine Cellars Site History: Parker Hill, 1984, client-commissioned research project, William F. Heintz Collection, pp. 27 and 28.

7. Stags Leap District Appellation Committee (John Shafer, Chairman), Petition to Establish the Viticultural Area of "Stags Leap," August 22, 1985, private archive, Stags Leap District.

8. "Napan Hurt When Horse Strikes Car," *Napa Register,* January 2, 1973, 2A.

root-attacking insect called phylloxera. This menace had already devastated the vineyards of France, an apocalypse so complete that in Stevenson's *Silverado Squatters* he movingly laments what he sees as the end of centuries of French winemaking altogether. Now hordes of these tiny bugs did their worst here. Within a few years of phylloxera's arrival, Horace Chase had lost 50 of his 57 acres of wine grapes. Winery owners throughout the Valley were turning to new crops, including watermelons, olives, almonds, and peaches (walnuts and prunes became widespread in the century that followed).

On the property we own today, the owner Jacob Ohl had taken to growing corn alongside his dwindling Zinfandel and Malvoisie grapes. Near where you'll find Stag's Leap Wine Cellars, a large population of hogs was newly in residence, helping to offset the owner's loss of grape income.[9]

Things got so bad that the Bank of Napa is listed in 1895 as the owner of a great deal of acreage throughout the Valley as the result of repossession.

In short order the dreams of many of those first wine pioneers were extinguished. After phylloxera, even with successful replanting between 1898 and World War I, the doom of the Napa Valley wine business was sealed with the era of Prohibition in 1919.

The landscape became dotted with ghost wineries. The mountain vineyards of Jacob Schram and the Beringers were reclaimed by the forest. Much of what had been a massive, thriving industry lay dormant, waiting for another cycle and another generation.

9. William F. Heintz, Stag's Leap Wine Cellars Site History: Parker Hill, 1984, client-commissioned research project, William F. Heintz Collection, p. 39.

FOUR

The Pendulum Swings

Home winemakers were allowed to produce as much as two hundred gallons a year for their own consumption during Prohibition. Selling wine grapes to these winemaking operations in basements across the country helped create a decent living for some growers in the Valley. There was a pretty lively illegal alcohol trade as well. According to our neighbor, Frank Perata, who lived on our property as a boy in the 1940s, there is an old moonshine that is still buried somewhere along the creek behind the winery. In addition, when Frank's father was tearing down a decrepit outbuilding, he found a secret storage area for wine barrels under the floorboards.

Slowly the stars began to align for Napa Valley with the end of Prohibition in 1933. Wine was still almost solely of interest to German and Italian immigrants. This continued to be a beer and whiskey country, so no one here was getting rich but at least making wine couldn't get you thrown in the slammer anymore.

Toward the end of World War II, the government built a prisoner of war camp along Silverado Trail (near where Conn Dam is located today) complete with barbed-wire fences and a guard tower. Perata remembers that the German POWs were rented out to local growers to tend walnut orchards and vineyards here in Stags Leap.

The war had a bigger effect here than providing cheap labor from the Third Reich; it sparked several things that helped create favorable conditions for a Napa resurgence. The postwar period saw big national economic expansion—the importance of this can't be underestimated. The gunpowder of every boom is money.

This creation of wealth coincided with an upswing in American interest in wine. Many military men and women who had been stationed in Europe returned home bringing new Mediterranean-inspired food and drink cravings with them.

By the late 1950s and into the 1960s, residents of San Francisco, movie stars, Bay Area connoisseurs, and others started visiting in the Valley in greater numbers to try wines at Robert Mondavi's new winery and at other places, such as Sutter Home and Louis M. Martini Winery.

By the early 1970s, Napa Valley wine was on the cusp of a very different era. The 1972 harvest garnered the highest prices anyone had ever seen for grapes. The overall crop value was $19.4 million, nearly $2.5 million more than the previous year.[1] According to an ebullient *Time* cover story on California's soaring wine industry, Napa Valley had "run out of vineyard land."[2] (Not true, but points for enthusiasm.)

Our family was showing up to a party that had just gotten started. However, as we would learn, in spite of all the actual and metaphorical California sunshine, *every* setback experienced by those first Napa wine pioneers—economic downturns, killer bugs, bad weather, and fickle public tastes—would circle back and challenge us as well.

1. Aldo Delfino, Agricultural Commissioner, *1972 Napa County Agricultural Crop Report*, Napa County Department of Agriculture, Napa, CA, 1973, accessed June 28, 2011, www.countyofnapa.org/AgCommissioner/CropReport.

2. Patricia Delaney, "American Wine Comes of Age," *Time*, November 27, 1972, 81.

FIVE

Arrival—1973

We met my mom in San Francisco and drove into Napa Valley on a sunny January morning. The hills were vibrant green, and the air was warm enough that you could wear a T-shirt. For a Chicago native this was a jaw-dropping introduction to the season they called winter out here. We drove north on the two-lane Silverado Trail out of the town of Napa, passing walnut orchards, hay fields, and vineyards. Cattle chewed their cud and stared at us from hillside pastures.

About seven miles north of Napa, Dad turned on the blinker, and we made a right onto a narrow drive that jogged around the base of a forested hill. The road split on the far side of the hill, and we went left.

The arrow-straight drive was flanked on both sides by row upon row of nut-brown, skeletal grapevines in winter hibernation. The roadway ended at a collection of odd little buildings, dominated by the part-adobe, part-stone house with a red tile roof. The rest were creaky-looking outbuildings. Beyond these structures, however, was an incredible sight—massive green hillsides shot through here and there with craggy, thrusting bedrock. And blocking out nearly half of the eastern sky stood towering cliffs called the Stags Leap Palisades.

When I'd imagined California, I'd thought of beaches, dune buggies, and oiled, bronzed skin. This was like nothing I'd pictured.

The house looked as though it had started as a modest stone structure that was later expanded, several times, by builders with more vigor than skill. Its tile roof seemed like a Mediterranean afterthought. The interior was all crooked floors and doorways, and its oddly scented rooms echoed, since there wasn't yet a stick of furniture in the place.

That first night, with the moving truck still several days away, we unfurled sleeping bags in the living room, stoked a fire in the fireplace—the house's only heat source—and pretended we were camping. My parents were buoyant and energized by this new chapter in their lives, and my brother and I couldn't help but become infected by their sense of adventure.

As I lay in my sleeping bag that night, I took in the foreign feel of this place. The sounds outside were like nothing I'd heard before—vast silences broken occasionally by the yelping of a coyote, the hooting of an owl, the rustle of oak leaves from the huge, shaggy trees just outside. With no streetlights for miles in any direction, the night sky out the off-kilter window was a rich, limitless blackness fogged with stars.

It wasn't Oak Street, and it was light years from Malibu. But already this felt like it could become home.

SIX

Grapes

I landed at my new school, St. Helena High, pretty easily earning a position right away on the varsity basketball team—something that would never have happened back in Chicago, where the competition was unbelievably fierce. I'm still friends with fellow teammates Cyril Chappellet and Jeff Jaeger. We beat our "archrivals," Cloverdale, in the first game, which was an auspicious start. Also, I was the new kid on campus, which had a little coolness attached to it, so life was good.

Not all the adjustments to country living were stress-free though. On my first night after basketball practice, I drove home from St. Helena and discovered that with no streetlights and very few cars out and about, Silverado Trail was pitch-black. I couldn't find any signs or landmarks in my headlights to help direct me home, and I drove almost to Napa searching for the entrance to our driveway. Finally I had to turn around and head north again, slowing down at every break in the trees, every cattle guard, and every possible turn. In an era before cell phones, the only thing I could do was drive up and down the Trail in this way, with a growing sense of panic, until I finally stumbled on our driveway.

By contrast, sunny school mornings started with a bang. My brother Brad and I would pile into a beat-up 1955 Jeep pickup that had come with the property. I'd throw its antiquated "three-on-the-tree" shift system into gear and gun the engine, taking Brad to Robert Louis Stevenson (RLS) Middle School in St. Helena before I'd head over to St. Helena High. Every morning he'd egg me on to "beat the bus"—a way of saying drive like hell down Silverado Trail to beat the school bus to RLS. Fortunately there were fewer cars on the road back then, which is probably the only reason we're both still alive.

While I was off shooting hoops and risking my neck in various ways, Dad was coming to grips with the reality of life as a grape grower. With the purchase of our property, he had inherited a contract with the St. Helena Cooperative Winery (which everyone simply called "the Co-op"). By next fall our grapes would need to be harvested and hauled up to St. Helena to be crushed and fermented. Most of the juice from our property, and throughout the Valley, was sold to Gallo and became a jug wine called Hearty Burgundy (which Dad remembers as being pretty good back then. And no wonder, with so much prime Napa Valley fruit in the blend).

The work started right away. At that time of year, in winter, the vines were ready to be pruned. When spring warmed the soil, we'd get the first wave of weeds and predatory insects.

For the short term, he hired a vineyard management company run by Ivan Shoch, one of the original investors in Robert Mondavi Winery, and learned a lot by observing how this hired crew cared for the soil and the vines—when they tilled between the vines, when and how they pruned, and so forth. He also took viticulture classes at University of California–Davis and Napa Valley College.

Long term, Dad realized that all those vines planted back in 1922 needed to go. They were a mix of red grapes, Carignane and Zinfandel, and white grapes, Sauvignon Vert and Golden Chasselas (which today is typically identified as Palomino), that had been planted by an Italian immigrant named Batisti Scansi. Not only were they past their prime, but the world of American wine was changing fast. The future looked to be less in mass-market wines in fat-bellied jugs and more in fine wines that had a specific place and grape variety associated with them.

This meant that over the next few years we'd need to replace the 30 acres of aging vineyards, while at the same time expanding our vines up onto the surrounding hillsides, where Dad believed we'd get the best quality.

This forced him into the dicey task of deciding which new grape varieties we would stake our future on. First he needed to get a fix on where the wind was blowing in terms of the marketplace. What wines were consumers buying today? What wines were they likely to gravitate toward several years down the road when our new vines were reaching maturity? Those factors had to be balanced against an educated guess as to which types of grapes would grow best on our site.

In 1973 this was a world in which a grape called Napa Valley Gamay occupied nearly 1,000 acres of the 12,000 acres planted to red grapes. (Today that variety claims fewer than 20 acres here.) There were 1,200 acres of Petite Sirah in the Valley and double that of Pinot Noir.

Zinfandel was a tempting choice because, first, even though the vines weren't in top condition, the variety already existed here on the property. Second, as a grape grower, Dad's income was tied to how much he'd get paid per ton of fruit. Besides being popular with consumers then, Zinfandel clusters tended to be big and heavy, which translated into a few extra dollars when you weighed and then sold your load at harvest.

Cabernet Sauvignon, meanwhile, seemed risky. Conventional wisdom at the time held that the Stags Leap area was too cool for Cabernet. We got excellent midday heat in summer, but with the northernmost tip of San Francisco Bay just eighteen miles away, afternoon and evening breezes delivered a consistent chill in the late-day air, even in July and August. It was widely believed that you needed to plant Cab in the warmer areas of Rutherford and Oakville.

The first person to go against the grain in that regard was our neighbor to the south, Nathan Fay, a grower who occasionally produced a little homemade wine for himself. He'd planted 15 acres of Cabernet Sauvignon in 1961, and he was followed about ten years later by Warren Winiarski at Stag's Leap Wine Cellars, after he bought the Heid Ranch adjacent to Nate's land. Dick Steltzner, of neighboring Steltzner Vineyards, had also planted some Cabernet by about this time.

Dad consulted with two local growers, Manuel Barboza and Laurie Wood, to get their take on this. Barboza had been the vineyard manager at neighboring Stags' Leap Winery since the 1920s and knew this part of the Valley like his own family. Wood, who owned a vineyard management company, came out to our property and dug test holes and studied the soil to confirm his initial assessment of the vineyard's potential.

Both men were convinced, despite popular belief, that the property held good potential for red grapes, Cabernet Sauvignon in particular.

Before Dad got into the Cabernet Sauvignon business though, Ivan Shoch approached him with a more direct route to some income in the grape business, which was the idea of planting the knoll at the western foot of our property to the white variety Chenin Blanc. While Cabernet Sauvignon appealed to the tastes of the new vintners in this region, the American public had yet to be won over. White wine, specifically Chardonnay, was overwhelmingly the top choice out in the marketplace, and a number of wineries were betting on Chenin Blanc as being the next big thing. Shoch had a contact at a local winery who was looking for more sources of this white grape, and Dad decided to sign on. The reason was purely financial. While he prepared to plant Cabernet on his previously unplanted hillsides, he had a guaranteed sale with Chenin Blanc. He hoped that by thinking first with his wallet, he would later have the freedom to follow his heart.

Being a newbie to this business, when it came time to set up an agreement for his future harvest price Dad did the unthinkable—he asked for a written contract. What he wasn't fully clued into was that grape contracts then were done on a handshake. Perhaps to indulge this citified newbie, the buyer agreed, and they drew up a contract for a price that was based on 1973 prices. Again, not a problem. Prices for grapes had been growing at an astounding rate for more than ten years. And in 1973 they had climbed higher still—the total value of the Napa Valley grape crop that year was $33.9 million, a staggering $14.4 million more than in the previous year. Cabernet Sauvignon sold for an average of $874 per ton. Chenin Blanc sold for $482 per ton.[1] It was like the gold rush all over again, and no one wanted to miss out.

1. Aldo Delfino, Agricultural Commissioner, *1973 Napa County Agricultural Crop Report*, Napa County Department of Agriculture, Napa, CA, 1974, accessed June 28, 2011, www.countyofnapa.org/AgCommissioner/CropReport.

SEVEN

Cabernet

Dad's approach to his vineyard life evolved rapidly. Unknown to me until much later, he'd come to Napa Valley hoping to start a winery fairly quickly. (For years I thought he'd wanted to come out here and live the life of a gentleman farmer, but he swears now he always intended to get into winemaking.) However, once he got into the middle of the business, he realized how much he had to learn. Ever the realist, he decided to gradually take over the vineyard work on his own—to avoid paying fees to a management company—and focus solely on growing and selling grapes. At least for now.

In addition to cultivating vines, he thought he should get a job that would give him some flexibility and steady income. After all those years hanging around educators and teaching math and spelling to us kids at home, he decided to become a teacher. To that end he started commuting to University of San Francisco to get his teaching credential.

His concerns about money were prompted in part by the fact that the U.S. economy took a nosedive in 1974, due to factors such as the OPEC oil embargo and related financial turmoil. We had a new genre of inflation called "stagflation," rising unemployment, and long lines at gas stations.

One thing you learn when the economy tanks is this: no one has to buy wine. It's one of life's glorious add-ons, which means that the financial vitality of the wine business is strapped pretty firmly to the nation's fiscal health. When the economy bottomed out, the grape bubble popped. Cabernet Sauvignon prices plummeted into the $400-per-ton range[1] and Napa growers wouldn't see 1973 prices again until 1985.[2] Chenin Blanc was now averaging $243 per ton. When the buyer came to purchase Dad's white grapes on our knoll, he very reluctantly paid those much higher 1973 prices thanks to that unwelcome written contract. The buyer informed Dad that everyone else was "taking it in the shorts," in other words, some (or perhaps quite a few) of those handshake contracts weren't being honored, which probably did much to curtail the practice.

Meanwhile Dad was beginning to take over the vineyard operations himself. He let go of Ivan Shoch's company and began to contract with Big John Piña, who worked with him more on an as-needed basis, which in the beginning was still quite a lot.

With Big John's help, Dad took his first running start at planting Cabernet Sauvignon in 1974. He had his eye on a south-facing 7-acre shoulder of the hillside located high up behind our house. A big part of preparing a site for planting, at least on Shafer property, is clearing rocks. My brother Brad and I spent every weekend that school year lugging rocks out off that hill. By hand. By the thousands.

The only thing worse than doing a job like this—for hours on end in the merciless sun—is doing it with your thirteen-year-old brother. He had a special love for chucking rocks at me and once even scored a bull's-eye on the back of my head. Dad referred to this kind of work as

1. Aldo Delfino, Agricultural Commissioner, *1974 Napa County Agricultural Crop Report*, Napa County Department of Agriculture, Napa, CA, 1975, accessed June 28, 2011, www.countyofnapa.org/AgCommissioner/CropReport.

2. Stephen J. Bardessono, Agricultural Commissioner, *1985 Napa County Agricultural Crop Report*, Napa County Department of Agriculture, Napa, CA, 1986, accessed June 28, 2011, www.countyofnapa.org/AgCommissioner/CropReport.

"contouring the land." Brad and I called it a lot of things much less poetic.

Planting a hillside is always a tough endeavor, but in Dad's case it was made more challenging because it was a rarity in that era. You couldn't buy a how-to manual for this sort of project or even type "how to plant a hillside vineyard" into Google. As such, it was a good bit of timing that Dad met Louis P. Martini at one of realtor Jim Warren's welcome-to-the-neighborhood cocktail parties. Louis invited Dad to ride out to their Monte Rosso Vineyard in the wilds of Sonoma County and showed him how they'd terraced their mountainous site, which Louis's father had expanded in the late 1930s. It was a wild ride in Louis's pickup through dense woods on a roller-coaster road, which Dad remembers as "someplace straight out of the movie *Deliverance*."

Louis P. Martini was a big guy with a broad forehead and a big smile, a quintessential product of the Golden State in its prime, all confidence, who'd grown up around crush pads and grapevines. I'm sure he and Dad hit it off for all kinds of reasons—in part because Louis had also been in the Army Air Corps in World War II and in part because he was just an engaging guy. His father, Louis M. Martini, had started in the wine business down in Livermore Valley, California, then moved to Kingsburg (south of Fresno), and had ultimately transitioned to Napa in the early 1930s.[3] Martini did not need the Romans to tell him there was something special about a hillside vineyard. He was clear on the difference between what you got on a hillside and what you got on the Valley floor.

He believed that because of the drainage and the exposure, hillside fruit produced more elegant wine. Quick drainage meant that the vines never had a lot of moisture to draw from, and the exposure to sunlight on the side of a mountain gave the grapes something they just didn't get

3. Louis P. Martini, "A Family Winery and the California Wine Industry," an oral history conducted in 1984 by Ruth Teiser, The Wine Spectator California Winemen Oral History Series, Regents of the University of California, p. 46.

anywhere else. Monte Rosso, with its south face, simply produced fruit with a difference you could see and taste.

After listening to Martini and talking with some other consultants, Dad got down to business. Early on, as we were terracing the hillside, it became clear we'd need to blast out several Buick-sized boulders. My sister Libby was living in San Francisco and working at Wells Fargo at the time, but helped out at the property as often as she could. At Dad's request she drove to Marin County and loaded up the trunk of her car with dynamite, terrified on the forty-five-minute drive to our vineyard that she'd get rear-ended.

A couple of blasting experts, who'd learned their craft in the Vietnam War, came by and busily drilled holes in strategic spots, dropped in sticks of the explosive, ran blasting wire all over the place, and in short order—kaboom!—sent up plumes of smoke and debris. In the blink of an eye, the boulders were gone, but the hillside looked like it had just given birth to about twenty thousand baby rocks. And Brad and I were back on the job.

On the advice of a recent U.C. Davis viticulture graduate, we further prepped the hillside site by "ripping" the soil—as subtle a technique as it sounds. Dad hired a guy who came out with an attachment on the back of his tractor that looked like a giant dinosaur tooth. The tooth punched down three or four feet into the earth and the tractor drove the length and breadth of our vineyard-to-be, tearing up the soil.

The technique of ripping is a fine idea when you're prepping a vineyard on a flat valley floor site, which at the time accounted for nearly every other vineyard in the area. However, we learned it is a disastrous idea on a hillside. Not long afterward, heavy November rains struck and we watched, sick at heart as soil and rock turned into rivers of mud, leaving clefts and small canyons behind. Fixing this took weeks of hauling soil back up the hill.

Unfortunately, we had quite a run of hard luck after acting on what we had hoped was good advice.

Mid-1970s: An early hillside planting on the Shafer estate.

Early on, knowing that we needed a well, Dad hired a geologist who surveyed the property and advised him to drill near the tiny stream-bed of Chase Creek, which meanders through our property. The well-drilling company came out and dutifully punched a hole in the earth and discovered a water source that produced a meager four gallons per minute. So Dad tried again—brought out another expert who told us to drill in a flat area of our vineyard just west of the house. The result was the same.

This time, though, the guy who was hired to drill the well said to Dad, "You really shouldn't be drilling down here anyway, you should be up there," pointing to the hillsides. "That's where the water-bearing rock is."

The idea of moving higher up to drill down seemed to defy logic, but having had his fill of geologists, Dad took the well-driller's counsel. That third attempt on the hillside resulted in hitting a spectacular 250-gallon-a-minute water source.

The challenges ramped up the following spring when we planted our rootstock.[4]

In this case we used a rootstock called St. George, whose namesake was a celebrated slayer of dragons. Despite its heroic name, there's one creature this rootstock had no power against—deer. Quite a number of stags (and does and fawns) leaped through a previously undetected hole in our fence, and they ate the rootstock down to raw nubs that barely peeked through the soil.

Dad attempted to bud (graft) the chewed up rootstock to Cabernet Sauvignon anyway, which resulted in a pitiful 20 percent "take."

Undaunted, Dad pushed forward with the next step a lot of people were saying he needed to take, which was to create an overhead sprinkler irrigation system (for his yet nonexistent vineyard).

At the time, most vineyards were located on the valley floor, where they could be dry-farmed, because the deep, rich soils stored a good deal of moisture from the winter rains.

Our hillsides, by contrast, came with a scant eighteen- to twenty-two-inch covering of porous volcanic soil and rock over a layer of weathered bedrock. So the soil, the underlying geologic material, and the steep slopes meant that any winter rain didn't hang around very long. By mid- to late summer the hillsides were as dry as ash, making irrigation mandatory if you wanted your vines to survive.

The secondary reason for an overhead sprinkler was the discovery—first made in orange groves—that during frost season you could protect

---

4. Rootstock is a grapevine root system that you source from a specialized wine industry nursery. You plant it in the soil, get it established for a few months, and then graft on a cultivar, or cane, such as Merlot, Cabernet Sauvignon, Chardonnay, Chenin Blanc, etc. This technique of grafting rootstock to a cane was developed in France as a way of outwitting phylloxera in the 1800s. It was discovered that the root systems of some species of wild grapevines from North America were resistant to the insect, and the French vignerons realized that they could graft their French vines onto American roots and thus establish vineyards that were phylloxera-resistant. Today a wide variety of rootstocks has been developed to resist disease and to offer desired results in a variety of soil types and climate conditions.

your vines from frost damage by coating them in water and letting a thin layer of ice form around them. It's counterintuitive, but it works, like creating a tiny igloo around each grape; the ice actually helps the vines stay above the critical temperature of 31.5 degrees Fahrenheit.

What made this approach affordable was the fairly recent introduction of inexpensive PVC pipe. Grape growers were never exactly rolling in cash from Prohibition onward, so by necessity they were always on the lookout for new ways to squeeze a penny. Previously, frost protection was performed with the use of smudge pots, basically metal chimney-type structures in which you'd burn diesel oil that created a warm, heavy, dark smoke that filled your vineyard—and the air—keeping the vines above freezing. Some growers simply burned piles of old car tires. On a frosty morning back then the Valley could be pretty smoky and smelly.

Overhead irrigation systems like ours took weeks to build, and with his engineering background I think Dad was intrigued by the calculations involved in getting the water pressure and distribution right. But rather than try to conquer this one himself, Dad hired a consultant to design and build a complex array of pumps, pipes, valves, and sprinkler heads that all connected back to our pond.

After weeks of scrupulous assembly, it was finally time to test the completed sprinkler system. Dad cranked it on and we heard an exciting swoosh of water cascading through the web of PVC pipe. Water began to first dribble out and then to shoot in streams of spray here and there and across the way as planned. There was a real sense of occasion and achievement. We were for real. We were finally in the wine business. Our crops planted (getting there), our trellises erected (sort of). This was the real beginning of—

Pow—

The sprinkler head closest to us exploded into the sky, hurled on a blast of high-pressure pond water. We were still taking that in when the next sprinkler head down the line fired into the air. Then another. And another and another. All the way down the line. Pow, pow, pow— sprinkler heads across the vineyard soared into the air like fireworks.

The sprinkler consultant had used the wrong pressure valves, and the whole thing came apart before our eyes.

With these and other setbacks, my mom started to call the vineyard site "John's Folly."

The final kicker came a couple of years later when Dad realized that we didn't need an overhead sprinkler system at all. First, he learned, since the vines were on a hillside they don't need frost protection. The frost zone exists in low-lying valleys and depressions in the valley floor, not at higher elevations. Second, the sprinklers were a terrible waste of water, dumping gallons upon gallons on the vineyard, when all we needed were small, controllable amounts. As soon as possible we switched to drip irrigation, a then-new system pioneered by the Israelis, in which you dole out micro-sips of water to individual vines.

We hadn't started with proper deer protection. We hadn't needed to rip the soil. We didn't need overhead sprinklers. It seemed at this point that rather than embarking on something that had been done since ancient times, planting a hillside was some kind of exotic experiment, which left Dad feeling his way forward in the dark.

EIGHT

Grape Future

In 1974 I graduated from St. Helena High and had to start thinking about "real life" and my future. I started paying more attention to what was going on in my dad's world. I'd cruise up our driveway, which cut through the vineyard, and there he'd be out on a tractor—which he was still learning to operate—in jeans and beat-up hat. He'd give me a big grin and a wave, and it was hard to reconcile this image of him with the dad I'd known back in Chicago—the corporate guy in the three-piece suit. I'd never seen him so happy. Dad, his grower buddies, and the consultants he worked with would drive around the Valley in their old Jeeps and their pickup trucks and they'd talk about the weather and grapes and local politics. This way of life appealed to me a lot more than the prospects of living in a city and sitting at a desk all day.

I was accepted into U.C. Davis and signed on to major in viticulture, the science of cultivating grapes. This meant a lot of math as well as a great deal of chemistry and plant biology—the hard stuff. At the same time I enjoyed picking up the basics of pruning and trellising in the school's teaching vineyard and reading up on the latest research on vineyard cultivation. Davis was, and is, the leading school for anyone interested in the wine business. In one or two of my undergrad classes I remember observing a group of graduate students in the front row

(I was usually found in the back) asking questions, making notes, and taking things way too seriously, in my opinion at the time. It was a group that turned out to include Cathy Corison of Corison Winery, Tony Soter, Soter Vineyards in Oregon, and Richard Ward and David Graves, both of Saintsbury.

The summer after my freshman year, I secured my first winery job. It was in Calistoga working at Kornell Champagne Cellars, a producer of sparkling wines, with the unforgettable Hanns Kornell. It was my first taste of responsibility. I'd have to get myself out of bed at 6 A.M., fix my own breakfast, pack my own lunch, and blaze up Silverado Trail on the forty-five-minute trip to Kornell, arriving a little before 8 A.M. If you were even a few minutes late, Hanns would give you a blistering earful, if he didn't simply fire you on the spot—which I saw him do a number of times.

Mine was the gruntiest of grunt jobs, made worse by the wearing of a mandated nerdy blue jumpsuit. Each day entailed jobs such as hauling hundred-pound bags of sugar into an upstairs storage area, cleaning up after another bottle of sparkling wine had exploded in the cellar, and working on the bottling line. (Never in all my life has the clock moved more slowly than when I worked on the bottling line at Kornell.) You learned never to be idle. The lowest form of humanity, as far as Hanns Kornell was concerned, was an employee with his hands in his pockets. If there was a minute in which you weren't occupied, you'd better grab a broom or you'd get a rain of fire from the boss.

Hanns Kornell terrified me. I'd never met anyone so tough. As a teenager in Germany he'd survived the Nazi's Dachau concentration camp and had come to the United States with only $2 in his pocket.

He'd beaten brutal poverty, he'd stared down Hitler; he wasn't about to take *anything* from a lazy college kid.

I had several surprises the following summer when he rehired me. Well, I guess the first surprise was that he rehired me. Beyond that, though, I realized that he actually seemed to like me (by now he'd nick-named me "Professor") and that under his rhino hide was a sweet, decent guy. One afternoon I was inside a fermentation tank, cleaning it out, and for some reason the small, round door swung shut. I panicked. It was dark, hot, and small, with a limited supply of oxygen; then from outside I heard a chuckle—"heh, heh, heh." It was Hanns's idea of an affectionate prank. Later I knew I was in his good graces, because he'd started saying in his thick German accent, "Hey Professor you should marry Paula (his high-school-age daughter)—stay and work with me!"

Years later I took my young children, Katie, Kevin, and Stephen, up to Kornell just to say hi. We walked in and the hospitality guy at the bar said he'd watch my kids while I walked around looking for Hanns. I poked my head in the cellar and got that familiar scent of wooden riddling racks and sparkling wine. I walked around outside and couldn't find him. As I was approaching the hospitality room again I heard the sound of giggling. I walked in and there was Hanns Kornell on the floor playing with my children. Then he looked up and said to his hospitality guy in that great accent, "Get these kids some chocolates!"

It was the last time I saw him. But to this day I still hear that voice in my head telling me to get my hands out of my pockets.

Throughout this period Dad was juggling two careers—education and grape growing. His first classroom stint was at a new continuation school in Napa called Temescal, created for students who, for a variety of reasons, weren't succeeding at the local high school. Most had gotten into trouble and had spent time in juvenile hall. Dad believed the work there was important and could have a positive impact, but it was not an easy year. For his efforts there, Dad got his tires slashed and his brake lines cut.

The following year he transferred to St. Helena High, where things went so well he was offered a full-time position. But by this time, Dad felt he was doing two jobs poorly and had to make a choice. Fortunately, the vineyard won.

NINE

Alfonso

If he was going to get serious about taking over his vineyards, one of the first things Dad realized he needed was manpower. His thought was to hire a foreman to live on-site to help with the increasing workload. When he asked around for recommendations, John Piña pointed him toward a young man on his own crew named Alfonso Zamora-Ortiz.

Alfonso had little or no vineyard experience, but he had worked in a nursery and possessed valuable insights regarding plant life—how to size up the health of a vine, when to prune, how much to irrigate, and so forth. None of his guidance came from reference works or a formal education; all of it came through observation, gut feeling, and experience. If he had Big John's respect, Dad thought, Alfonso was certainly worth trying out.

Alfonso had fairly recently come to the Valley from his home in the Mexican state of Jalisco and didn't speak much English. Dad wasn't terribly fluent in Spanish, although he'd been studying it in night classes at Napa Valley College. Yet they managed to communicate through gestures and half-sentences and a sense of humor.

Working together, Dad and Alfonso picked up on the basics of things like running and maintaining a tractor, discing between vine rows, and using sprayers and dusters. They took on the tasks of laying out and terracing the new vineyard blocks, repairing fences, and digging postholes for the new trellis systems.

Early on they tried to tackle the weed problem with the use of a French plow. Dad drove the tractor pulling the plow, while Alfonso walked behind and steered the plow's blade around the base of the vines to clear the unwanted weeds and wild grasses. It was not a perfect system, and they had their share of gouged vine trunks.

Worse was when Dad drove the tractor pulling the discer between the rows. The spacing was unforgiving, allowing only a few inches between each side of the discer and the head-pruned vines, whose fifty-year-old trunks were as thick as posts. More than once in less-watchful moments Dad took out an entire vine. Among growers this is called "tractor blight."

Meanwhile, it came time to make a second run at grafting grapevines onto the budwood now sprouting optimistically again on the vineyard block, which was stuck with the name John's Folly. The fence had successfully been mended, keeping out all the hungry deer. When it came time to "bud over," as it's called, rather than go to a nursery and purchase Cabernet budwood—as is standard practice today—unbeknownst to Dad, Big John did the far more practical thing, and something that had happened in the Valley for decades—he got some for free. Besides helping to manage our vines, Piña also worked for a lot of other people, including Milt Eisele, taking care of his vineyards in Calistoga. This had become a well-known site, thanks to the fact that Phelps produced a rock-star wine called Joseph Phelps Eisele Vineyard Cabernet Sauvignon. It was one of the early Cabs, like Heitz's Martha's Vineyard, which were head-turners and showed the rest of us what Napa Valley was capable of producing.

When it was time to make a second attempt to bud John's Folly to Cabernet, John Piña simply cut the requisite number of canes, or vine branches, from Milt's vineyards (without mentioning it to Milt) and brought them over to our property.[1]

Dad did not discover this act of cane-sharing until some weeks later when he bumped into Milt at a cocktail party and Milt let Dad know he was not terribly pleased.

This time, without any interference from leaping stags, the grafts took beautifully to the budwood, and we were at long last in the hillside vineyard business.

1. Years later Bart Araujo purchased Eisele Vineyard, and the vines were unfortunately struck by our old microscopic nemesis, phylloxera. Needing to replant, Araujo contacted me to see if they could have some of our Eisele budwood. Of course I said yes, and Araujo Estate Wines recovered from phylloxera with new budwood from their original vine cuttings. Four or five years later, we needed to replant a small block of our hillside vineyard, and I called Bart and asked if we could have some canes, and he graciously agreed. Back and forth it goes.

TEN

1976

By 1976 Dad and Alfonso were hard at work replacing the property's old vines one block at a time, while simultaneously prepping and terracing new blocks of vines on the hillsides. On our property the vineyard blocks run from about 1 to 9 acres in size. We divide them up based on their geographical structure, whether they face south, southwest, or west.

Fortunately I was at U.C. Davis during most of this period so now the rock hauling duty fell squarely on Brad and whomever Dad hired to assist.

My dad had to move at a careful pace. If he tore out too many of those old vines too quickly, he'd have no income as he waited for the new ones to produce their first sellable crop. This was when he planted some Chardonnay on the lower, flatter portion of the property we call Bench, believing rightly that the popularity of this white would continue to grow and that for a grape grower it'd be a good source of income. With the economy still in the doldrums and grape prices languishing, it was imperative to pay attention to the bottom line.

Uppermost in his mind, though, was Cabernet Sauvignon. He still nursed the dream of one day building a winery and making a world-class Cabernet wine from the vines he'd fought to get established in the hillside soil. Some of this was fueled by his friendship with our neighbor, Nathan Fay.

As mentioned earlier, in 1961 Nate Fay had been the first grower to plant Cabernet in the cooler Stags Leap area. Besides selling grapes to local wineries, he kept a little fruit each year for himself and made some Cabernet for friends and guests to enjoy. One evening Mom and Dad, along with Joe and Alice Heitz, were invited to dinner with Nate and his wife, Nellie. With the meal, Nate poured his homemade 1968 Cabernet, which Dad remembers to this day as a stunning wine—rich and delicious with lush dark fruit. It was this same vintage, also tasted at Nate's house, that had prompted Warren Winiarski to purchase land next door and make his first Stag's Leap Wine Cellars Cabernet in 1972. For Dad, though, the timing for such a move still wasn't right. Unlike a number of our neighbors, such as Winiarski or Mondavi, he did not want to jump-start a winery with borrowed money and then find himself beholden to a group of investors. That could turn into a corporate stranglehold as bad as the one he'd extricated himself from back at Scott Foresman. Building a winery didn't have to happen tomorrow. If the timing was right, he thought he might be able do it on his own. So he chose to wait for the game to change.

On May 24, 1976, the biggest thing on everyone's mind in Napa was the heat and the ongoing drought. The previous winter had been the third driest on record. Early May saw a 100-degree heat wave that led the California Department of Forestry to declare "fire season" a month earlier than normal. There were early jitters about wildfires and for good reason—fire crews were busy as one blaze after another burst to life in the dry grasses and underbrush. The city of Calistoga was desperate for ways to cut water consumption by one-third or it risked running dry. All of this looked like a continuation of 1975, which had started with very little moisture during the winter and spring and had culminated in a summer of prolonged extreme heat, which had depressed the entire agricultural economy of the Valley—not just grapes but everything else from tree fruit to cattle. Prices for Cabernet Sauvignon in 1975 dropped more than $100 per ton[1] *below* 1974's abysmal per ton price of $454.[2] As the drought continued into 1976, grape growers were deeply worried that the decline in grape prices would continue as well. Nothing here on May 24 indicated that Napa would declare its emancipation from France in this bicentennial year.

On that day in Paris a wine tasting at the InterContinental Hotel was taking place, which would prove a pivotal moment for Napa vintners. British wine merchant Steven Spurrier had set up a tasting of what he considered the best wines of France and of Napa Valley. From France came white Burgundies: Puligny-Montrachet Les Pucelles Domaine Leflaive, Domaine Leflaive, Batard-Montrachet Ramonet-Prudhon, Beaune Clos des Mouches Joseph Drouhin, and Meursault Charmes Roulot. The reds were legendary Bordeaux wines: Château Haut-Brion, Château Mouton Rothschild, Château Montrose, and Château Léoville-Las-Cases.[3] The bottles were covered, the esteemed French judges tasted through the lineup, tallied the points, and discovered to their consternation that they had handed the top spots to two Napa Valley wines—a Cabernet Sauvignon from our neighbors at Stag's Leap Wine Cellars and a Chardonnay from Chateau Montelena in Calistoga. *Quelle horreur!*

I've heard that once the bottles were unveiled, some of the judges in their arch-dismay tried to change their rankings. But it was too late. A month later the tasting was reported in *Time* magazine, which dubbed the event "The Judgment of Paris." It was a story with superb appeal to Americans, who a) take delight in seeing a victory go to "the little guy" and b) enjoy French snobbery taking a poke in the eye.

1. Aldo Delfino, Agricultural Commissioner, *1975 Napa County Agricultural Crop Report*, Napa County Department of Agriculture, Napa, CA, 1976, accessed June 28, 2011, www.countyofnapa.org/AgCommissioner/CropReport.

2. Aldo Delfino, Agricultural Commissioner, *1974 Napa County Agricultural Crop Report*, Napa County Department of Agriculture, Napa, CA, 1975, accessed June 28, 2011, www.countyofnapa.org/AgCommissioner/CropReport.

3. George M. Taber, *Judgment of Paris: California vs. France and the Historic 1976 Paris Tasting That Revolutionized Wine* (New York: Scribner, 2005), 186–95.

The effect of the Paris tasting was palpable pretty quickly in Napa, although it didn't take the form of any kind of public celebration. In part, the outcome of the tasting was simply a great psychological boost for all those who had believed in Napa and moved here in the prior five or ten years to grow grapes and make wine, believing fervently in this region's potential to stand on the world stage, only to be largely ignored outside the West Coast. It was a way vintners could tell themselves they were not crazy for pouring their lives into Napa Valley. In a fairly short time wine critics and collectors from the East Coast and from the United Kingdom starting showing far more interest in what we were doing. In terms of gaining respect in the fine wine world, I think we would have rolled that boulder up the hill at some point, but Spurrier's Paris tasting got us there perhaps as many as ten years sooner.

The buzz created by the Judgment of Paris had an effect on my dad. The idea of starting a winery was driven more forcefully to the front of his mind. How could it not? From our property a pro golfer with a strong drive could practically land a ball in Winiarski's Cabernet vines. Just beyond that, Clos du Val's 1972 Cabernet had also been selected by Spurrier for the tasting—an honor in its own right—and had come in eighth in the red category.

All around the Valley talk swirled of new wines and wineries. The Trefethen family and the Raymond family both released their first wines that year. Spottswoode got rezoning approval from the St. Helena City Council to reactivate wine production on their historic property. Newly constructed wineries opening their doors included Grgich-Hills, Cakebread, Robert Keenan, and Smith-Madrone, with more in the various stages of development, such as Pine Ridge Winery and Duckhorn. It was also the year that corporate America returned its attention to Napa Valley. Coca-Cola purchased Sterling Vineyards in Calistoga for $8 million, the largest corporate purchase since before the crash in '74. The biggest purchases prior to that had been Heublein acquiring Inglenook in 1969 and Pillsbury buying Souverain in 1972.[4] In addition, the prices for grapes such as Cabernet Sauvignon finally edged higher. After hitting a low of $339 per ton in 1975,[5] the $473 per ton of 1976[6] gave growers like Dad the sense that the momentum that had stalled in the early '70s was picking back up.

Dad's friend and fellow World War II B-24 pilot Ernie Van Asperen[7] was on the verge of starting Round Hill Winery and also provided encouragement. He knew Dad had been studying winemaking at Napa Valley College and talked him into producing some homemade wine out of grapes from our fifty-year-old Zinfandel vines. Dad did the whole thing by hand—picked the grapes, crushed and fermented them, and so on. He had a great time doing it, and this too nudged him to take a few steps in the direction of developing a winery. He teamed up with winemaking consultant Larry Wara and began to flesh out some ideas.

By the autumn of 1977, the Cabernet vines on John's Folly were a couple of years old, and Dad finally harvested fruit that was truly his own. He sold most of that first crop to Mike Robbins at Spring Mountain Winery (whose 1972 Cabernet had also scored well at the Paris tasting). But he hung on to a small amount and made ten or twenty gallons of wine in his basement, funneling it into cleaned-out bottles that were still labeled "Mondavi Red Table Wine." In one corner of the Mondavi label he penciled in the historic words "Shafer 1977 Cab."

4. Charles L. Sullivan, *Napa Wine: A History from Mission Days to the Present*, 2nd ed. (San Francisco, CA: Wine Appreciation Guild, 2008), 293.

5. Aldo Delfino, Agricultural Commissioner, *1975 Napa County Agricultural Crop Report*, Napa County Department of Agriculture, Napa, CA, 1976, accessed June 28, 2011, www.countyofnapa.org/AgCommissioner/CropReport.

6. Aldo Delfino, Agricultural Commissioner, *1976 Napa County Agricultural Crop Report*, Napa County Department of Agriculture, Napa, CA, 1977, accessed June 28, 2011, www.countyofnapa.org/AgCommissioner/CropReport.

7. It wasn't until writing this book that I realized how many of Dad's friends had been in the Army Air Corps during World War II: Louis Martini, Nathan Fay, and Ernie Van Asperen. They should have gotten together and released a wine called "Wing Commander."

After Robbins had a chance to try the wine from Dad's hillside fruit, he called and offered a ten-year grape contract. But at long last John Shafer's dreams pulled rank on his practical side. Selling this fruit was out of the question. This was the Cabernet Sauvignon on which he wanted to build a winery.

ELEVEN

Hillside Cabernet

In 1978 it felt as if a spell had been broken. The year started with near-normal winter and spring rains, which pulled us out of the long drought of the previous years. The year went on to become one of those growing seasons when everything goes right: a summer of warm, sun-flooded days with chilly evenings, offering no rain pressure as harvest approached. The sort of year grapes and winemakers thoroughly love.

By early September Dad was in countdown mode. Every morning he was up before dawn gathering sample grapes and testing the sugar and acidity levels. Finally, he knew it was time to harvest. Of course to do that he needed a picking crew. He started making phone calls to all the vineyard management companies. The first two or three, including his buddy John Piña, couldn't help him. Their crews were already scheduled. He kept trying, calling up and down the Valley looking for a group of guys who could come out and pick his 7 acres of Cabernet. Time and time again the people on the other end of the phone line said, apologetically, they couldn't help him, because their guys were already busy. Dad grew more anxious each time he struck out. Somewhere there had to be a crew.

In this new era of post-Judgment of Paris optimism—with increasing planting and rising prices—all the older, more established wineries in the Valley had first dibs on hiring picking crews, and an upstart vintner such as John Shafer, who didn't even have his first vintage in the barn yet—for that matter, didn't even have a barn—would just have to wait.

The temperatures were rising. It went from hot to hotter. The sugar levels in the grapes were spiking. With each passing hour, Dad felt sicker and sicker looking up the hill at that 7 acres. The grapes were getting too ripe; sugar levels were rising past the then-benchmark of the 22.5 degrees to 23 degrees Brix range.[1] Past that sugar reading was the edge of the viticultural earth. It was like one of those ancient maps, where the cartographers simply wrote *"Hic Sunt Dracones"*—"Here there be dragons"—when they reached the limits of known lands. In a similar vein, who knew what happened after 23 degrees Brix? It could *not* be good.

When he finally rounded up a crew—three days too late—with sugar levels of 24.5 degrees and 25.5 degrees Brix, Dad figured he'd just make the best of it.

His crew picked seventeen tons, which Dad hauled up to St. Helena to be crushed and fermented at Markham. Then he had the newly fermented juice trucked to Van Asperen's winery, Round Hill, where it was put into oak barrels, two-thirds of which were French and one-third of which was American.

During my Christmas break from U.C. Davis, I joined Dad and the crew at Round Hill as they racked the wine. Racking is an age-old method of clarifying a wine by pumping it from one barrel to another, separating the liquid from the solids and sediment. In this case we were moving the wine from barrel to barrel and then cleaning the old barrels out for further use. It's a time-consuming process.

At lunchtime Dad and I were sitting outside with the crew under some trees, eating sandwiches and trying some of this Cabernet we'd been racking all morning. It was the first time I'd had a chance to try

---

1. Brix is a measurement of the sugar level in grapes that is expressed as degrees.

Dad's wine and to do so with a crew like this made me hope like crazy that he had put together something drinkable. I knew he'd picked it later than anyone advised and that it had been trucked around the Valley in various states. My heart rate picked up a little as Round Hill's winemaker and all the guys in the cellar crew tried it…and nodded, tried it again and…really seemed to like it. It was still just three months old, had been roughed up from racking and riding around in trucks, and it hadn't gone through malolactic fermentation (a second fermentation nearly all red wine goes through), so it wasn't ready for prime time by any means, but it sure seemed to have some beautiful potential—great aroma, lots of dark, rich fruit, and tannins that, in spite of its extreme youth, didn't seem green or overwhelming, which you'd more or less expect of a wine that young in that era. It's a moment that's always stayed with me. The sense of relief Dad and I shared was huge.

The wine's tour around the Valley wasn't quite finished. After the wine was racked, Dad borrowed a flatbed truck from Joe Phelps and hauled the forty-odd barrels from Round Hill back here to our property and placed them in the old stone cellar located below Alfonso's house.

The weather wasn't through with him yet. Thanks to a bone-chilling cold stretch in January, he couldn't coax his first-ever Cabernet through malolactic fermentation, a process that requires a certain amount of warmth. Finally, not knowing what else to do, he wrapped the barrels in electric blankets and parked space heaters all around, hoping to warm the barrels enough to create the right conditions for malolactic fermentation. Even so, it wasn't until April or May that he got the second fermentation. The whole enterprise seemed unlikely to deliver optimum results. (To this day Dad still refers to the '78 Cab as the "electric blanket vintage.") After that he had to do what every other winemaker has done for the last eight thousand years—wait and see.

TWELVE

Family Winery

Whether the 1978 Cabernet was a success or not, Dad was irreversibly on course to start a winery. While that first vintage was still in the barrel, the winery was christened—on paper at least. One day at U.C. Davis, I received in the mail the paperwork for our family's general partnership, which Dad had organized and outlined with his usual diligence. Under his plan, my brothers, my sister, Mom, and I would all be partners in this venture called "Shafer Vineyards." I remember reading through the documents with a sense of admiration for Dad's careful logic in laying it all out and for creating a way that all his kids could receive some financial benefit if things went well. And believe me, I wished him well. We all did. However at that point it didn't look like any of us was destined to work with him. My brother Bill was at Harvard doing graduate work in architecture. Libby was in San Francisco employed as a financial counselor at Wells Fargo. Brad was just starting college but was already looking in the direction of going into law. And while I had majored in viticulture, by the end of my four years I'd changed course and had decided to go into teaching. After my stint at Kornell Winery those two summers, I'd started working with kids—at a group home in Sacramento, then at a camp for developmentally disabled teens in Shasta County, among other things—and really felt a strong pull in that

direction. Looking back I realize a lot of youthful idealism and romanticism was involved, picturing my career in the classroom as a way to
change the world. By 1979 I was at Davis for one final year getting my
teaching credential.

I get some surprised looks these days when I mention this early career
direction. But it's important to remember that while I was now a partner
in Shafer Vineyards there wasn't much here that I could envision as a career. Mom and Dad had built their own house in 1974, which commanded
an inspiring view of the Stags Leap area, but everything else about Shafer
Vineyards looked much as it had when we had arrived in 1973. Dad was
renting out the little adobe house. There was no new winery yet. He
had just one vintage in barrels, which still hadn't finished fermenting.
Shafer Vineyards was little more than an idea dressed up with a bit of
optimism.

The other thing worth knowing is that John Shafer was not Frederick
Shafer, his father—Dad took no interest in dictating to any of us what our
majors should be in college, nor what we should do with our lives. He
simply wanted us to pursue things that we were passionate about, just as
he was pursuing his own dream. The truth is my dad and I did not bond
over grapes or vineyards or wine or any of that. When I came into early
adulthood, Dad and I found a great friendship over golf. I'd come home
from a break at Davis and he and I would head down to the Chimney
Rock Golf Course (now sadly gone). Certainly it was not a world-class
course, but I cannot begin to count the fun memories golfing there with
my dad, playing for a dime a hole. Eventually Brad got involved, and this
triggered a great decades-long rivalry in which "the trophy" has been a
silver bar (a little smaller than an iPhone)—now etched all over with
memorable phrases and comments—that we have traded back and forth
over the years as the golf gods have smiled on us or not.

By the summer of 1979, I'd been recruited to teach math at a junior
high in Tucson, Arizona—my mom's old hometown. To bide my time
and make some money before my first adult job, I worked as a tour guide
at Robert Mondavi Winery, which was a bit like being at the center of a

tornado. At a time when Napa Valley was the second most touristed place in California (just behind Disneyland) this was easily the most popular winery, certainly in terms of the sheer volume of visitors I saw that summer. The place was already iconic. Its summer concert series was a cultural hub of the Valley. Robert Mondavi himself was a charismatic figure and an old-school, big picture guy, who'd gotten in front of every microphone he could find since the 1940s to movingly extol the glories of Napa Valley and its wines.

I think one of his longest-lasting contributions to the success of the wine industry was that he helped promote the idea that wine is food and as such is a basic part of lunch and dinner. In my opinion, the reason this proved so pivotal is due to a deeply rooted split in the American mind. We're a nation shaped to a significant degree by Puritans and were later influenced by some heavy-duty religions that picked up where Puritanism left off, banning or frowning upon dancing, drinking, theater-going, and even fiction reading. From early on, some part of the U.S. character had been uncomfortable with the idea of pleasure for pleasure's sake, which is what wine represented. At the same time, we're also influenced by founders such as Thomas Jefferson and Benjamin Franklin who enjoyed an easy relationship with what the Puritans might call decadence, as well as by the spirit of the kinds of rugged, gun-toting, rough-riding free spirits who settled frontiers, for whom reckless pleasure, including large quantities of alcohol, was second nature. The era of Prohibition was the ultimate playing out of America's love/hate relationship with alcohol. The concept that Mondavi and others here promoted changed the nature of that debate. If people were persuaded to think of wine as part of a meal, a moderate glass or two with your steak and potatoes, then that removed the taint of seamy hedonism. It helped split it away from beer and liquor, which were consumed at frat parties and nightclubs, where moderation and connoisseurship didn't factor in. And yet it remained pleasurable, albeit more modestly so.

Mondavi was among the first to employ chefs at a winery and to bring in culinary guest stars, such Julia Child, Wolfgang Puck, Jeremiah

Tower, and Alice Waters, who would put together memorable wine and food combinations.

With time, a number of wineries, wine educators, writers such as M.F.K. Fisher, and chefs at the Culinary Institute of America in St. Helena would take this a step further by advocating the idea that specific pairings of wine and food further elevated your gustatory experience. This continued to broaden the acceptance of wine in this country, as it appealed to that part of the American psyche, which valued hard work and industry. To do food–wine pairing at home seemed to entail the reading of books, the securing of ingredients, and the memorization of piles of data. In short, you could turn your wine drinking into a project, making wine not just civilized but a good use of your time.

Of course, five miles from the Mondavi whirlwind, Dad was in a whole different universe. He wasn't trying to change the culture; he was simply trying to get his winery built, as were so many others at that time. Between 1977 and 1981 the number of wineries here soared from 51 to 110, according to historian Charles Sullivan.[1] It was a boom that hadn't been seen here since the late 1880s. New wineries debuting in this era included Far Niente, Whitehall Lane, Mumm Napa Valley, Flora Springs, and Opus One.

With precious little level land, Dad made his first foray into construction by carving a pad for the winery facility out of a hillside. Operating as his own general contractor, he hired a crew of carpenters with a good local reputation. These were men from a little town called Angwin, located high atop Howell Mountain. This is a predominantly Seventh-Day Adventist community, which means that our winery was built by devout teetotalers.

It's probably fortunate that the urge to establish the winery was based on the successes of the 1977 and 1978 harvests, because 1979 was a chal-

---

1. Charles L. Sullivan, *Napa Wine: A History from Mission Days to the Present*, 2nd ed. (San Francisco, CA: Wine Appreciation Guild, 2008), 322.

lenge. A great deal of heat descended on us when the grapes were ready to pick. Once again, Dad couldn't get a picking crew here when they were needed.

When he finally secured a crew, Alfonso and I also jumped in and helped pick grapes, and we were lucky to get them in before the rain—a nice bit of timing. Other vintners were not so fortunate, and as a result the vintage was not highly regarded.

While winery construction continued, Dad trucked our fruit to Rutherford Hill Winery, where winemaker Phil Baxter oversaw the crushing, fermenting, and, later, the bottling of that vintage. He'd done much the same for Joe Phelps a few years earlier when the Phelps winery was still under construction.

Phil was considered one of a new, young breed. He'd studied winemaking at Fresno State, graduating in 1969 along with Richard Arrowood of Chateau St. Jean, Joe Cafaro at Keenan, and Jerry Luper at Chateau Montelena. He'd started at Krug and then taken a job at Souverain Cellars. Pillsbury had purchased Souverain in 1972 but bailed in 1976, when the economic picture was pretty pitiless. Bill Jaeger and Chuck Carpy bought the property, renamed it Rutherford Hill, and kept Phil on as winemaker.

In spite of difficulties with the vintage, Phil did a great job with the wine. When it was released, our '79 Cabernet was ranked among the better wines of the year and won a gold medal at the Los Angeles County Fair.

By 1980 a lot of things were happening at once—the winery facility was nearing completion and that year's harvest was looming. Meanwhile Dad had two vintages of wine on the way. He knew we would be releasing the '78 Cabernet in the spring of 1981, which meant that by the last quarter of 1980 he would have to start the demanding task of selling a brand-new wine to a world that might or might not be interested. His plan was to focus first on breaking into the California market, then moving into New York, and finally, for personal reasons, getting our wines in the Chicago area.

All of this meant that Dad was now heading up vineyard operations, overseeing winemaking, acting as his own general contractor, and would soon be the national sales director. If he wasn't careful he'd soon find himself doing four jobs badly. With Alfonso able to take on more of the vineyard side and Mom dealing with day-to-day administration, Dad knew he needed a winemaker. And he found one—a promising young man, who was the assistant winemaker at Freemark Abbey, one of the Valley's more prestigious wineries at the time.

Winery construction finished just prior to the 1980 harvest and on September 17 Dad crushed his own fruit here for the first time. That inaugural load of grapes was Chardonnay from our Bench vineyard block. In spite of it being a muggy, overcast day, spirits here were high. Dad asked Father Tom Turnbull, an Episcopal priest, to bless the grapes—an annual tradition at a number of local wineries. It was a thrill for Dad to turn on his own crusher–destemmer for the first time and in the following days to inhale the fragrance of new wine in our own cellar.

And yes, for those with an eye for detail, we, like almost everyone else, did destem and crush Chardonnay just like we did red varietals. It would be one of many things we would rethink over the years.

THIRTEEN

Selling Wine

The 1980 growing season had been declared a great one—one of the best in a long time—in the media even before a single grape was picked. We had winter rain at the right time, steady temperatures throughout the summer, and then some heat when we needed it. So Dad knew the grapes were fine and he could check that off his list of things to worry about. We had a young, new winemaker who'd learned his craft at a celebrated winery. Check. The winery itself was built and we had 1,100-gallon oak ovals in which we aged our Chardonnay and 2,200-gallon oak uprights in which we aged some of our red wines, as well as a few stainless steel tanks for fermenting. We also had an actual barrel room, where the remainder of the reds would age in old American oak bourbon barrels. Check, check, and check. Dad felt like the vineyard and winemaking sides of the business were squared away.

He knew that by fall he had to go back into sales mode for the first time in many years; but this time, instead of selling textbooks for Scott Foresman, it would be wine from his own hillsides. Wanting to know how other wineries went about their sales efforts, he quizzed a number of people, prompting a memorable conversation with Joe Cafaro, at Robert Keenan. According to the story Dad tells, Joe described his sales approach as working like this: "I go to the winery, fix myself a cup of coffee, sit at my desk and wait for the phone to ring." Keenan was a hot new kid on the block that had quickly established itself on the map of winedom. Their phone was definitely ringing. Shafer's was not, and Dad knew that sitting at his desk was a can't-miss strategy for failure.

About this same time, Dad was contacted by a new wine marketing company in town called Wilson Daniels that was experiencing big growth riding the wave of the late '70s winery boom. Their offer was to manage all aspects of sales and marketing for a monthly fee. Dad knew that a lot of the new wineries were signing on for their services, but he turned them down, convinced that in spite of the added effort it would require of him, the winery would benefit in the long term from us making our own face-to-face contacts with customers and trade and creating and distributing our own marketing materials. He believed then, as now, that the operation of a winery is a three-cornered stool made up of vineyards, winemaking, and marketing. To outsource in any of those areas was to risk everything. Much of this strategy of course came from his experience in sales and marketing in the publishing world back in Chicago. Beyond that, he felt it was a simple fact of human nature that no one was going to be as motivated as he to get the winery off the ground.

He put together his sales plan, which meant initially going after California, New York, and Illinois. (To his disappointment Illinois did not take off as hoped. He eventually realized that all his friends back in Hinsdale would rather drink vodka than wine, no matter whose name was on the label.) He targeted California, because it was such a large market right here in our own backyard. Wine consumption rates were much higher here than in most other states, and consumers overwhelmingly favored California-made wines. Next he would focus on New York, because it was the hub of the media world. If you could establish a reputation there it had a built-in ripple effect, influencing hearts and minds throughout the country.

On one of his first sales trips he flew down to Los Angeles and in a single day he visited a dozen wine shops, taking with him just one bottle of the '78 Cabernet. At each stop he'd introduce himself to the owner, pull the cork, and pour a careful sample of the wine. He and the buyer would chat a bit and at the end of the day eleven of the twelve stores ordered a case or two of the wine. He was elated.

On my Christmas teaching break in 1980, I drove home from Tucson and learned of the reception Dad was getting with the wine, not only in Los Angeles, but in other California markets as well. It was great to try the 1978 Cabernet in its finished form. I hadn't tasted it since that day with the Round Hill cellar crew, and enjoying it again now with Mom and Dad confirmed the potential it had exhibited early on. Dad announced that after breaking into New York, he wanted to open up Texas and Colorado but he'd have to take things one market at a time.

I had an announcement of my own. I'd decided to quit teaching. I told Mom and Dad that I'd given it a decent shot; I loved the profession itself and enjoyed my time in the classroom. But I'd cooled pretty quickly to the politics of the school district, the school itself, and even the department in which I worked. Dealing with overbearing parents was no great treat either. Like many others, I'd been drawn to teaching by the romanticized idea that I could help change kids' lives and thus make some small difference in the world. But I sized up the situation pretty quickly and realized that if I stayed on as a teacher, it would have to be for far more realistic reasons.

Dad had spent time in teaching as well and understood all of this. When he asked what my plans were, I said I was going to come back to Napa Valley and put my viticulture degree to work. Once again I was feeling the call of blue jeans and pickup trucks.

"I already have a winemaker," Dad said. "I don't have a job for you."

"I don't want to work for you anyway," I laughed.

We both knew the situation. At the time of this Christmas conversation he'd still not released his first wine and the winery's future was nothing but uncertain.

My plans were to come back and work as someone's cellar rat, which was all I was really qualified for at the time. On top of that, there was little precedent in our family for going into business together. True, we had a general partnership, but for the moment that was simply a piece of paper with our signatures on it.

On my mom's side, I had some awareness of a family business story playing itself out. Her brother, William Small Jr., in Tucson, had inherited the newspaper, the *Tucson Citizen,* which his father (my grandfather) had bought during the Depression. When Uncle Bill heard that I was planning to leave Arizona to return to Napa, he called me up and said, "We need to talk." During my time in Tucson I'd gotten to know him and my Aunt Susan, as I'd go over to their house for dinner once or twice a month. Bill was awfully nice to a long-haired twenty-four-year-old whose main interests were sports and an active social life.

His message was that he wanted me to go into the family business with a clear idea of what could happen. And it was not a warm and inviting picture. His was a classic second-generation story. When Bill was in his forties, his father, William Sr., had handed him the reins of the newspaper, saying he was stepping aside and retiring. What that turned into was Bill getting unrelenting phone calls from his father, who would be looking through that day's paper, unhappy about this editorial or that headline or the cutline under a front-page photo. In addition to all the pressures of work during the day, Bill found himself the target of endless nightly harangues from the newspaper's former boss—his dad.

I told Uncle Bill that I wasn't returning to Napa Valley to work at Shafer Vineyards but he said, "It could happen. You need to go into it with your eyes open."

I appreciated him taking the time to do this. He was a sweet guy and he was looking out for me. While I did not find myself in his position, family businesses in general can be difficult ventures. Those that work well do so by design—with clear ground rules, a lot of thought, a willingness to compromise, and a sense of the big picture versus the gaffe of the moment.

By the end of the school year, I'd made contact with Randy Mason, who hired me to work at his new winery near Yountville called Lakespring. Technically my title was assistant winemaker, but in reality I was a cellar rat, pulling hoses, running pumps, spraying out fermentation tanks, and shoveling stems and pomace. It was winery boot camp, and I loved it. I learned more from Randy in my time at Lakespring than I could have imagined. It was an on-the-job, nonstop, move-your-tail-or-get-run-over kind of place.

Over at Shafer Vineyards, things were picking up too. As it turned out, the 1978 Cabernet was far from a disaster, in spite of bumping around the Valley on flatbed trucks and getting wrapped in electric blankets. Once it was released in May 1981, for a gutsy $11 a bottle, it won a prestigious taste-off at the San Francisco Vintners Club, placing it higher than some of the best wines of that era. Dad was on the road all the time now, getting placements in restaurants and retail shops. One writer even called Shafer "an instant success."

About that $11 price tag. Coming up with a suggested retail price for your wine is on one hand exceedingly easy and on the other can be a source of terrible second-guessing, third-guessing, and sleeplessness. First, if you'd like to stay in business, at the very least you have to cover your current costs—your picking crew, barrels, bottles, and labels. You have to put gas in your tractor and pay for the electricity that operates your well. You have to pay for airline tickets to Los Angeles and New York in order to sell your wine. You have to buy shoes to replace the ones you wore out schlepping your wine samples from one city to the next, and on and on.

Beyond that, you have to make a profit, because it costs money to counteract the Second Law of Thermodynamics, which states that left to themselves things tend to go from a state of order to a state of disorder (I'm paraphrasing). Left to their own devices, vineyards go into sprawl mode and don't produce good fruit, equipment wears out, trellis systems fall over, and your septic system backs up. Anything you've ever paid for will give out or go bad in the near future, so profit is essential. Entropy is expensive.

Beyond all of the tangibles comes the fuzzy math of perception. This is where the fretting and sleeplessness come into play. If you get greedy and put a ridiculously high price on your wine you risk a) not selling it, as well as b) a stormy, brand-damaging backlash from consumers, retailers, and media. Yes, your phone will ring, but not in the good way. If the price on your wine is too low, then you risk a situation in which the consumer standing in the wine aisle at the grocery store or retail shop will simply assume that it's of low quality. Your price is your confidence level. You're saying, "This is how much you will enjoy what's inside the bottle." If 80 or 90 percent of the people who drink the wine agree with your assessment (via the price) then you've hit the right spot. However, getting there, especially on your first release, is tough. For Dad it involved his gut, his business goals (i.e., the position he wished to occupy in the world of fine wine), and a quick check of what his competitors were doing. When we released our Cabernet for $11, Pine Ridge had just released their 1978 Cabernet for $7. Meanwhile Joseph Phelps put their 1977 Backus Cabernet on the market for $15, and Mondavi had released their 1976 Reserve Cabernet for $25. That was about the range, so you can see Dad didn't try to shoot for the moon, but he put us in a solid, justifiable position.

If you can ever say there was an official debut of the 1978 Cabernet it was the Napa Valley Vintners 1981 Wine Symposium held in late February at Silverado Resort. This was a first for the Vintners, and in some ways was probably a precursor to the current Premiere Napa Valley barrel auction also held at the end of February. It was a three-day event with seminars, tastings, luncheons at wineries, and dinners with keynote speakers. Rather than go big and bus in hundreds of people, they wisely kept the event to fewer than 130 key people in retail, restaurants, and hospitality. At a cost of over $700 per person, it wasn't cheap, but the vintners had done their homework, and the event was considered to be a success.

At one of the evening tastings, Mom and Dad arranged their bottles and glassware at a table covered in a white cloth, and for the first time found themselves in the position of pouring their own wine. Because Shafer was the new kid, all the big shots of winedom—members of the trade, wine writers, other vintners—were coming by to try Dad's first release. As the evening wore on, quite a number were coming back for a second and third taste, which didn't sit well with my mom. After she whispered in irritation to Dad that a particular customer was back for a third or fourth sample, Dad let her know that if people came back more than once, it was a good thing.

Besides simply coming back for more, many that evening engaged Dad in conversation on how well-developed, structured, and yet soft the Cabernet was, especially for its young age. The question that came up repeatedly was, "How much Merlot did you add?"

Dad would reply, "None." In response he'd receive a look of frank disbelief. Adding Merlot was standard practice—how else were you going to get a Cabernet that was drinkable on release? The truth was that he made it with 100 percent Cabernet because he didn't have any other Bordeaux varieties on hand at the time. There was some Zinfandel and Chardonnay on the property, but nothing he would have considered blending into his Cabernet. As the evening progressed, taster after taster kept prodding him about the Merlot percentage in the blend. He felt some real discomfort realizing that people actually thought he was lying.

One of them, a wine buyer named John Barclay of Scott's Seafood in San Francisco, was especially persistent. Returning a second or third time, he slipped behind the table, lowered his voice, and swore himself to secrecy if Dad would let him in on it: "How much Merlot did you blend?"

What Dad later came to believe was that the buyers were identifying the most prominent attribute of Cabernet Sauvignon grown in the Stags Leap District: silky, supple, velvety tannins that don't require softening with the addition of another varietal such as Merlot.

It was that character, so clearly identified in his mind with this region, that would prompt Dad four years later to head up a committee of neighboring growers and vintners in petitioning the government to designate this region with the Stags Leap District appellation.

FOURTEEN

Libby

In the late 1970s my sister Libby was a financial analyst in San Francisco. Dad called her one day and said, "Now that we've got all this wine, someone's going to have to sell it."

She agreed to come to Dad's shaky new enterprise to help with sales and work with Mom on the winery's administrative side. To immerse herself in this industry, she took a job as a tour guide at Beringer, where she worked for a year meeting wine consumers of every imaginable stripe. Concurrently, she worked at our winery two days a week.

As the winery expanded its sales reach, Dad started to bump up against shipping regulations, compliance issues, the art of staying on distributors' radar screens, and keeping government inspectors happy—they were really swimming in it. Dad suggested to Libby that she get an administrative job at a small winery like ours and see how they handle a lot of these things.

She secured a position at Robert Keenan Winery on Spring Mountain, where she learned a great deal. Between this and getting some good accounting help, the winery got more on track. Over time Libby began to show more promise in the area of sales, although her approach for securing placements could be unorthodox.

When she came to work in the Valley, my sister was single, in her late twenties, and enjoyed meeting people and getting out and about. On at least one occasion, her social life proved beneficial to the winery.

At one point she was going out with three different guys—a pretty deft juggling act. One was the Valley's most sought-after artisan brick-layer, another was the scion of a family attached to a candy fortune, and the third was the tennis pro at Silverado Resort, a fellow named Giuseppe.

During their acquaintance, Giuseppe wrote to his brother Giorgio back in Sicily and said, "If you can get over here, I can get you a job." Before you knew it, Giorgio was living in the Valley and had a job as a waiter at Silverado Resort.

One day David Stevens, director of the prestigious Masters of Wine program in London, visited the resort for dinner and Giorgio was his waiter. Stevens ordered a particular bottle of wine to accompany his meal, and Giorgio said, "No, no, no. You want Shafer's 1978 Cabernet."

Stevens said, "Who is Shafer?"

Giorgio insisted that he order our wine, and apparently they went back and forth until Stevens relented and said, "All right, but it's on your head."

The outcome was that Stevens loved the wine, and he took the time to visit us. We brokered a deal to get some of our 1979 Cabernet to him in London, where the wine was placed in the Savoy Hotel as well as other outlets.

Libby loved reminding my dad of this: "You know who's really responsible for getting our wine into the Savoy Hotel—it was all me, Dad!"

FIFTEEN

New York

While California was welcoming our first wine and our initial foray into London came as something of a lark, New York was another matter. Getting restaurant buyers and retail shop owners in Manhattan to pay attention to Shafer proved difficult. The East Coast wine establishment was still much more oriented toward Old World wines, specifically those of Burgundy and Bordeaux. Wine-buying habits ingrained over a couple of centuries had hardly been erased in the four years since the Judgment of Paris. The second thing that worked against us was that the only New York distributor that would have us was a company that primarily sold pharmaceuticals and secondarily represented California wine (a peculiar hybrid you'd never find today). Within a year Dad and every other West Coast winery in its portfolio received a letter that said we were all being dumped. The company was getting out of the wine business and, given that, you could assume that our wines had not been actively represented. (The second distributor we signed on with went bankrupt within a year. Strike two.) The third thing that Dad realized pretty quickly was that nearly every California winery came to New York hawking a Cabernet and a Chardonnay, placing us in a tight spot in terms of differentiating the name "Shafer" from the hundred other brands that had emerged in the past three or four years. How many California Cabernets and Chardonnays would consumers buy? And this was the reason that Dad was more receptive than I expected to an out-of-the-blue idea of mine.

SIXTEEN

Chain Saws

Randy Mason had been vineyard manager at Chappellet from 1973 through 1979 and was hired away by the Battat brothers (Harry, Frank, and Ralph) to start Lakespring. Their first harvest was 1980, so when I came on in the summer of '81, Lakespring was still a new operation. In the cellar I was working with Cabernet and Chardonnay, as well as Merlot, a grape that was new to me.

Before 1980 only a few Napa Valley wineries produced a Merlot. The two I can recall were Louis Martini, who unveiled the first wine bearing the Merlot label in 1973 or so, joined not long after by Sterling, where winemaker Ric Forman was an early Merlot proponent. Both were produced on the lighter side of the spectrum, and I think they were good, but for whatever reason the wines didn't make a big splash. Of course this was a grape that had been a part of the blend in Bordeaux for centuries, and here in California it was grown widely, but it was thought of similarly, as merely a blender, meaning it was grown to be blended in varying percentages with Cabernet Sauvignon. The whole approach to Cab then—when it was picked and how it was produced—meant it could have a tannic edge like a hacksaw. Blending in some Merlot was crucial to making the wine softer and more enjoyable.

The first Napa Valley Merlot that made people pay attention came out in 1980. It was Duckhorn Vineyards' inaugural wine, a 1978 Merlot produced predominantly with fruit sourced from Three Palms Vineyard just outside of Calistoga. This is a vineyard where Sterling had sourced some of its Merlot fruit in the early '70s, but Dan and Margaret Duckhorn took the varietal in a different direction. Working with their winemaker, Tom Rinaldi (today with Provenance), they blended it with 15 percent Cabernet for some backbone, which they had sourced from a Howell Mountain vineyard and some from our Stags Leap neighbor Dick Steltzner.[1] They aged it in 100 percent new French oak, and it was a beautiful wine—blew everyone away. For the first time, it looked like Cab's sidekick could not only stand on its own but also had a shot at grabbing the attention of the fine wine market here in the United States.

After trying the Merlot we were working on at Lakespring, I became a zealous convert. When you do it right, Merlot is a gorgeous, delightful, sensual wine. Just ask all those collectors who're shelling out the price of a new car for a case of Château Petrus. When I visited Mom and Dad, I started talking about Merlot and, frankly, started bugging Dad to get with it and plant some. I was aware that some of our neighbors had already taken steps along this line: Carl Doumani at Stags' Leap Winery had released a 1977 Merlot. Clos du Val, Rutherford Hill, and others were releasing '78 Merlots.

Dad was making the transition from thinking like a grape grower to thinking like a vintner. You could see the physical manifestation of this on the hillside. In the early to mid-1970s, even though he was a grower, he dreamed of one day making a world-class wine, which is why he

1. Margaret and Dan Duckhorn, "Mostly Merlot: The History of Duckhorn Vineyards," an oral history conducted in 1996 by Carole Hicke, The Wine Spectator California Winemen Oral History Series, Regents of the University of California, accessed July 22, 2011, www.archive.org/stream/mostlymerlotduckoohornrich/mostlymerlotduckoohornrich_djvu.txt.

planted his first south-facing hillside block, John's Folly, to Cabernet Sauvignon. However, wearing his grape grower's hat, when he and Alfonso had planted the vineyard blocks we called Upper and Lower Sunspot on the hillside, he'd budded to Zinfandel for purely financial reasons. Zin was a popular variety with a track record for producing big, heavy clusters that translated handily into dollars-per-ton.

Now he was taking a vintners' perspective. We were in the business of selling wine rather than selling grapes. One of the thoughts still rolling around in his head was this realization that every Napa winery owner was heading to Manhattan with a bottle of Cabernet in one hand and a bottle of Chardonnay in the other. What would happen if you showed up with something new? Such as a bottle of Merlot?

Mind you, Merlot was no slam dunk. Wineries were trying any number of different varietals out to see which would capture the public's attention. It was an era when for all we knew Johannesburg Riesling or Napa Gamay was going to be the next big thing. Get ten winemakers in a room on this topic and you'd get fifteen different opinions.

As far as consumers were concerned, white wines were king. No matter how much Napa vintners and winemakers loved Cabernet Sauvignon and gloried in its many virtues, the United States was buying two bottles of white for every bottle of red.

If Dad had gone strictly by the trends in the marketplace, he'd never have planted Cabernet and he surely wouldn't have bothered with something as untested as Merlot. He would have poured his efforts into whites. But often the key to success in the wine business is to think past the current cycle and take a gamble on what consumers are going to latch onto five years down the road. Many small wine producers will play this game of roulette simply by planting what they like, what appeals to them personally, and then work at winning people over. Sometimes this strategy works well. Sometimes it shuts you down.

As Dad mulled over these prospects, his pragmatic nature reasoned that we could always sell any Merlot fruit we planted or use it in blending if it didn't pan out as a varietal bottling.

Initially he was talking about just planting a little bit. A few rows here and there, playing it safe. I didn't think he should play it safe at all, but instead take a running jump at producing a Shafer Merlot. (Easy for me to say, right?)

Over the course of a few weeks, as we continued talking about this, Dad started eyeing a 3-acre block that he'd planted to Zinfandel in the mid-1970s. If he were going to take a gamble on planting to Merlot, a parcel of that size would do it.

Back in his corporate days, decisions like this would have required months of intensive research, pricey consultants, and endless memos and subcommittee meetings. In the case of nascent Shafer Vineyards, it required just two steps. The first was finding the right Merlot budwood to graft onto the old vines, and the second was simply working up the nerve to cut all those income-producing Zinfandel vines down to their trunks.

The first step turned out to be exceedingly simple. Sloan Upton, who owned Three Palms Vineyard, was a good friend and when Dad asked if he could get some Merlot budwood, he said that'd be fine. So Dad drove north on Silverado Trail up to the vineyard and as luck would have it, they'd just pruned. He simply walked through the vine rows and collected a few bundles of canes that were lying on the ground.

The second step involved a couple of deep breaths. And chain saws.

On a chilly February morning in 1982, a crew of guys stood around gunning their chainsaw engines next to those Zinfandel vines. They waited for Dad's signal.

Above the noise Dad shouted to me, "Are we really going to do this?" I just smiled and nodded.

Dad laughed, "Do you know how long a decision like this would've taken at my old job?"

He gave the high five sign and within moments the vineyard block was filled with the smell of chainsaw smoke and newly cut wood. Afterward his crew grafted the Three Palms Merlot onto the Zinfandel trunks using a process called T-budding. This way we were grafting the Merlot onto an already developed trunk and root system. While there would be no fruit that year, if all went well, Dad had the chance of harvesting a light crop eighteen months later in the fall of 1983.[2]

2. When Dad budded those vines to Merlot, there were 660 acres of that variety in production in Napa Valley (Stephen J. Bardessono, Agricultural Commissioner, *1981 Napa County Agricultural Crop Report*, Napa County Department of Agriculture, Napa, CA, 1982, accessed July 8, 2011, www.countyofnapa.org/AgCommissioner/CropReport).

Within ten years that acreage was over 1,700 (Stephen J. Bardessono, Agricultural Commissioner, *1991 Napa County Agricultural Crop Report*, Napa County Department of Agriculture, Napa, CA, 1992, accessed July 8, 2011, www.countyofnapa.org/AgCommissioner/CropReport).

In 2005 Merlot hit a peak of more than 7,000 (David R. Whitmer, Agricultural Commissioner, *2005 Napa County Agricultural Crop Report*, Napa County Department of Agriculture, Napa, CA, 2006, accessed July 8, 2011, www.countyofnapa.org/AgCommissioner/CropReport).

SEVENTEEN

Napa Vintners

With his first wine officially released, Dad had signed on to join the Napa Valley Vintners Association, which was on the verge of a new project then called the Napa Valley Wine Auction.

The inception of the Napa Valley Vintners took place in the spring of 1943, when Louis M. Martini invited fellow winery owners John Daniel Jr. (Inglenook), Charles Forni (Napa Valley Cooperative Winery), and Louis Stralla (Napa Wine Company) to an informal outdoor lunch in the Monte Rosso Vineyard. They must have had a good time sharing wine and talking about the wine business, because it became a regular thing with this group. A little over a year later, in October 1944, these vintners drew up an Agreement of Association and named the new organization the Napa Valley Vintners. Shortly thereafter, the original founders invited other vintners to join them: Georges de Latour, Robert Mondavi, Elmer Salmina, Charlie Beringer, and Roy Raymond.[1]

They got to work promoting Napa. Records show that by 1948 the Napa Valley Vintners were welcoming visitors here by sponsoring

---

1. Napa Valley Vintners, History and Time Line, accessed July 18, 2011, www.napavintners.com/about/ab_2_overview.aspx.

splashy promotional activities that showcased the wines and the beauty of the place. For example, seven hundred Harvard University graduates were hosted by the vintners in 1949, and two thousand guests from General Electric enjoyed a Western-style barbecue with local wines at the Napa County Fairgrounds in 1952. I suspect the Napa Valley Vintners were involved in helping to secure funding for the production of the 1959 film *This Earth Is Mine*, which was shot throughout the Valley—an early example of product placement. The film starred Rock Hudson, who had been one year behind Dad in high school, when he was a kid named Roy Fitzgerald.

The first rumbling of the Napa Valley Wine Auction started in 1979 as an idea created by Robert Mondavi, Margrit Biever (who married Mondavi in 1980), and San Francisco writer and socialite Pat Montandon.[2] Based on a distinguished, century-old auction in Burgundy that benefits Hospices de Beaune, the initial plan was that Napa Vintner wineries would donate wines for this new event, and the proceeds would be donated to the two local hospitals—St. Helena Hospital and Queen of the Valley Hospital in Napa.

The concept was presented to the Vintners, who further refined it; jobs were handed out via subcommittees and so on. Forty-four wineries are listed in the 1981 auction catalogue, among them names you'd certainly recognize, such as Silver Oak, Stony Hill, Markham, and Cuvaison. There were also a few names that have since disappeared, such as Cassayre-Forni, today the site of Swanson Vineyards, and Charles F. Shaw, now the reigning monarch of the value wines known as "Two Buck Chuck," a brand name in the portfolio of brands owned by Fred Franzia. At the time, Shaw was a Napa Valley up-and-comer, whose Napa Gamay did well at the auction.

Because we'd just joined the association, the Shafer lot of one case of 1978 Cabernet Sauvignon was listed not in the main catalogue section but as a "Private Donation."

2. *Napa Valley Wine Auction Catalogue* (St. Helena, CA: Napa Valley Vintners, 1981).

The planning and publicity worked—260 bidders from across the country paid $100 each for bidding paddles. The members of the Vintners Association, along with private donors, offered a whopping 504 lots.

The auctioneer was Michael Broadbent of the redoubtable London auction house then called Christie, Manson & Woods. In his opening remarks, Broadbent set the tone for the day, saying with a smile to the gathered bidders, "If you can't afford a barrel, you shouldn't be here."

Fortunately, they came ready to open their wallets. Lot 1 was a bottle of 1937 Beringer Vineyards Cabernet Sauvignon, which was snapped up for $400 by a young man named Marvin Shanken, who'd recently taken charge of the publication, *Wine Spectator.* The prices that followed continued to amaze. A jeroboam of Chappellet's 1969 Cab went for $6,000. A barrel of Mondavi's 1980 Special Selection Cabernet sold for $9,200. We were thrilled when Broadbent's gavel came down at $600 for a case of our 1978 Cabernet. This represented $50 per bottle for a wine we had released a month earlier for $11.

Broadbent kept the bidding moving swiftly and good-naturedly despite the blistering heat—those who were watching the mercury say it reached 107 degrees. As the auction continued, he first removed his coat, then his tie, and eventually his shoes.[3]

The headline-making moment of the day came with Lot 339, a case of wine curiously named "NapaMedoc." This was the placeholder name Robert Mondavi and the Baron Philippe de Rothschild had given their still-new joint venture, which eventually became Opus One. A number of paddle holders had come to the auction for the sole purpose of being the day's winning bidder on this case of Old-World-meets-New-World 1979 Cabernet made, according to the auction catalogue, "under the direction of Tim Mondavi and Baron Philippe's winemaker, Lucien Sionneau." No one had tasted the wine, but it had buzz on its side, being the first of its kind—a collaboration between a French first-growth family

3. Gerald D. Boyd, "Napa's Auction Has a Smashing Debut," *Wine Spectator,* July 31, 1981, 1.

and one of America's most prominent wine families. The bidding was among the most intense of the day. Several bidders, including Mel Dick of Southern Wine & Spirits, were intent on taking home this historic prize.

In the end it was New York wine merchant Charles Mara who paid $24,000, breaking the record for the amount anyone had ever paid for a case of California wine ($2,000 per bottle).

In spite of the high temperatures of the day, the auction was considered a major success, bringing in a total of $324,142. Later that year the Hospices de Beaune Auction, the model for our event, totaled $1.1 million. We clearly had a long way to go before reaching that kind of benchmark.

EIGHTEEN

Arson

On the Monday morning after the success of that first auction, Napa Valley woke up to yet another day of blasting heat. I drove over to Lakespring and walked into work and the first thing Randy said was, "It's fire weather."

Altogether we'd had eight or ten days of unrelenting 100-degree temperatures, along with constant, strong north winds and low humidity. It was like taking a giant blow-dryer to the already parched grass and underbrush that covered the eastern slopes of the Vaca Mountains where Shafer Vineyards and other wineries and homes were nestled.

At lunchtime Randy and I went outside to eat and, sure enough, to the north on the Vaca side of the Valley, we saw a slender column of smoke. By the time we'd finished our break, the smoke had grown thicker and darker, and it was moving south, pushed by the unremitting winds. In the distance we heard sirens.

By 2 P.M. the smoke was massive, and Randy said to me, "You should go home and see if everything's okay."

When I got back to the winery, I drove up to Mom and Dad's house, where it was clear this wasn't going well. Smoke and silken ash were heavy in the air, blown at us from the north in advance of the fire.

We later learned that an arsonist had dropped five homemade incendiary devices at points along Silverado Trail and another five on Soda Canyon Road. These two roads hug the foothills of the Vaca Mountains, where the native grasses were as ready to burn as confetti. The fire quickly spread and grew to monstrous proportions—a roaring twelve-mile wall of flame—blocking the sun with churning smoke and filling the air for miles with a rain of char and particulates.

Within hours it destroyed Demptos Cooperage and more than fifty homes at Silverado Resort. It would also threaten nearly every winery on our side of Silverado Trail—Altamura Winery (today the site of Darioush), Signorello, Clos du Val, and Stag's Leap Wine Cellars among them. On our side of the Valley, there was such a massive column of smoke you'd almost think we'd been hit by an atomic bomb.

About two hours before the fire reached us, we thought we were saved when a forestry official drove up in a fire engine.

"What're you doing here?" he asked us, surprised to find anyone. "You need to grab what you can and clear out. This house is going to go."

They didn't have enough firefighting equipment to help us, he said, and flew off down our drive.

We didn't know what to do. Abandoning the house seemed wrong. But what? We had a garden hose and started soaking the ground around the house as well as the roof.

When Dad built the house on a hill overlooking the winery, he realized he should plan for potential grass fires. Fortunately he had taken a couple of measures against this possibility. One was to build it with a stucco exterior and a tile roof. The other was to position a twelve-thousand-gallon water tank up the hill, so he could take advantage of gravity flow in case of a power outage during a wildfire. So we had plenty of water to work with but had no idea if we could actually save the place.

I think it hit my mom hardest. The thought of losing the house was traumatizing. She and my brother Bill, an architect, had first sketched out the design for my parents' home on a napkin over dinner. Add to that the potential loss of irreplaceable photos and the prospect of heir-

A massive wildfire in June 1981 threatened to destroy the Shafer home and winery.

looms turned to char. If we had to abandon the house, we'd only get the chance to take a few precious things with us. Everything else would be destroyed.

Then something completely unexpected happened, truly a miracle. A guy named John Lloyd drove up in his old pickup. John owned the Phillips 66 gas station in Yountville, which he ran with his sons. He jumped out of his truck with two flares in his hands.

"You want to save your house?" he hollered to my dad.

"Of course," Dad said.

"Well come on." Lloyd led us down the western slope below the house. "We've got to light some backfires," he said, igniting the flares.

"Isn't that illegal?" I blurted.

John Lloyd turned and gave me a classic look of what-kind-of-city-boy-jackass-are-you?

"Just grab a hose," he said.

Lloyd started fires in a ring around the house, while I soaked the areas directly adjacent to the structure and in this way we burned a wide, protective space all around.

The smoke blowing from the north grew thicker, darker and hotter. At last the flames came thundering at us, climbing up the gorge just to the north of Mom and Dad's house. Trees were exploding in the heat.

Thanks to John Lloyd's backfires, the flames came to within about fifty feet of the house and then, running out of fuel, circled around in a wide arc on both sides. Cinders carried by the wind landed near the winery and lit up dry brush between our irrigation pond and the crush pad below, causing some panic. But those flames quickly burned themselves out, running into the cement of the crush pad in one direction and our vineyards in the other. Fortunately the rest of the winery, Alfonso's house, and the old adobe house were protected by our vineyards, which had been irrigated and were in full leaf. In addition, back then there was no grass or underbrush between the vine rows (as we have today), so with only bare earth and green foliage to choose from there wasn't anything for the fire to consume. The conflagration continued its ferocious way south toward Stags' Leap Winery.

It was a bizarre scene. Wildlife everywhere trying to escape the heat and the flames. Rattlesnakes were all over the road. We saw deer, wild turkey, jackrabbits, quail—all the creatures that call these hills home— in full flight. It was both tragic and very eerie in the deep copper-orange light of the dying day.

Even eerier was watching the fire's progress after the sun went down. All night long you could see the blaze continue south and to the east, where it was moving toward Pritchard Hill in the direction of Chappellet and Long Vineyard. We stayed up until dawn, keeping watch on the house and the winery, afraid that stray flying embers or hot spots we thought were dead would spark to life.

The next morning Mom stood at the edge of their hill looking south. In the smoky early light of day, as far as she could see down the Valley, there were only two colors—black and green... black, where everything had been burned away, and green, where vineyards stood. Just below her, on the knoll, the ground was blackened where we'd set the backfires. And then farther below were our gloriously green late-June vines.

For a long time Mom had been much less enthusiastic about jumping full force into the wine business. She'd come out to Napa with the idea of something more along the lines of semi-retirement—raise some grapes, enjoy a new home, play golf three times a week, spend time with family and new friends. Dad, meanwhile, had fallen hard for life as a grape grower and then as a vintner. He wanted to plant as much of the property as possible and ramp up production. He loved every aspect of this business. And this caused a number of disagreements and compromises between them. She'd put the brakes on further planting, and he'd reluctantly agreed.

But looking at that patchwork of black and green stretching into the distance, she realized that vineyards provided a safe, natural firebreak. She went back to the house and told Dad she thought they should plant the area around the house as soon as possible.

When it was all over, the firestorm had burned 23,000 acres in Napa County, consuming some sixty-five structures, livestock, pets, game, timberland, and brush. The damage totaled more than $35 million, and the arsonist was never caught.[1]

A couple of days after the fire, our winemaker suggested to Dad that when they planted the knoll to protect the house, he should name that hillside vineyard block "Firebreak." And that's been its name ever since.

---

1. Marsha Dorgan and David Ryan, "Fire on the Mountain," *Napa Valley Register* June 22, 2006, accessed July 14, 2011, http://napavalleyregister.com/news/local/article_91228a84-916f-5cf9-9172-4ba3954dcoed.html.

NINETEEN

Trouble

After the harvest of 1982 Dad called me up and asked if I wanted to play a round of golf at Chimney Rock. I met him a day or so later, and I could tell something was wrong. A couple of holes in, he finally told me that there were problems in the cellar. The 1978 and 1979 Cabernet Sauvignons had been very well received by consumers and the wine trade. The *Wine Spectator*, which did not score wine in that era, had nonetheless listed them among noteworthy new releases and listed both among a handful of "Recommended" wines. At the time the *Spectator* was more like a semi-monthly, tabloid-style newspaper, with just one page dedicated to a listing of new releases.

The canary in the coal mine was the 1980 Cabernet, which was crushed and produced at our own facility with our own winemaker. It was a lesser wine. Dad had chalked that up to difficulties with the vintage. Even more than today, winemakers were at the mercy of the climate, because they knew less about how to react to the curveballs Mother Nature threw, such as unexpected frost, heat, rain, and humidity. (By the time our 1980 Cabernet was released, *Wine Spectator* was then handing out scores and awarded it a disappointing 73.)

More and more often Dad's winemaker was showing up late for work or he'd disappear for hours in the middle of the day for no good reason.

Ultimately the increasing unreliability and the shaky work ethic were symptoms of a deeper issue. Dad eventually realized that his wine-maker had a serious drinking problem. Dad sat him down and offered to stand by him if he'd get help, go to Alcoholics Anonymous, and get cleaned up.

Dad really liked his young winemaker. We all did. Looking back I think the guy was a tortured soul. He'd been a medic in Vietnam during the war, and I think he'd come back having been tested and traumatized in ways we had not fully appreciated. And you know what? It could have been me. When I turned eighteen in 1974, I had registered for the draft and received a letter from the draft board letting me know that I had a very, very low number, which meant that I was going to be called up soon. I was nervous. By that time there were no doubts about the horrors faced by grunts in the Vietnam War—night after night on the evening news in black-and-white footage we'd all seen the ravages of the conflict. Fortunately, my draft number came up during the winding down of the war, and I wasn't called up. But if the timing had been a little different, even by a few months, the story of my own life could have been very different.

None of this was lost on my parents. If anyone had a soft spot in his heart for veterans, it was my dad. But when Dad made his offer of sup-port, the winemaker turned him down. Said he wasn't interested. What else could Dad do? He had to let the guy go, which was gut-wrenching.

Standing out there on the golf course I could see that Dad was deeply concerned. I knew what was coming next and mentally prepared my response.

"I'd like you to come be our winemaker," Dad said.

"Not a good idea," I said. "I'm not ready. You need someone who's got experience. A Phil Baxter, a Randy Mason."

Every day at Lakespring I watched Randy, whom I liked and respected tremendously (still do), and who had ten years on me in the wine busi-ness. The knowledge Randy carried around in his head, the issues he dealt with, and the chaos he managed boggled the mind. The more I learned, the more I knew I didn't know. In a way it mirrored Dad's experience when he'd come out here in '73 thinking he'd plow right into building a winery. The reality of the business had spun him around—rightly so—the complexity, the cost, and the risks.

No, if Dad's winery was wounded, I did not want to be the guy who came in and finished it off—which is surely what I'd do out of simple inexperience.

Dad of course had a counter to this. "Doug, it's a small valley," he reasoned. "Who am I going to hire? Anyone I interview for a winemaking position will know that I've got a son waiting in the wings. Anyone with half a brain will know we're not talking about a long-term proposition."

Over the next few weeks he persisted, asking me a couple more times. I just as persistently refused. Finally at Christmas, he wouldn't let it go. I didn't want to see my dad high-and-dry, which is how he felt. At the same time, I knew I wasn't ready. I wasn't the right guy. And I didn't want to walk into a situation in which the failure of the winery would ultimately rest on my shoulders.

"We'll hire a winemaking consultant," Dad said. "And we'll get an assistant winemaker."

Long pause. I shook my head, feeling more checkmated than anything else. "All right," I said.

TWENTY

January 1983

Almost ten years to the day that our family had first driven onto this property, I walked into the cellar as winemaker. It should have been a great day, a reason for celebration, but I was knotted up inside. Something wasn't right.

I looked around the interior of the cellar. The ceiling was about forty feet high to accommodate the series of fermentation tanks. I looked at the 1,100-gallon German oak ovals that even then were beginning to fall out of favor in the winemaking world, as were our 2,200-gallon oak uprights. We also had a few stainless steel tanks for fermentation and racking, which had become standard equipment in the Valley by this time. So it was a mix of new and old.

I'd seen the cellar before, of course. But now it was mine to run, which was not comforting. In a weird way it reminded me of something that had happened on our move out to California a decade previously. Dad, my brother Brad, and I had made it through two or three days of snowstorms in the Midwest and arrived in Reno, Nevada, where it was finally sunny and clear. Dad decided that he wanted to teach Brad and me a life lesson about gambling, so, even though we were underage, he gave us each twenty bucks and told us to play the slots until the money ran out.

"You go in knowing how much you can afford to lose and when it's gone, you walk away," he told us. Only the lesson hadn't worked as Dad planned. After stuffing a few quarters into a slot machine I hit a jackpot. Not thousands or millions, but a lot. The machine lit up and started ringing like a fire truck and quarters were gushing out. At that moment I realized some security guards were moving across the casino floor in my direction and I started stuffing quarters into my pockets like mad. Dad, my brother, and I beat it for the door and made it out and had a pretty good laugh about it once our heart rates slowed down.

Now here I was, ten years later, standing in this cellar. And it was like Dad had turned me loose in the casino. I felt underage. My gut told me I shouldn't be there. But this time, there wasn't anybody there to throw me out.

As I walked by the tanks I realized that something didn't smell right. Literally. I climbed a metal staircase and made my way along a catwalk that allowed me to open the round door at the top of one of the stainless steel tanks. My first shock was that this 1982 Cabernet should have been put into barrels months ago. Worse still, it was sitting in a partially filled tank, a terrible bit of neglect, since this invites oxidation and multiple kinds of spoilage.

The wine should have smelled like cassis and blackberry, but instead it had a funky, musty smell. Even though the interior of the tank was dark, something looked strange—the color and the texture of the surface looked uneven. I pulled a flashlight out of my jacket and shone the beam around inside, playing it across the top of the liquid. It took a moment for my eyes to focus, but even longer for my mind to come to terms with what I was seeing. I was stunned to realize that in the beam of my flashlight I was seeing two inches of mold floating on top of the Cabernet. Nothing in my background had prepared me for anything like this. I didn't even know mold could grow in such an environment. I closed the door on the tank and checked the others. They all had mold.

Everything about the cellar showed signs of neglect. The floors hadn't been washed. There was mildew on the catwalks. The insides of the tanks were stained and filthy with leftovers from harvest, several months previous. The lab was in disarray. Equipment was broken and lying around, needing to be repaired or replaced. Rule one of any cellar is keep it clean—sterilize your bottling equipment, hoses, tanks, floors, and pumps. Be obsessive about it. A dirty cellar makes dirty wines—and I'd never seen a cellar in such a state.

The next weeks were hellish. One of the chief problems was that all the wines, and therefore the cellar itself, was shot through with *Brettanomyces* (often simply called "Brett"). It is considered spoilage yeast, which at high levels can give a pungent, cheese-like, mousy, barnyard-like, manurial, or even metallic character to the wine. At very low levels it can impart complexity to a wine's aromas and flavors that has a consumer fan base. In some French wines it's considered part of the traditional flavor profile. On the other hand, some consumers and critics simply consider the presence of any level of Brett a defect. So there's always debate whether it's a good thing or a bad thing. There was no room for debate in this case. It was dreadful. And rooting it out required weeks of intensive labor.

First I racked all the '82 Cabernet out of the filthy tanks, leaving all the nasty stuff behind, got the wine into barrels, and sulfured it to stabilize it, meaning that at that point I'd stopped any further growth of Brett.

Then I cleaned out those large oak uprights and ovals, whose interiors were caked in tartrates, which are white crystals that form as part of the winemaking process. It's the basis of cream of tartar in your spice rack. Using hand sanders, Alfonso and a couple of guys and I ground through layers of tartrates to get down to the wood. It's nearly impossible to truly clean wood, since it's so porous, but I thought that if we could sand off a layer of wood inside the tanks, we'd be in better shape. For hour after hot, cramped hour the crew and I were holed up in those wooden tanks, first breathing tartaric dust and then fine wood particles. We had to be careful not to create any sparks, because that kind of wood dust can be explosive.

We relentlessly racked the wine from barrel to barrel. We sterile-filtered and did everything possible to clarify and clean up the wine. As we racked we systematically sanitized the barrels as we emptied them, again working to kill off as much Brett as possible.

One of the real nightmare jobs was cleaning the insides of our stainless steel tanks. Those partially filled tanks were the worst, because wine and grape skins and crud had dried on for the past six months. To get to the ceiling of the tank I had to wiggle a twelve-foot stepladder inside and get it stable—which was nearly impossible because the floor of the tank is convex. Then for hours I'd have to scrub. Imagine the worst oven pan in your kitchen—the one that's got a couple layers of old baked-on soot. You know how tough it is to stand there at the sink and bear down on that thing with a scrubbing pad until it slowly starts to come clean. Imagine now that pan is twenty-five times that size and it's above you. You have to stand on an unstable ladder, scrubbing at arm's length, with bleach running down your arms and dripping into your face. All day. I remember once it was 7:30 in the evening and I'd been scrubbing this tank for hours. I was exhausted. My skin was burning from the bleach. My arms felt like they were going to fall off and I just wanted to cry. In fact, I may have, I can't remember. Those weeks are all a blur.

Finally though, with the help of Alfonso and some of our vineyard crew, we'd bleached the cellar from floor to ceiling. And I could officially declare it clean.

In addition to managing the crisis-level kinds of issues, I still had to deal with the normal insanity of running a cellar. Every day I was showing up at 5:30 A.M., firm in the knowledge that I had twelve to fourteen hours ahead of me. One thing that contributed to the long hours was the fact that I'd hired a cellar rat who took more interest in his night life than in showing up for work in the morning.

The job facing me next was racking, filtering, and bottling the 1981 Cabernet. I tasted the wine several times with our winemaking consultant. He said the wine seemed fine. It seemed fine to me, so we got it out of barrels and into bottles.

Unfortunately, six months down the road we tasted the wine again and it wasn't doing well. It wasn't an abomination, but because I'd had to filter it so heavily, and probably because of the vintage and the kinds of fruit that had gone into it, it tasted like a cheap red wine. One of those one-note, thin wines that should be sold for $2.50 a bottle rather than the $11 of previous vintages.

Dad wrestled with what to do. As someone whose orientation had always been long-term, he knew that if he released a poor wine after an initial good showing, he'd burn through all the goodwill and brand-building he'd been working at like a madman. Everything could go down the drain, because as a winery in its youth—with almost no track record and only fragile customer loyalty—you're only as good as your last release.

On the other hand, if he couldn't sell an entire vintage of Cabernet, he risked a financial beating the winery might not survive. The timing could not be worse. Things in the wine marketplace had taken a hit. Because of the strength of the dollar, wines from Europe were getting cheaper and thus more attractive to consumers. Especially on the East Coast, sales of wine from California had slowed way down, reversing a growth trend of nearly a decade. In some markets Dad felt like he was working twice as hard to sell half as much.

It added up to a grim picture, but he fairly quickly made a decision— we would not release the '81 Cabernet under the Shafer label. It was a tough call, but I admired him for it.

Rather than take a total loss, Dad struck deals with brokers, selling the vintage for pennies on the dollar as privately labeled wines. That meant our first step was to soak the Shafer label off thousands of bottles. We filled a large drainage pan from the crush pad with warm water and a little ammonia, and we scrubbed each bottle clean by hand. Once Dad made deals with various entities we relabeled everything. In one instance we made a deal with a restaurant in Orange County for a couple hundred cases that became their house red. Closer to home we sold a bunch of cases to Bohemian Grove in Sonoma County, the ultra-exclusive wooded getaway for the political and corporate elite, such as Henry Kissinger, Walter Cronkite, and Malcolm Forbes (so I'm told). They may have been highly selective about the company they kept, but thank God they didn't seem terribly particular about what they drank.

TWENTY-ONE

1982 Cabernet

Of course I hadn't inherited one wine but two. At some point during the various other debacles, I started tasting through the different lots of 1982 Cabernet. Some of it was from our own property—by now it was planted throughout—and some of it was from fruit that we'd purchased, which meant most of it came from within a two- or three-mile radius of the winery.

After each harvest, once the wines have been "put to bed" in their barrels, a winemaker tastes through the various lots to see what he or she has to work with from that vintage. Inevitably, there's a spectrum. Some of the wine may be less interesting or less complex than you'd like, and you slate that to sell to the bulk market. Other lots may be good to very good, and with any luck you'll discover that some of your wines are outstanding. When I tasted through lots of '82, I found all the things I'd expected to find, until I finally came to the Cabernet produced from our hillside block called Sunspot. At the time it was one of our newer plantings to Cab. Dad and Alfonso had originally budded all of Upper and Lower Sunspot to Zinfandel in the mid-1970s. However, once it became clear that his future lay in becoming a wine producer, Dad had T-budded Upper Sunspot over to Cabernet, which is where his heart had always been.

John Shafer (left) and Doug
Shafer (right) in the barrel room
circa 1984.

(Lower Sunspot for a few years was budded over to Merlot. Today of
course it's Cab.)

I still remember standing in the barrel room, taking a sample of wine
from one of the Sunspot barrels with a slender glass tube called a "wine
thief." I poured a small amount into a glass and tasted it. My first imme-
diate thought was, "Okay, here we go." The wine had an attractive, per-
fumy aroma. In the mouth it had richness and concentration and even
softness at this youthful stage. My next thought was, "It'd be a shame to
just blend this with all the other lots of Cabernet together." You'd blend
out what was truly special about this lot.

I had Dad taste a few lots with me, including the Sunspot, and by
doing so showed him the differences I was finding.

"I think we should produce two Cabs," I told him. "And I think this
one [pointing to the sample of Sunspot] should be our reserve."

Bottling that one on its own would be a way of spotlighting what had the potential to be a beautiful wine, and it'd be a way of harkening back to the success of the 1978 and 1979 Cabernets, which were made with fruit solely from our hillsides.

He agreed it was a good idea and we decided we'd keep the '82 Reserve in barrels a year longer than the other Cabernet.

TWENTY-TWO

Other Labels

The upshot of all this maneuvering in the cellar was that Dad at some point had to announce to the world that there would be no 1981 Shafer Cabernet. He just said we'd had trouble with the vintage and it wasn't up to our standards. And the world continued to turn on its axis. Meanwhile we produced a one-off bottling of 1981 Shafer Red Table Wine, which was a blend of Zinfandel, Merlot, and a little bit of salvageable Cabernet. I think we may have purchased some additional wine from our neighbors.

In some ways it wasn't a bad time to experience a shortfall. There was a lot of extra wine throughout the Valley, and throughout California for that matter. Vine planting had outstripped consumption, which now ran smack into that increased competition, mentioned earlier, from the French.

Frank Prial, in his *New York Times* wine column (August 3, 1983), did not mince words: "There are signs that the growth of the wine market in the United States may not for many years, if ever, live up to the optimistic projections of five years ago.... California at the moment is awash in unsold wine, and another bumper crop of grapes is almost ready to be picked. The market, to use a marketer's euphemism, is flat."[1]

1. Frank J. Prial, Wine Talk, *New York Times*, August 3, 1983, accessed July 30, 2011, www.nytimes.com/1983/08/03/garden/wine-talk-074412.html?ref=frankjprial.

Ouch.

One response to this perfect storm was to do exactly what we'd done—take what you had in your barrels, blend it together, give it a generic name—like "red table wine"—and price it to sell. Heitz was doing this with a white blend simply called Chablis. In similar fashion Mondavi released Robert Mondavi White. Phelps jumped in with both feet and produced a nonvintage called Vin Rouge, in which they'd blended Pinot Noir and Cabernet Franc from three different vintages. These were all wines that showed up on the shelves for $4 to $5, and the great thing was they were all nice wines. The consumer was the winner.

Another idea that had caught on was that of creating a second label. This had been common practice in France for quite a while. Château Latour, for example, offered a second label called Les Forts de Latour. As additional backup they occasionally released a third tier simply called Pauillac, the name of the commune.

Among our neighbors, Caymus Vineyards had introduced a second label called Liberty School; Clos du Val had Gran Val, while Stag's Leap Wine Cellars had introduced Hawk Crest. Dad began drawing up plans for our own second label, named Chase Creek for the little Napa River tributary that wound its way through our property.

While he was doing this, I was in the thick of it on the crush pad. The 1983 harvest was a crush in every sense. We got a perfect little surge of heat up to the nineties in early September and sugars in all varieties were climbing steadily. In my notes I have our harvest starting on September 9, crushing six tons of Merlot—then we were hit with day after day of 100-degree heat and in my notes, in a slightly hysteric scrawl, are the words, "Still hot. Everything coming FAST!" And on that day my little crew and I (including my brother Brad) crushed twenty-eight tons, and the next day it was thirty tons. In one tank I had to slow down fermentation because the press was so tied up for another couple of days. By the fifteenth we'd crushed one hundred tons. It was like a giant wall of grapes coming at us. Fortunately, the temperatures slid back down into the eighties and nineties, the sugars in the fruit dropped, and things calmed down a bit, to the point that we were even able to custom-crush someone else's Chenin Blanc. On October 21 it was all over.

It was the first year we harvested Merlot, and it was the last year we picked Zinfandel. The stalwart grape that had been so popular in the 1970s had steadily been losing ground in the marketplace. After that harvest we tore out all our Zin and replanted entirely to Cabernet.

TWENTY-THREE

Elias

By early March 1984 I had put up a notice on the jobs board at U.C. Davis advertising for an assistant winemaker (I'd finally lost patience and fired my first assistant, whose track record for showing up late or not at all showed no signs of change). A week later I was in the barrel room topping off barrels when Dad walked in with a candidate—a skinny young guy who looked like he was about fourteen years old. He introduced himself as Elias Fernandez. In three weeks he was going to graduate from U.C. Davis with a degree in fermentation science. He and I chatted for a while, and he seemed smart and decent. I checked his résumé, and for someone his age he had a hefty bit of experience: employed at Martini for three summers, did a stint at Cuvaison, and worked crush at Schramsberg. Then he handed me his transcripts—his grades—which was a little unusual.

Turns out he and I had taken a lot of the same chemistry and biology classes, and in every case he'd gotten better grades than I had. Unless you're a wing nut, you *want* to hire people who're smarter than you are. Even as a neophyte in the employment world I understood this.

Dad asked him a couple of questions, such as where Elias saw himself five years down the line, and Elias responded by saying he wasn't

Six-year-old Elias Fernandez peeks out of his mom's
picking bucket (1968).

sure. At this point he just wanted to put what he'd learned to work and
start making wine. Then Dad asked what kind of salary he was looking
for, and Elias looked a little uncomfortable and said he didn't know and
didn't really care. He just wanted to make wine. A singular focus, this
guy.

A few other applicants were interested in the job, so Dad and I said
we'd call him in a few days.

Truth is he was easily the top candidate from the start. The more we
found out about his background, the more certain we were that he'd be
a great addition to our team.

If anyone can claim to have winemaking in their bones, it's Elias.
Both his parents were farmworkers, who met in the tomato fields of the
San Joaquin Valley and later moved to Napa, settling in St. Helena.

Early 1990s (left to right): Cellar worker Enrique Del Campo, winemaker Elias Fernandez, and winery president Doug Shafer prep a load of red grape must to be pressed.

His father was from the great state of Michoacán in Mexico, while his mother's family had lived here in Napa Valley for at least a couple of generations. Some of Elias's earliest memories are of working outdoors at his parents' sides. By his teens he knew well what it's like to fill picking bins with fruit in the hot sun and to get stung by wasps and have to keep working. He had pruned grapevines in early morning light while his fingers ached with cold.

His dad primarily did vineyard work and for many years was employed by Laurie Wood as part of his vineyard management crew. His mom had picked walnuts, tomatoes, and other crops that were plentiful in the Valley in the late '60s and '70s. She later worked for the Davies family of Schramsberg and was very close with Jack, Jamie, and their kids.

Living in St. Helena, Elias had attended elementary school, middle school, and high school with kids who would one day grow up and play prominent roles in the Valley—Hugh Davies, the Novak kids from the Spottswoode family, the Duckhorn kids, Mark Aubert (today a talented and highly sought after winemaker), Mark Neal of Neal Vineyard Management, Armando Ceja of Ceja Vineyards, Alexis Chappellet, and kids from the Raymond family and the Carpy family, who'd farmed Napa Valley grapes and produced wine since the 1800s.

During the summer of 1977, between his sophomore and junior years of high school, Elias landed his first real job, a summer position at Louis M. Martini. In the miserable heat of that drought year he stacked hundreds of cases of Martini wine in boxcars. This was when the train still went to Martini. He fixed broken pallets, taped case boxes, hand-labeled bottles that were destined for export with special tags, and helped repair a roof. He filled in on the bottling line and even taught himself to drive a forklift. In short order he started to learn the hundreds of little tasks that go into running a cellar. Mind you, none of this inspired him with the romance of the wine industry. He was punching a time clock and making some money and had zero interest in a wine-related future.

He worked at Martini in this capacity for three summers prior to his college years.

From early on Elias's mother had insisted that he do his best in school and set his sights on getting a college degree. She got him started playing the trumpet in third grade, made sure he did his homework, and encouraged him to join the track team in high school. By the time he graduated, his trumpet skills helped him earn a Fulbright music scholarship to the University of Nevada, Reno.

There were several "firsts" in his life at this point. He was the first person in his family to go to college. It was his first time living outside Napa Valley and thus his first time living in a completely different climate, where he encountered snow. And it wasn't necessarily a good thing. He remembers kids pulling the fire alarm at 3 A.M. and everyone having to evacuate the building and stand in the snow freezing their tails off.

On school breaks he'd drive home in his 1967 Ford Mustang and he'd head north up Silverado Trail or Highway 29 and take in the Valley with new eyes. The truth for most teenagers who grow up here is that the rural, small-town life of Napa Valley is about as fabulous as school detention. They can't wait to leave and go somewhere exciting. But after six months in Reno and after reconsidering the itinerant life of a musician, Elias started to think he'd like to try for something that would allow him to make his home here. And for the first time, he thought about wine.

He talked to his mom about this idea, and she in turn spoke with Laurie Wood, now a longtime family friend. Laurie, always a realist, was pretty skeptical about job opportunities in the wine business. This was 1979—the same year I was heading outside the Valley for my teaching stint in Arizona. There were certainly jobs on the bottling lines and in the vineyards. But Laurie said that careers as skilled as winemaking offered slim pickings.

Elias gave this some thought but went ahead and investigated what U.C. Davis had to offer. Ultimately, he transferred there in the fall of 1980 to pursue a degree in fermentation science. For a kid from the country (even after that year in Reno), it was an adjustment. His first chemistry class was held in an auditorium with five hundred other students. By contrast, his entire St. Helena High graduating class numbered just over one hundred.

He studied hard for that first chemistry test and thought he'd done pretty well. Then he got his score—a D-minus—and he felt sick.

On a chalkboard, after the test, his professor drew in descending order the letter grades A, B, and C. Under the C he drew a line. He said, "Anyone with less than a C-minus should seriously consider dropping this course."

Under no circumstance was Elias quitting. He wanted to become a winemaker and to do that he needed a lot of science.

Rather than taking the professor's advice, he got a tutor and studied harder. He ended that first chemistry class with an A-minus.

Davis wasn't all uphill though. Elias's viticulture instructors would take the class out into the teaching vineyard to introduce students to the basics of training the vines on trellises or pruning the vines. Elias already knew this stuff. Everyone else would be looking at the teacher saying, "Wait, how do you do this?" And he'd just be flying, halfway done pruning the first row.

That summer he again worked for Martini, still doing the same collection of odd jobs. Carolyn Martini recruited him to volunteer on the winery's behalf at the first Napa Valley Wine Auction in 1981. He remembers his disbelief as he toted wine to the tables and at the dizzying dollar amounts being called out as bidding paddles popped up all around him. (Of course he couldn't have dreamed of the bids for wine he'd make twenty years in the future.)

During the next school year wine started to be less about science and more about pleasure, exploration, and friendship. Some of his most unforgettable evenings were those Friday nights spent with classmates, all winemakers-to-be, tasting wines of the world. Those evenings started off with wine but of course led to conversations long into the night about their goals, their lives, and a universe of ideas. People from this class include Mia Klein today of Selene, Pam Starr of Crocker & Starr, Laurie Hook of Beringer, Scott McCleod, until recently at Rubicon, and Marco Cappelli, who was with Swanson and now makes wine at Miraflores and Toogood wineries.

Elias worked the first part of the summer of 1982 at Cuvaison in the cellar under winemaker John Thatcher, who early on in the winery's history had been assistant to the original winemaker, Philip Togni. For the first time Elias saw an approach in which the wine was treated, as he describes it, "like a newborn infant."

Unlike in the Martini cellar, he didn't see giant oak ovals or large red-wood or cement tanks. Fermentation happened in spotless, shiny stain-less steel tanks, and then the wine was gently pressed and pumped right away into individual, new French oak barrels. That summer working with Chardonnay, all the cellar jobs, such as bottling and racking, were performed in ways he hadn't seen before. When the wine was moved in barrels, the barrels were moved gently and carefully. The tanks were topped with inert gas to prevent oxidation. Every possible step was taken to preserve the wine's character and authenticity.

Elias remembers Thatcher as serious, energetic, and thorough—as well as stressed out. At the time Elias didn't know much about the life of a winemaker, except that for some reason there seemed to be a lot of pressure.

The second part of the summer Elias spent in an internship at Schrams-berg. It was his first experience on the crush pad during harvest. Be-cause they were making sparkling wines and were looking for high acid and low sugar, picking started in July, about a month before the Valley's still-wine producers. This time he was working with winemaker Greg Fowler (who went on to work for Mumm and is now senior vice presi-dent of operations for Constellation Wines) and his assistant Rob McNeill (who later took Fowler's place at Mumm).

At Schramsberg they were also looking for ways to treat the grapes more gently and for a better response to what was happening to the wine at the chemical level. When the five-ton gondolas lumbered in from the vineyard, rather than dumping the grapes into the hopper that then au-gured the grapes into the press—a common practice that caused a great deal of juicing of the fruit—they had a system for vacuuming the clusters out of the gondolas. With one end of a large hose, grape clusters were sucked out of the gondolas and they were then deposited into the press from the other end of the hose. Elias was the lucky guy chosen to work inside the press, filling its large round drum. He held the hose and aimed the flying clusters first at one side, filling it, then at the other. Finally, he'd climb out the top of the press and fill the center. While this was probably a decent early attempt to avoid juicing the grapes,[1] it sounds like Elias spent the summer in a space capsule filled with heat, stickiness, flying grapes, and bees.

Schramsberg's focus on whole-cluster pressing was atypical for the time. They understood something many of us making still wines hadn't learned yet, which was that the white wine would exhibit cleaner, purer flavors with less skin-to-juice contact, unlike red wine, which benefits from integrating the tannins from the skin of the grape for structure and long-term aging.

After the fruit was pressed, Elias had the chance to work with the juice in the days that followed, first after the solids had a chance to settle out in the large stainless steel tanks, and then as it moved through fermentation. Tasting throughout the process, he got to see the progression from juice through the first stages of the wine.

What Elias experienced by moving from his summers at Martini in the late '70s to the more exacting artisan environments at Cuvaison and Schramsberg in the early '80s was a key transitional phase in Napa Valley winemaking. What he was participating in—what we all were seeing to one degree or another—was the budding of a new era, a Valley-wide search for something better, something that was still beyond our reach, but very close. Overall, the 1980s here were about getting things right in the cellar, whereas the 1990s would be about getting things right in the vineyard.

---

1. Later most wineries learned to avoid juicing the fruit on the way to the crush pad by switching from five-ton gondolas to the use of half-ton picking bins; most wineries specializing in sparkling wine use even smaller, handheld bins.

Elias went back to Davis, worked hard, and eventually distinguished himself as the first Latino to earn a degree there in fermentation science, with honors no less.

· · ·

I called Elias back a week after he interviewed with us in March 1984 and offered him the assistant winemaker position. He accepted right away, which made him the first person in his graduating class to land a job. As Laurie Wood had suspected, employment like this was not plentiful in the Valley, and Elias says that the majority of the class of 1984 did not finish the school year with employment offers. Scraping their nickels and dimes together, a good number of them took off to do grunt work of various types in French wineries to learn what they could of vineyard cultivation and winemaking in Bordeaux and Burgundy.

Napa Valley had a complicated and (mostly one-sided) fractured relationship with France, and Europe in general. For most of the twentieth century we had been the Rodney Dangerfield of wine regions, never getting any respect. With the Judgment of Paris we had claimed a spot on the fine wine world map—a gift given to us by none other than the French themselves. While that tasting gave us a psychological boost and turned the heads of Francophile connoisseurs everywhere, we had still not recovered, I think, from our own decades of insecurity. There was still something homespun about the Valley. In the mid-1970s there were only three or four restaurants that aspired to much beyond simple, hearty, lunch-counter fare. The Louis Martinis and the Nathan Fays and the John Shafers had only been to Europe—in the 1940s—out of patriotic duty, not because they were devout foodies or wine aficionados. The Valley at large had not yet spritzed itself with the eau de toilette of aristocracy that seemed to be so easily worn by the First Growths of France. It helps explains why having Euro-cred was a thing of such significance for the new wave of vintners and winemakers who had arrived here in the late '60s and onward. Any time spent among the Bordelais—any way to French-up your résumé—was worth mentioning in the presence of media and consumers, because it was simply not enough to be Napa Valley.

If truth be told—and of course this is all from the easy view of hindsight—I think the Old World was intrigued by what we were doing. Baron Philippe de Rothschild of Château Mouton had first approached Robert Mondavi in 1970 about establishing the partnership that so electrified the first Napa Valley Wine Auction. The Swiss conglomerate Nestlé bought Beringer in 1971. Moët & Chandon, the Epernay-based keepers of Dom Pérignon's sparkling flame, established Domain Chandon here in 1973; a monied Swiss family purchased Cuvaison; Christian Moueix, the owner of Château Petrus and other properties in Pomerol and St. Emilion, began making Cabernet Sauvignon from Napanook Vineyards fruit in 1982. The DeWavrin family of Château La Mission Haut-Brion and Château Laville Haut-Brion in Bordeaux were part owners of Conn Creek Winery and went on to found Chateau Woltner on Howell Mountain. Later, Taittinger would start Domaine Carneros in the 1980s, and the Skalli family of France would build St. Supéry. The list goes on. Yes, we were less than nobility, and in fact we were probably cowboys, but what these Europeans suspected—and what the rest of us hoped—was that we might be the next big thing.

Meanwhile, in 1984 none of us at Shafer Vineyards had been to France or were likely to see any sort of leisure travel outside of Napa Valley any time soon. We had too much to do.

That first day that Elias showed up for work, I decided to test this new assistant, wanting to know right away if he was a keeper or not. No more Mr. Nice Guy for me. I handed him a brush and a bucket of bleach and asked him to scrub the undersides of the catwalks (a way of keeping the cellar as sterile as possible). It's a nasty job—and one of the first that I had been given at Lakespring. It's hot, you're looking up for hours, trying not to get this stuff in your eyes, meanwhile it's running down your arms. He worked at it all day without complaint and did a stellar job.

Within a few weeks I began to get a sense for Elias. He always showed up on time. Any job I asked him to do, he performed with diligence, worked fast, and came back asking what was next. In short, I learned that I could count on him, which was an enormous relief, given how overwhelmed I'd been. He was also pretty quiet. He'd give his opinion about something if I asked but not usually without a prompt. He told me much later that he was simply absorbing everything around him and often didn't feel qualified yet to throw out his views or ideas. With all these qualities, plus just being a good guy, we hit it off pretty quickly and I hoped we could hang on to him.

As the harvest of 1984 grew nearer, Dad, Elias, and I would head out before first light to gather grapes from the various vineyard blocks and bring them into the lab to stay on top of their development. We'd keep grapes from each block separated in plastic baggies. Then we'd squeeze some juice onto the glass pane of a refractometer and check for the sugar level. We'd check in with our consultant, who would make recommendations of when to pick, which was actually a fairly simple process, since we only harvested based on sugar, trying to pick each cluster when the fruit hit that magic number of somewhere between 22.5 and 23 degrees Brix.

That year, as more of our newer Cabernet plantings came into maturity, we were harvesting more fruit than ever before. And we were plagued with every kind of misfire. Early on I was driving Dad's pickup pulling a full three-ton gondola of Cabernet grapes down the steep end of Sunspot. It's a tough maneuver, because you're making a tight corner and the slope is pretty unforgiving. I took the corner a little too fast— and when I say "fast," we're talking tortoise speed versus glacial speed— and the gondola jackknifed on me, sliding down the hill toward the pickup. I hit the brakes and cranked the steering wheel, trying to regain control. I could see that gondola coming toward me, closing in like a pair of scissors, and there wasn't a thing I could do about it—boom— it smashed right into the driver's side door. That pickup took a lot of abuse.

One thing that helped me hold onto a shred or two of dignity is that I wasn't the only one screwing up.

When we'd bring fruit off the hillside in a gondola, we'd pull it to the crush pad and park it in front of the destemmer/crusher. Then one of us would drive the forklift in, getting its arms under the gondola. Next we'd chain the gondola to the forklift, lift the gondola, and dump the grapes down into the hopper of the destemmer/crusher. One day Dad was in the pickup and pulled a gondola-load of grapes to the crush pad, and we went through the rigmarole of dumping the grapes. But somehow, in all the activity at the crush pad, and with so much on his mind, after the grapes were dumped, and the gondola was lowered, Dad hopped in his truck and drove off the downhill slope of the crush pad pulling the gondola—and dragging the still-attached forklift *sideways* with him. Meanwhile, as he was driving along, he realized the truck was driving funny and thought maybe he'd left the parking brake on. Then he noticed everyone shouting at him to stop.

A lot less funny was the trouble we were having with our press. It was a new piece of German equipment that, Labor Day weekend, decided to work at less than half speed. We discovered the problem late in the day after having just crushed several tons of Chardonnay, a situation that did not allow us to stop and go get a good night's sleep and come back to deal with in the morning. After the fruit was crushed, it was imperative to press it the same day, because at the time we wanted the Chardonnay juice to get some contact with the skins. Too much contact though—overnight for example—would overly infuse the juice with tannins from the skin, making the juice astringent and unpleasant. We called the local service rep for the press manufacturer, but he'd gone out of town for the holiday weekend. The way the press was working, we had to punch some buttons every twenty minutes to make it run through its next cycle. Realizing this was going to take all night, my mom made beds in the office for Elias and me—sleeping bags, pillows, everything but teddy bears. We took turns, getting up every twenty minutes, pushing buttons, and lying back down. Good thing we were young.

TWENTY-FOUR

Napa Valley Wine Technical Group

We weren't alone in the kinds of winemaking challenges facing us. These same difficulties were making cellar crews sweat blood and bullets throughout the Valley. Back in the 1940s Andre Tchelistcheff, Beaulieu Vineyards' brilliant winemaker, believed quite rightly that the more vintners and winemakers talked to one another and shared ideas, the better the wines of the whole region would become—the concept that a rising tide floats all boats. With this in mind Tchelistcheff organized the Napa Valley Wine Technical Group as a forum that would allow people in the industry to pool knowledge on what they were struggling with, to share new approaches, and to give feedback on new equipment—solid, practical information that would help the Valley as a whole.

Tchelistcheff kicked this thing off just after World War II by inviting Bob and Peter Mondavi, both then of Krug, John Daniel of Inglenook, Louis M. Martini, and others to join the group.[1]

By the 1980s, the Technical Group was meeting once a month at a restaurant in Calistoga for drinks and a dinner that always included "the swinging beef"—a massive, hanging, half-carcass of roast cow that

---

1. Charles L. Sullivan, *Napa Wine: A History from Mission Days to the Present*, 2nd ed. (San Francisco, CA: Wine Appreciation Guild, 2008), 247.

almost took on mascot status. Over dinner there'd usually be a presentation by a U.C. Davis researcher or perhaps a winery owner on something we might all be dealing with: stuck fermentations, *Brettanomyces*, oxidation, problems with yeast, or issues with malolactic fermentation. Another evening might feature tasting through a trial of four different blends or wines that had been aged in barrels with different kinds of American and French oak. For years Elias and I didn't miss a meeting—it was a vital source of up-to-the-minute data, approaches, and opinions regarding the things we were often in the middle of trying to understand and resolve.

Talk about young turks—some of the regulars in this era were Nils Venge, then with Groth, Ken Deis, then with Flora Springs, Joe Cafaro, Bo Barrett of Chateau Montelena, and Randy Mason and Craig Williams, then with Joseph Phelps. Most of them were about five to ten years older than Elias and me, but they weren't just peers, they were friends, so a meeting of the Technical Group was always a good time. Beyond that, for Elias and me, the group played a crucial role in helping us get a handle on our cellar.

TWENTY-FIVE

The Food–Wine Era

During and just after the brutal harvest of 1984, our winemaking consultant would come by and taste the initial wines and let us know how much acid we should add to the wine. We were picking on sugars, meaning that we were nailing that 22.5- to 23-degree Brix sweet spot, because the winemaking consultant and our U.C. Davis training told us we should, just as Dad had been told he should and was mortified when he'd missed it in '78 and '79. We'd been instructed to pick at 22.5 degrees because that's what everyone did then. I suspect this went back to how wine was made in Bordeaux. In a really good year they *might* get up to 22.5 or 23. In many vintages, when it was too cold and cloudy, they had to pick at lower sugars and in the cellar had to perform *chaptilization*—meaning they added bags of beet or cane sugar to get the juice up to 22.5 or 23 degrees.

This was a period called the "food–wine era," in which Napa wineries had collectively tried to back away from a bolder, richer style that our vineyards were prone to make given our sunny, warm climate. This more French style was how it was supposed to be done. We picked at low sugar and then we'd add acid—this was accomplished by mixing powdered acid and some wine in a five-gallon bucket and then pouring it into a tank filled with Cabernet, Merlot, or whatever wine you were working with.

In our lab, all the numbers—the pH, acid, alcohol—everything looked exactly right. We were hitting those numbers dead center. But the resulting wines were thin and weedy and vegetal. We didn't like them and didn't drink our own wines at home. Frankly, none of it was exactly leaping off the shelves in retail shops.

In June 1985, the wine critic Robert Parker, who had a growing and committed following, took many of us in California to task for heading over the food–wine era cliff like so many lemmings. In *The Wine Advocate* he wrote, "The growers that are smart, those that have been making light, bland wines under the guise of 'balance and finesse' will abandon their misguided and ill-informed and abysmal efforts at making light, rather feeble wines and return to the winemaking philosophy that won California cabernets international fame and recognition in the mid-seventies—rich, intense, full bodied wine with considerable flavor interest. After all, ladies and gentlemen of California's viticultural regions—isn't intensity and concentration of flavor as well as balance and harmony how vintages and wines are judged?"[1]

It depended on who you asked. In London, even while sales of California wines were steadily growing, there was a pretty consistent complaint that our wines were too big.

In June 1981, Philip Hiaring, editor of *Wines & Vines* magazine, had written, "Interesting to note the reaction of many English drinkers to California wine. They say the wines in general are too 'alcoholic' and aggressive in nature due to intense character." He went on to point out that the alcohol levels in California wines and those of Bordeaux and Burgundy were actually very close, if not often identical, and that, in his opinion, the British were not reacting to more alcohol but rather to more extract.[2]

---

1. Robert M. Parker, "Domestic Cabernet Sauvignon and Merlot: New Releases," *Wine Advocate* 39 (June 1985): 16.

2. Philip E. Hiaring, "Wise & Otherwise," *Wines & Vines*, June 1981, 16.

All of which sounds very much like the kinds of debates still bouncing around today. It's basically the "California wine stinks" versus "California wine is beautiful" argument. While the eras and media have changed (print to online), some people still get very worked up about this particular topic.

In August 1985 *The New York Times* wine writer Frank Prial weighed in on the food–wine movement. In a column called "Cabernet Sauvignon's Identity Crisis," he wrote:

> Cabernet has fallen on hard times. Once America's unchallenged leader in red-wine prestige and desirability, cabernet sauvignon is going through a kind of identity crisis. What sort of wine should it be, anyway? Big and rich and mouth-filling, with lots of body, color and alcohol? Or should it be lighter, leaner, more "sculpted," which is a word Robert Mondavi likes to use for this newer style of wine... To some California Cabernet producers [the new popularity of lower-priced French wines] was the signal to go to a lighter style—less alcohol, easier on the palate, more in keeping with the trend to lightness... Somebody even came up with a name: "food wine"... Suddenly, all the big cabernets were bad and everyone was rushing to develop the new style. Unfortunately, quite a few of them did not succeed. Thin and bland, the new wines made a lot of people nostalgic for the bad old days of macho reds.

Prial concluded his piece by writing,

> Cabernet Sauvignon is still the premier red grape of California, and probably always will be. But one can hope that someday the idea of a mandatory cabernet style will be obsolete. In the best of all possible worlds, there would be instead just a fascinating variety of extremely good red wines.[3]

Speaking for a moment as a wine consumer, I fall pretty squarely in with Prial on this one. It's like the old Almond Joy commercial, "Sometimes you feel like a nut, sometimes you don't." Depending on the evening, the meal, the group of friends, or just my mood, I may feel like a

---

3. Frank Prial, "Cabernet Sauvignon's Identity Crisis," *New York Times*, August 4, 1985, accessed July 22, 2011, www.nytimes.com/1985/08/04/magazine/wine-cabernet-sauvignon-s-identity-crisis.html.

Chablis from Burgundy or a Pinot Noir from Russian River, a Sancerre from the Loire Valley, a Sauvignon Blanc from New Zealand, a lean, graceful Bordeaux, or a rich, elegant Napa Valley Cabernet. I like choices and feel fortunate to live in an era when there are so many great ones at so many price levels. It would be a frumpy little world if all wine were to adhere to a single style.

In any case, Parker ended his June 1985 assessment of the new California releases by saying, "There are some very nice new cabernets on or coming on the market, but there is also a glut of mediocre cabernet out there at prices that are quite ridiculous." He then went on to award a lot of scores in the mid-70s through the mid-80s.

However, two wines I'd had a hand in making—the 1982 Cabernet, which he scored a 67, and the 1982 Cabernet Reserve, which he awarded a 64—came in for some special attention. "Shafer has consistently made good cabernet," he wrote, "but these two offerings in 1982 are disappointingly poor efforts...the Regular wine is dark ruby in color but excessively stemmy with hollow flavors and a bitter finish. The Reserve is even worse, very vegetal and stemmy to smell, full bodied and alcoholic, but little true varietal flavor is present. Both wines should be avoided."[4]

Well that stung a bit. But more than anything, as a young winemaker, what was I supposed to make of this whole new world of critical review and scores? There is no enology class at U.C. Davis called "The World of Wine Critics and You."

The same wine, the Reserve, that Parker had warned his readers away from was selected for high praise from *Wine Spectator, Bon Appetit, Chicago Tribune*, the *California Grapevine, Connoisseurs' Guide to California Wines*, and *Vogue* (of all things). Dan Berger, writing for Copley News Service, called it "a stunning wine" and "an absolute delight."

Parker's score generated some controversy. People who liked us called Dad and wrote to him with equal measures of support for our

4. Robert M. Parker, "Domestic Cabernet Sauvignon and Merlot: New Releases," *Wine Advocate* 39 (June 1985): 23.

winery and outrage for the young Mr. Parker. Other people wrote letters directly to *The Wine Advocate* and cc'd Dad.

The truth is, while Dad nor I considered it a perfect wine, neither of us thought it deserved quite that level of drubbing. We suspected Parker may have gotten an off bottle or that the Cab had gotten beaten up in its travels. Put a bottle in the back of a delivery truck in the middle of a hot summer afternoon, and you can pretty thoroughly cook the life out of it within an hour or two.

Not knowing how else you're supposed to react to this sort of thing, Dad wrote Parker a nice note, inviting him to retaste the wine and sent it along with another bottle or two to Monkton, Maryland (where Parker lives and works). This is the only thing you can really do in a situation like this. You send your letter and then forget about it, because most wine critics don't revisit or reevaluate their critiques.

In issue 40 of *The Wine Advocate* that August, we were surprised to see that our Reserve was making an unheard of reappearance. Under the heading "Mistaken Identity," Parker wrote: "[In the previous issue] I had some unkind words to say about Shafer Vineyards 1982 Reserve Cabernet Sauvignon. In fact it was tasted twice and found to be overtly vegetal and herbaceous. Well, after several angry letters from consumers (John Shafer of Shafer Vineyards was remarkably restrained, given my review) I put the wine in two additional blind tastings. Bottle variation exists, but in the second group of tastings, the Shafer Reserve tasted like a completely different wine ... rich blackcurrant, spicy bouquet, deep, dense, full bodied, moderately tannic flavors and impressive potential. It is a big, rich wine that I Recommend."[5]

Through all of this I was learning pretty quickly not to let scores and reviews make or break my day—that's the fast track to emotional ruin. The most healthy way to react to this kind of thing is to learn what you can—some critics are more helpful than others in this regard—and then simply focus on your grapes and what's going on in your cellar.

5. Robert M. Parker, "Mistaken Identity," *Wine Advocate* 40 (August 1985): 31.

Make the best wine you can with the vintage Mother Nature throws at you and try to learn and improve as you go.

Wine is like music, in that I may like the Rolling Stones, and you may like Lady Gaga or C.P.E. Bach. Doesn't really matter. It's all about personal taste. After decades in this business I've been told everything imaginable about our wines. One member of the British wine writing establishment informed me over dinner a year or so ago that our wines are "heresy." Fortunately, a good number of people have let me know that they believe our wines are beautiful and well made and have contributed to many thoroughly enjoyed evenings.

Once a critic wrote that one of our wines exhibited a strong V.A. (volatile acid) character, when I knew from the lab report that the wine had in fact almost zero V.A. (no wine is completely free of this). Another took us to task for a wine with some *Brettanomyces* when a year or two earlier they had given a neighboring winery a score in the high 90s for a wine with five times the amount of Brett (which I determined, out of curiosity, by a lab analysis).

The real classic, though, was when a bit of under-the-radar marketing came back to bite us. At some point in the mid- to late 1980s, Dad got an interesting guerilla marketing idea. He contacted Williams-Sonoma and Crate & Barrel, offering them free Shafer dummy bottles for the wine racks displayed in their stores. Both retail chains were pleased to work with us. Obviously we didn't want to ship hundreds of bottles filled with wine, so we filled them with colored water. They looked good in the store racks and introduced many thousands of customers to the Shafer label.

Then we received a letter one day from a woman who'd purchased a bottle of our wine at a retail shop and had saved it for a special dinner with her boss. When she pulled the cork on this magical evening, the letter writer discovered to her horror that the liquid inside looked, smelled, and tasted *nothing* like wine. She was terribly upset that we had the audacity to sell such a plainly flawed product.

Of course we were as confused as she was. However, after a bit of investigation we believe that what happened is that the owner of the retail shop had helped himself to a Shafer bottle out of a rack in Crate & Barrel. Then he sold it in his shop to the woman, who simply wanted a nice bottle for dinner with her boss. I'm not sure we ever convinced her that we weren't some kind of quasi-criminal operation, so it turns out you're even judged by your stolen dummy bottles.

Essentially, as the producer, you must try to be as Zen as possible about the evaluation of critics and consumers.

TWENTY-SIX

Hillside Select

By about the midpoint of 1985 Dad and I had been out on the road introducing our 1982 Reserve Cabernet Sauvignon to countless consumers and
retailers. We would taste the wine with distributor partners, with restaurant buyers, and at big charity tastings, and no matter the venue, we were
peppered with the same question, "What does reserve mean?"

It was a valid question. By that time a growing number of wineries
throughout California were latching onto this term in various iterations,
such as *vintners reserve, barrel reserve, special reserve,* and so on. There was
and still is no regulation of the term, no particular benchmark you have
to hit in terms of quality, no oversight. Anyone can print the word "reserve" in gold letters—be it unabashed plonk or the most elegant wine
in the world—and it has no real meaning.

In our case we believed that "reserve" did in fact mean that this was
the best-of-the-best from our hillside vineyards. Try telling that to a
skeptical New York retailer who's heard that same story about a thousand times too many.

Dad and I got tired of responding to this question over and over again.
The answer was to come up with a name that no one else used, that told
a consumer something authentic about the wine and gave a sense of its
pedigree and quality.

After tossing around lists of ideas, I finally suggested "Hillside Select," since it's a true reflection of what's in the bottle; each vintage we select only the best possible grapes from our hillside vineyards—the fruit with optimal color, ripeness, and richness—with which to produce the wine. Thanks to Dad's publishing background, he had the foresight to trademark it.

By working quickly we were able to get the name approved by the Bureau of Alcohol, Tobacco and Firearms,[1] and onto our 1983 vintage bottles. When we christened the wine with this new name we naturally had high hopes for its future.

Unfortunately, we would have to pass through a period of darkness and difficulty with this one and our other wines before we'd get to enjoy feelings of a job well done.

---

1. In January 2003, the name was changed to the Bureau of Alcohol, Tobacco, Firearms and Explosives.

TWENTY-SEVEN

The Good, the Bad, and the Very Bad

On the Wednesday before Thanksgiving Day 1986, Dad, Elias, and I uncorked a bottle of the '85 Merlot and the newly bottled '84 Cabernet to see how things were progressing and were a little freaked out to discover that both wines reeked aggressively of rotten eggs. Bottle variation can be a real phenomenon, as Parker had pointed out, and pinning my hopes on that very slender possibility we opened more bottles—but one after another noxiously exhibited the same problem.

This was far worse than the day I had walked into the cellar in 1983 and discovered the mess I'd inherited. The wines sitting in front of me now, smelling like garbage, were not the product of someone else's neglect. These were the product of Doug Shafer working as hard he could. These were the results of sixty- and seventy-hour weeks and pulling all-nighters with touchy equipment and of reading and discussion and attending Technical Group meetings.

It was the very nightmare scenario I had feared from the beginning playing itself out in its most awful form—the fear that by accepting the job of winemaker, I would single-handedly bring down the family business.

A day later I called up our winemaking consultant and arranged for a conference at his office with bottles of wine to review and discuss. Dad told me he had phoned Louis Martini and asked him to come over, taste the wines, and give us what guidance he could. I was mortified that this legendary vintner would be exposed to this wine and was more than happy not to witness his reaction.

After I left to meet with our consultant, Martini arrived and apparently it was the usual bonhomie between the two of them. Dad opened a bottle each of the Merlot and the Cabernet and Martini diagnosed the problem after the first sniff.

"Oh, you've got a few sulfides," he said in an almost cheery, welcome-to-the-club kind of way. It was no more alarming than if Martini had noticed that Dad had a ladybug on his arm.

For me, however, this was a dark crisis. I thought the best first step would be to change our consultant. After some discussion as to who we'd most like to work with, we hired Tony Soter. Tony had been winemaker at Chappellet and at Spottswoode, whose wines we admired a great deal.

The first thing that Tony brought to the situation was a total lack of panic—he was a cool, calm presence. That alone helped.

The issue we were facing was a hydrogen-sulfide problem that often doesn't become fully manifest until after the wine's been in the bottle awhile. There was only one possible fix—and it was a massive, wrenching undertaking. All the bottles had to be uncorked by hand, dumped back into tanks, blended, filtered in a variety of ways, and then, if it all worked, rebottled.

It was a complex process that took weeks, and the whole time it felt like my guts were being stretched and twisted. I couldn't eat and could only sleep a couple of hours a night. All I could get down was coffee, and I started losing pounds that I didn't need to shed. Meanwhile, from uncorking thousands of bottles by hand, my right forearm started growing to Popeye-sized proportions.

We found a company that actually specialized in buying used bottles like this—washed them, sterilized them, and resold them. I remember asking the guy when he came to pick them up, "Is there really enough of this kind of thing to base an entire business on?" He just laughed and said, "You'd be surprised."

Besides the sulfide issue with the wines already bottled, with Tony's help we began to dig deeper and realized we had the beginnings of the same problems with wines still in the barrel, such as the 1984 Hillside Select.

Once we got the wines cleaned up through filtering, racking, back-blending, and so forth, we soon realized that Tony wasn't just going to help us run a clean, tidy ship. This guy was a quiet radical. He brought a completely different mind-set to viticulture and winemaking. Rather than keeping us in the lab crunching our numbers, he fanned the flames of the revolutionary idea that a wine has two primary jobs—to bear the stamp of the place from which it comes and to taste good. Working backward from these goals, Elias and I realized, would mean re-engineering nearly everything we'd ever done in the vineyard and in the cellar. With Tony's encouragement we threw out our enology textbooks (metaphorically) and every preconceived notion of how wine was supposed to be produced. We had to unlearn the old approaches and begin to discover how to make wine with our senses, paying attention to what the vines needed in order to be balanced and healthy, focusing on what the wine needed in the cellar.

To begin with, Tony took us out into our vineyard and he'd point at a vine and ask us if it looked healthy—was the foliage the color it should be? Were the leaves droopy? Were there too many shoots per vine? Were there too many clusters per shoot? The idea here was that if you have a healthy, balanced vine, you're much more likely to have ripe, balanced flavors in the grapes you harvest.

When it came time to decide when to pick our grapes he urged us to stop being slaves to our lab numbers. Sugar was only one of several elements to get into balance. The gospel according to Soter said that before we picked up a single lab instrument, before we did anything science-related at all, we first needed to do what should have been obvious all along—hike through the vineyard blocks and taste the fruit and look at the vines.

If the fruit tasted green and unripe, so would the wine. If the grapes tasted ripe and juicy and delicious, then likewise, so would the finished wine. He taught us to pull apart the grapes and look at the seeds and then give them a good crunch in our teeth. If the seed was still green with a lot of pulp clinging to it, and if it mushed when you bit down on it, you'd wind up with raw, green tannins in the wine. If the seed was brown and crunchy, like you'd poured it from a box of Grape Nuts, you'd get ripe, well-structured tannins.

The key to delicious, compelling wine was ripeness. With this idea in mind, a sugar level of 22.5 wasn't the automatic signal to start picking. Instead, your Brix could fall within a range of numbers, such as the levels at which Dad had unintentionally picked back in 1978 and 1979—with excellent results.

Over time, as a consultant, Tony would put his imprint on a number of Napa wineries including Stonegate, Spring Mountain, Sequoia Grove, Stag's Leap Wine Cellars, Niebaum-Coppola, Viader, Dalla Valle, and Araujo.

After two years of overhauling our orientation, Tony told us we'd learned everything he could teach. Our response was a minor panic attack, asking him to please consider staying on as a consultant. I offered him three times what we'd been paying him, and Tony said, "I won't take your money; you don't need me anymore."

For ten years afterward I called Tony every Wednesday before Thanksgiving to thank him from the bottom of my heart for helping us.

It was exciting for Elias and me to finally reach the point where we felt such a sense of confidence that we could start taking risks and fine-tuning our approach both in the vineyard and in the cellar—learning especially to recognize when not to intervene.

It had been apparent early on that the Cabernet Sauvignon from this site offered something special. The juice tasted mouthwateringly good the day we picked and even better days later; the new wine was black, viscous, and opaque. Beyond the flavor and mouthfeel, we had begun to realize how dependable our hillside vineyards were, year after year, without fail. They consistently produced wine we considered outstanding.

What we discovered is that the wine from these hillsides wanted to be lush, rich, and elegant—a far cry from what we'd produced in the food–wine era, a style that was dictated in part by an insecurity about the bolder flavors of Napa Valley fruit versus the fruit harvested in the Old World.

And by the way, those red wines that we had to dump, fix, and re-bottle? The December 15, 1987, issue of *Wine Spectator* scored the Cabernet a 93 and the Merlot a 90.[1] I remember reading these results and turning to Elias and saying, "This is a weird business."

---

1. *Wine Spectator*, December 15, 1987. 1984 Cabernet review: www.winespectator.com/wine/detail/source/search/note_id/48417; 1985 Merlot review: www.winespectator.com/wine/detail/source/search/note_id/3848.

TWENTY-EIGHT

The War of the Apostrophes

The property next to ours, with its castle-like, 1890s-era manor house and surrounding vineyard, had passed through various hands over time. During World War II it had served as a rest camp for naval officers and was the setting for at least three Hollywood movies, including *This Earth Is Mine*. During the later 1940s and into the 1950s it remained a visible landmark in Napa Valley as a well-known resort. After passing to new ownership in 1956, the place closed down as a guest facility and went into quiet decline. Yet at least some grape growing continued on the ranch, as it did elsewhere in the Stags Leap[1] area, until the 1960s and early 1970s, when the local wine industry experienced the resurgence we covered earlier. At that time much of the area's orchard and dairy land was converted (or in many cases reconverted) to vineyards.

In 1970, among the influx of new growers and vintners, Carl Doumani purchased this property and began producing wine under the Stags' Leap Winery label. Carl had done well in restaurants and property development in Los Angeles, where he bought his first bar when he

---

1. Throughout the book, and in this section in particular, the name *Stags Leap* appears in its various permutations—Stag's Leap, Stags' Leap, Stags Leap, and Stagg's Leap. When quoting directly from an original source, I have maintained the form used by the writer. For my own usage, however, I default to the apostrophe-free version.

was a twenty-year-old. Once Carl had moved here, Robert Mondavi reached out to him about the grapes on his site, which sparked an interest in the wine business.

In that same year Warren Winiarski bought a site a bit farther south in Stags Leap, adjacent to Nathan Fay's Cabernet vines. Like Dad, Warren was from Chicago, though his background was in academia rather than in the corporate world. He had a degree in political theory from the University of Chicago and had studied for a year in Naples, Italy, where he developed a lifelong love for all things related to wine. After teaching political theory for a few years at the University of Chicago, he eventually packed up his family and moved to Napa in 1964, where he worked for Lee Stewart at Souverain, learning the basics of winemaking. He then broadened his knowledge at Robert Mondavi Winery, where he had the chance to taste wines sourced from vineyards throughout the Valley, since Mondavi purchased fruit from far and wide. In the fall of 1969, while trying to decide where to stake out his own future here, Warren had a chance to taste Nathan Fay's 1968 Cabernet and was so profoundly impressed by the flavor and texture of the wine that he knew he'd found the right spot. He purchased a 52-acre prune and apple orchard next to Nathan's place and set about creating a vineyard, naming it Stag's Leap Vineyard, which became the initial fruit source for Stag's Leap Wine Cellars.

It seems a foregone conclusion that these neighboring wineries with names set apart by little more than an apostrophe, helmed by two headstrong characters like Warren and Carl, would eventually clash.

In their first lawsuit in 1972, Carl sued Warren to halt the latter's use of the name "Stag's Leap." Warren defended on the basis that it was a geographical term referring to a general area in Napa County and as such Carl had no exclusive rights to the name.

Carl lost that round with Judge Devoto of Napa Superior Court stating in his decision on April 12, 1973, that, "The Court is satisfied from all the evidence that 'Stag's Leap' is a generic or geographical name" to which Carl had no exclusive rights.

The judge, recognizing that Stags Leap covered a substantial area and that the name was already in public domain, allowed both wineries to operate under their respective versions of the name.

Valley observers likely figured this would be the end of it. However, less than a year later, the tables were turned when Warren sued Carl to establish his own exclusive right to the terms "Stag's Leap Vineyards" and "Stag's Leap Vineyards and Wine Cellars."

Carl then cross-complained against Warren, asserting his own exclusive rights to various Stags Leap names. This litigation churned through the court system for the next nine years, during which time both wineries sold their respective Stags Leap wines.

In the middle of all this, in 1981 when Dad was preparing to release his first wine, the 1978 Cabernet Sauvignon, it was clear that the wine had survived nail-biting conditions at harvest, being hauled around the valley in the back of a truck, electric blankets, and other indignities. Somehow the wine gods had smiled, and Dad believed that his out-of-the-starting-gate Cabernet had turned out to be pretty good.

Feeling celebratory, he would informally invite friends and neighboring vintners as they were available to come over to try the wine. Warren Winiarski—still in the midst of his court case with Carl—dropped by at Dad's invitation to taste the wine and catch up on local news. Warren had a great palate and cared passionately about fine wine, so naturally Dad hoped it would pass muster with him.

The tasting started off friendly enough. Dad uncorked a bottle and poured a sample for them both, and I'm sure Dad was pleased that this neighboring vintner, one of the top dogs at the Judgment of Paris, liked the wine and said the sorts of engaging things a new winemaker hopes to hear. Then Warren picked up the bottle and read the label, which included the words, "These grapes were grown in the Stag's Leap area of the Napa Valley." And at that point things got a little chilly. Warren let Dad know that in his opinion Shafer Vineyards had no business using the term "Stag's Leap" on his label and managed to convey the idea that he would stop him from doing so, if need be. I wasn't there and Dad says he doesn't remember exactly who said what, so I don't know how it all played out. What I do know is that it didn't end in a shouting match or anything silly like that. Overall I think Dad felt that Warren was simply being overzealous in this regard, thanks to all the time he'd spent in courtrooms arguing to be sole owner of the place-name.

At that point Dad already had his '79 wines (both a Cabernet and a Zinfandel) bottled with the Stags Leap reference on the label. However, after that, the words "Stag's Leap" disappeared from our labels. John Shafer had no stomach for costly, time-consuming legal entanglements. He saw no value in a short-term spat that offered an iffy outcome. Instead, he would bide his time, give it some thought, and eventually create a new long-term, unassailable approach for highlighting where his grapes originated.

Meanwhile, after years of back and forth, the court sent both Carl and Warren home empty-handed on the name issue with a ruling in 1982 that mirrored the Judge Devoto conclusion nine years prior: "All parties concede 'Stag's Leap' is a geographical name. A geographical name may not be exclusively appropriated as a trade name...here there was evidence all parties used the name "Stag's Leap" in combination with other words connected with grape growing or winemaking before Winiarski filed his complaint on December 19, 1973. The court specifically found none of the names claimed by the parties acquired secondary meaning before this date."[2]

In other words, a geographical name cannot be solely owned by any one entity. The only time that might happen, according to the decision, is if it had acquired "secondary meaning," which is to say if the name "Stags Leap" had become so entirely associated with a single business that it eclipsed an association with all others.

In spite of all the legal wrangling between the two, which had been dubbed "The War of the Apostrophes," Carl and Warren appeared to

2. Stags Leap District Appellation Committee (John Shafer, Chairman), Petition to Establish the Viticultural Area of "Stags Leap," August 22, 1985, private archive, Stags Leap District.

hold no great animosity toward each other. Afterward, at some point, they created a joint lot of a wine called "Accord," which sold at the Napa Valley Wine Auction. Carl told a newspaper reporter that he and Warren had gone on a vacation together[3] and they even joined forces in 1984 to sue Gary Andrus at Pine Ridge, when Pine Ridge released a Stags Leap Cuvee.

3. Thom Elkjer, "Loveable Rogue," *San Francisco Chronicle,* April 7, 2005, www.sfgate .com/cgi-bin/article.cgi?f=/c/a/2005/04/07/WIGOPC1NEI1.DTL&ao=all.

TWENTY-NINE

The AVA

The Warren and Carl imbroglio represented a small-scale version of much larger events that were coming together in the early '80s having to do with the role of vineyard sites in the evolving world of California fine wine. For a long time in this country, there were really only two kinds of wine: red and white. Occasionally you'd see them dressed up with names like Hearty Burgundy or Chablis, but wine was essentially known by its color. By the 1960s and into the 1970s a shift was occurring, and consumers began to associate quality with the names of specific grape varieties. White wine drinkers started to ask for Chardonnay. Those who preferred reds zeroed in on Zinfandel and Cabernet Sauvignon. By the late '70s and early '80s a small, but growing, number of consumers equated distinctive wine character with specific areas in California. And thanks to improved approaches to grape growing and winemaking, Napa Valley was rising to the top in terms of quality.

While it was a new idea that special places in the United States could produce wines of distinct character, it was an old story in Europe. The strongly held belief among vignerons and many wine consumers is that these areas produce distinctive characters in wine—the basis for the concept of *terroir.* In Spain, Rioja was classified in 1926. In France, the Institut

National des Appellations d'Origine, which administers and regulates appellations, was established in 1935, with Côtes du Rhône receiving the first appellation of origin recognition in 1937. Italy, Portugal, and other countries largely based their system on the French model, called *appellation d'origine contrôlée* (AOC).[1]

Over the ensuing decades, wine consumers had come to equate value with these regions. Within a larger AOC such as Bordeaux sprang up smaller regions, such as Medoc, which distinguished itself in terms of quality, leaving vintners in the United States eager to create appellations in similar fashion and work to build their own localized prominence.

In 1978 the Bureau of Alcohol, Tobacco, and Firearms (BATF), an arm of the U.S. Treasury Department, had announced that it was finally open for business with regard to establishing official American Viticultural Areas (AVAs). The agency took great pains to make clear that by certifying these newly named districts, it was in no way weighing in on the quality of wine produced there. AVAs would be based on geography, climate, and historical validity, as in the French model. Unlike the French model, though, vintners in a given U.S. appellation would not be required to use only specific grape varieties.

Fewer than five months after making this announcement, the BATF heard from the Napa Valley Vintners and Napa Valley Grape Growers, who jointly submitted a petition dated January 17, 1979, asking to define the Napa Valley Viticultural area as the watershed of the Napa River.

By the watershed, they meant of course all the land that contains tributaries feeding the river; essentially this meant from the ridgeline of the Mayacamas Mountains on the west to the ridgeline of the Vacas on the east, meeting more or less at Mt. St. Helena in the north. From a geological standpoint it seemed solid enough, however, a group of vintners and growers, who became known as the Eastern Growers Group, formed

---

1. Jancis Robinson, *The Oxford Companion to Wine* (New York: Oxford University Press, 1994), 329, 502, 799.

in short order to ensure that their properties east of the Vacas would be included in the new AVA. These were the Pope, Capell, Gordon, Chiles, Priest, and Wooden valleys.

To help hash out the issue, the BATF held a public hearing on April 28 and 29, 1980, in the Oakville-Rutherford Room of the Holiday Inn in Napa.

Day one kicked off with an introduction from Chuck Carpy regarding the original petition set forth by the 35 members of the Vintners Association and the 160 members of the Grape Growers Association. Chuck talked about how long these groups had hoped to form a Napa AVA, citing a letter dated 1971 that he'd written to the BATF regarding this concept.

But most of the people who showed up to speak at the hearing were the Eastern Growers Group and their supporters, who were eager to convince the BATF to enlarge the boundaries of the AVA beyond those outlined in the original petition.

Among those supporters was Robert Mondavi, who said his family's winery had for years purchased fruit from these areas and blended it into various Napa Valley–labeled bottlings, specifically mentioning Pope Valley fruit.

When Tim Mondavi took his turn at the microphone, he pointed out that their family's winery had been very pleased to buy fruit from "Carneros, Yountville, Oakville, St. Helena, Calistoga, Pope Valley, Chiles Valley, Wooden Valley and Gordon Valley." Tim told the BATF hearing officers, "It is definitely our feeling, and apparently that of the consumer, that these wines exhibit the character of the Napa Valley."

The Mondavis were joined by many other supporters, including Brother Timothy, Master Winemaker at Christian Brothers, who spoke in specific support of Gordon Valley, Capell Valley, and Priest Valley.

As a visual aid, Donald Gordon, a longtime eastern grower, presented a bottle of wine labeled 1954 Napa Valley Beringer Rosé made from Gordon Valley fruit.

The larger wineries expressed worry that they would have far less flexibility in buying grapes for their Napa Valley wines if the AVA boundaries were dictated by the watershed and that ultimately quality would suffer.

Near the end of the hearings Dick Maher of Beringer, representing the original petitioning group, took a turn at the podium to clarify their position, saying that they had simply proposed the Napa Valley watershed as a minimum area—stressing the word "minimum"—and that if the BATF "has no objection to geopolitical boundaries, the Napa Valley Vintners and the Napa Valley Grapegrowers do not object to the inclusion of the eastern boundaries."

As he was winding down the hearing, Stephen Higgins, a BATF hearing officer, hinted at what the agency had in mind down the road, telling the assembled vintners and growers that beyond a Napa AVA, they saw a future for subappellations within the larger area. This would spark lots of conversations among growers and vintners in areas such as Oakville, Rutherford, Mt. Veeder, and Atlas Peak, giving them the idea of creating their own Medoc-like AVAs within Napa Valley.

Higgins then closed by giving Napa winedom an idea of the task that lay before the BATF. The problem was, he said, "No one knows what the Napa Valley is."

"And," he continued, "if Brother Timothy will allow me, I remember the story about the little boy who was drawing a picture and a man asked him what he was drawing a picture of. And he said, 'I'm drawing a picture of God.'

"[The man said], 'That's impossible. Nobody knows what he looks like.'

"And the boy said, 'Wait 'til I'm done and you'll know.'"[2]

---

2. William F. Heintz, Napa Valley Hearing before the Bureau of Alcohol, Tobacco, Firearms and Explosives in the Matter of: Proposed Regulatory Definitions of "Appellation of Origin," held Monday, April 28, 1980 and Tuesday, April 29, 1980, 1980 client-commissioned research project, William F. Heintz Collection.

The Napa Valley AVA, including the eastern valleys, was approved by the BATF nine months later and became effective February 27, 1981.[3] Higgins's closing comments at the end of the Napa public hearing proved to be prescient. The tricky business of determining what an AVA looks like would continue to bedevil the process, as we and others would discover.

3. Department of the Treasury, Bureau of Alcohol, Tobacco, Firearms and Explosives, "Napa Valley Viticultural Area," 46 *Fed. Reg.* 18 (January 28, 1981).

THIRTY

The District

The first subappellation out of the starting gate was Los Carneros, a clean, beautiful growing area along the edges of San Pablo Bay, which is the northernmost tip of San Francisco Bay. Wine grapes had been grown here since the late 1800s.

In the fall of 1980, even before the Napa AVA was approved, Beaulieu Vineyard submitted a petition to award Carneros AVA status. Their concept was to keep Carneros entirely within the boundaries of Napa County. The BATF published notice that December in the *Federal Register* that they'd received the petition and solicited public comment—which they got. Growers on the Sonoma County side did not appreciate being cut out simply because they were on the wrong side of a county line that was invisible to Mother Nature.

The agency held a public hearing in Santa Rosa, California, to listen to a variety of growers and vintners from both counties air their ideas and concerns.

One of the biggest concerns voiced by vintners on the Napa side was that if the AVA extended into Sonoma they would not be able to use both Carneros and Napa Valley on their labels, but would be forced into a difficult choice between one or the other.

Some suggested that Carneros be split into two AVAs, a Sonoma Carneros and a Napa Carneros.

Finally, there was lots of back-and-forth regarding the boundaries—should it end here at these railroad tracks? Should the line go here along this creek? A Sonoma group was formed to hash out the boundary questions on their side.

The result of all this was that the BATF published a ruling in June 1982 that extended the proposed AVA well inside Sonoma County. In fact, two-thirds of the region would be Sonoma.

The final result, after nearly three years of study, discussion, and back-and-forth, was that the BATF approved the AVA, making it effective September 19, 1983.[1]

A model for the AVA application process was quickly beginning to emerge (in Napa as well as in other wine-producing regions around the country). It looked like this: Group A would get together, come up with AVA boundaries that seemed ideal to them, which might follow structures like ridgelines and streambeds and take a right turn at the big, gnarled oak tree over yonder and so on. The boundaries would, naturally, include their own properties. Group A would submit their lengthy petition with a host of supporting documentation, and then a Group B would form, a bit ruffled, refusing to be cut out of the action because their vineyards happened to lie just past the big, gnarled oak tree. There would be a one- or two-day public hearing at a local hotel conference room, where maps and photos would be examined by the BATF and where testimony would be heard from a long line of retired grape growers reminiscing about how before Prohibition pickers would load up wagons with fruit from this or that beyond-the-gnarled-oak-tree vineyard site and haul it to a respectable Group A winery, where that fruit became part of the blend that made this would-be-AVA's reputation.

---

1. Department of the Treasury, Bureau of Alcohol, Tobacco, Firearms and Explosives, "Establishment of Los Carneros Viticultural Area," 48 *Fed. Reg.* 161 (August 18, 1983).

The second Napa area to request AVA status was Howell Mountain, which offered a much more kumbaya scenario regarding how the whole process could work. The BATF published notice in the *Federal Register* of the original petition by a small group of growers and vintners in August 1984. Howell Mountain is a lush, forested mountain northeast of St. Helena; hillside vineyards had first been planted there in the 1880s. It also included the little village of Angwin, a largely Seventh-Day Adventist community of vegetarians and teetotalers, which has coexisted peaceably with the surrounding vineyards and wine community. The agency received not a single comment, written or otherwise, and the thing sailed through. It was approved just four months later, and the AVA became effective January 30, 1984.[2]

Howell Mountain offered some hope that the wine industry here and the BATF were on track working the kinks out of the system. By mid-1984, when I heard Dad and Dick Steltzner first talking about creating such a petition for Stags Leap, I couldn't help but wonder if theirs would go the direction of the more contentious Napa and Carneros approvals or Howell Mountain's without-a-hitch version, or if it would run a whole new course we couldn't yet anticipate.

Dad, for a long time, had felt there was something special about the Stags Leap area. It started when he tasted Nate Fay's 1968 Cabernet (in similar fashion to Winiarski)—a homemade wine that was elegant and polished at a young age. The idea was brought home again to him at the Vintner's Symposium in 1981, when so many of the people who tasted his 1978 Cab had persisted in asking how much Merlot he'd added. As time went on his belief was reinforced as more and more wine experts expressed similar ideas.

In June 1983, Anthony Dias Blue wrote in the *San Francisco Chronicle*, "There is a thread that connects these wines and it is the Stag's Leap regional personality. All the wines have velvety texture—a lushness

2. Department of the Treasury, Bureau of Alcohol, Tobacco, Firearms and Explosives, "Howell Mountain Viticultural Area," 48 *Fed. Reg.* 252 (December 30. 1983).

that is nicely balanced by a firm acidity. They are big without being clumsy and awkward."[3]

In 1984 *Connoisseurs' Handbook of California Wines* called Stag's Leap a "superb viticultural pocket" which is "one of California's most important wine-growing microclimates."

The first official meeting to discuss petitioning for AVA status took place here at the winery on August 23, 1984. To kick things off, Dad called a group that he knew would work well together and see things from a similar perspective: Joe Phelps, Nate Fay, and Dick Steltzner. Dad and Joe went way back to the days when Dad had borrowed Joe's truck to haul around his inaugural vintages in barrels. Dick and Dad had been pals for a long while—Dick had been the first to encourage Dad to make some homemade wine in the lead-up to creating the winery. And Dad and Nate Fay were on such good terms they'd actually discussed—fairly earnestly for a while—the idea of starting a winery together.

In that first meeting the group discussed, tentatively, what the boundaries would be. Steltzner passed around a rough outline, a hand-drawn map, based on airflow, soil type, and temperature. The Vaca Mountains to the east and cluster of northern and western hills formed a kind of box canyon on this side of the Valley enclosing a number of vineyard sites owned by Phelps and Mondavi, among others, along with wineries including Shafer, Stags' Leap Winery, Stag's Leap Wine Cellars, Clos du Val, Pine Ridge Winery, and a 15-acre portion of Silverado Vineyards.

Next they each volunteered to reach out to potential stakeholders with the basics of the AVA proposal. Nate said he'd talk to Robert Mondavi, Warren Winiarski, and Ernie Ilsley (a neighboring grower). Dick would contact Carl Doumani, Keith Bowers (U.C. Davis Farm Advisor), Bernard Portet of Clos du Val, and Gary Andrus of Pine Ridge. Joe Phelps and Dad agreed to speak with reps from the fifteen or so wineries that were known to have purchased Stags Leap fruit.

3. Anthony Dias Blue, "Cabernet's of Stag's Leap," *San Francisco Chronicle*, June 1, 1983, 20.

As a last item of business they voted to name Dad as chairman of the committee.

Building a case for the Stags Leap AVA would be, they knew, a big task. To satisfy the BATF, they'd need to establish that the name Stags Leap was a generally understood and accepted grape-growing and wine-producing area. Documentation going back to the 1880s would need to be gathered. They would need to interview old-timers who could testify to the historical authenticity of the name.

The Appellation Committee would need to prove that the soil types were unique within the surrounding area, which would mean getting documentation and testimony from geologists and soil experts.

Data would need to be gathered regarding climate—establishing the somewhat nebulous idea that the combination of wind, rain, temperatures, clouds, and sunlight here offered grapes something different from what they would experience a few miles to the north or to the south.

All of this would require a great deal of lawyering. One of the first things the group did was to hire an attorney who would prepare the petition, handle the replies and related correspondence, manage various conferences and calls, and follow through the BATF's administrative rule-making process until a final ruling. There could be a great deal of work related to responding to counterpetitions and a host of tasks to prepare for and participate in a public hearing. In March 1985 Dad and the Appellation Committee hired Richard P. Mendelson, then in the San Francisco office of Jackson, Tufts, Cole & Black.

Mendelson was clear with Dad from the start that he saw the Stags Leap AVA process as a "potentially volatile situation."

One of the early concerns was that the whole petition process could get fouled up because of that legal action I mentioned earlier involving Carl Doumani and Warren Winiarski joining together to sue Pine Ridge Winery over its use of the Stags Leap name on one of their new wine releases. The BATF could potentially look at the tangled legal status of the name and say "this isn't our department" and turn the whole thing over to the U.S. Patent and Trademark Office for review and then we would be in here-there-be-dragons territory.

Mendelson had been involved in the Temecula AVA petition process in Southern California. In that case, Callaway Winery—whose full name was apparently Callaway Vineyard and Winery, Temecula, California—had opposed the petition by local growers and vintners, saying it amounted to a trademark infringement. In an opinion submitted to the BATF Callaway wrote, "We see it [the Association's petition] as an attempt to ride the coattails of the name which has become a valuable, meaningful appellation for wine consumers."[4]

Dad met with Carl to get his take on the creation of an AVA. And it seems that he was pretty disinterested from the start. Carl has been called a very likable rogue more than once, which I think he appreciates. He does his own thing, and sitting through a bunch of committee meetings probably did not appeal to him. Ultimately, he didn't see the creation of a Stags Leap AVA as offering him any meaningful advantage in selling his wines. Plus, at that particular time, he was looking at selling his place, which meant he could potentially leave the whole issue to a new owner.

Even so, Carl did hang around the process for a short while. In fact, one time Elias and I were in the cellar cleaning tanks and equipment, and through the glass wall that separated the working winery from a conference room, I remember seeing Carl, Warren, Gary Andrus, Dick Steltzner, Joe Phelps, and my dad all sitting around a table talking about the AVA. Half the guys in that room had sued one another at various times, and yet they had the decency and business smarts to put that aside and work together in the same room.

Initially Warren Winiarski was not warm to the AVA idea either. First of all, it was complicated. How the legal challenge between Carl, Warren, and Gary played itself out could have an impact on the future

---

4. Department of the Treasury, Bureau of Alcohol, Tobacco, Firearms and Explosives, "Establishment of the Temecula Viticultural Area," 49 *Fed. Reg.* 206 (October 23, 1984).

of the AVA—it could certainly impact the eventual name. Richard Mendelson had warned that if a judge found in favor of Carl and Warren in regard to the Pine Ridge case, it could create a situation in which only Carl's and Warren's wineries could use the Stags Leap name and the AVA would have to be called something else altogether.

Warren wrote a letter to Dick Steltzner in March 1984 that spelled out where he stood at that time: "my position regarding any viticultural district is strongly influenced by what such a district would be called . . . Under the circumstances [given that the proposed name was Stags Leap], I cannot support your activities."

He did, however, close by saying that he looked forward to further discussions. Dad met with Warren a few times as things progressed, and he remained optimistic that they could figure this thing out and that ultimately Warren would throw his support behind the endeavor.

In the meantime, though, work on the petition continued without a commitment from Warren.

The Appellation Committee finally submitted its petition on August 22, 1985; it was signed by Dad as chairman on behalf of growers including Peter Candy, F. S. Foote, Ernie Ilsley, Monte Reedy, Angelo Regusci, Norman Robinson, Charles See, Jerry Taylor, and Susan Vineyard. Wineries represented included Clos du Val, Robert Mondavi Winery, Joseph Phelps Winery, Pine Ridge Winery, Shafer Vineyards, and Steltzner Vineyards.

Not long after the petition was sent to Washington, D.C., something significant changed—Gary Andrus, Warren, and Carl settled their differences out of court. Gary would be allowed to use the Stags Leap name on his wine label as long as he agreed not to turn it into a brand.

This brought the interested parties together again, and after further discussion the group decided to rewrite portions of the petition, which they resubmitted in December 1985. This amendment asked that the AVA be named Stags Leap *District* (rather than simply Stags Leap), which was hoped would help differentiate the name of the AVA from the name of Carl's and Warren's wineries. Believe me all the vintners in that group were, in their own ways, just as sensitive about protecting their own brands as Carl and Warren. Here at our winery we have gone into high legal gear a number of times when other wineries have attempted to use any of our trademarked properties, such as the name Hillside Select.

Your brand is your promise to the consumer. It's your reputation. It's the encapsulation of your core values. At a winery of our size it's not just a logo. It's those long hours I spent in the early '80s trying to make wine and learn the art of winemaking at the same time. It's the weeks Dad spent in airports and in rental cars to sell our wine. Our brand is the hundreds of times Dad, Elias, and I have gotten up in freezing, pre-dawn hours to taste grapes in the vineyard. It's the all-nighters. It's the vintages that wouldn't let us sleep. It's the days I missed with my family because of a sales schedule that had me in New York or London or Hamburg or on a cruise ship in icy rain. When someone attempts to steal our brand it's personal, as though some part of my family has been assaulted.

So yes, vintners get pretty testy when it looks like someone else is messing around with their brand.

The upshot of this new petition was that we found common ground. Warren signed on and lent his support to the endeavor, and we moved forward.

A new wrinkle occurred around December, when the first amendment was sent to Washington. It was becoming clear that one of our neighbors, Silverado Vineyards, was likely preparing a counterpetition, which would argue that the western border should extend all the way to the Napa River and include all of Silverado's vineyard property, rather than only the 15 acres within the borders of the then-current AVA.

Silverado had opened its doors in 1981, originally calling itself (very briefly) Trymill Winery, which I believe was a combination of the names of its owners Lillian Disney Truyens, the widow of Walt Disney, and Ron and Diane (Disney) Miller. For a long time locals referred to it simply as the Disney winery, which eventually died out, as its owners have never really attempted to capitalize on any Disney connection. The winery, to its credit, has done a very fine job standing on its own merits.

Jack Stuart was the winemaker and general manager at the time, a smart and very likable guy, who had earned his degree in literature and creative writing at Stanford University before moving into winemaking. He poured his skills of persuasion into convincing the Stags Leap Appellation Committee that the boundaries ought to be moved.

In a letter to Dick Steltzner, Jack wrote: "[the] committee on the viticultural district has seen fit not to include Mrs. Disney's Cabernet plantings in the first drawing of the proposed district. This exclusion is wrong from the point of view of historical evidence, geography and climate, soil and local and national reputation."[5]

He went on to contend that grapes purchased from the Disney property, going back to the nineteenth century, had always been referred to as from Stags Leap and that the soil types on the site were identical to other sites owned by Carl Doumani, Dick Steltzner, and others in the proposed Stags Leap AVA.

By May 1986 Jack Stuart had discussed his position at length with the group and had even shown a draft of the counterpetition they were indeed drafting. In the end he won them over. The original boundaries had been based on the idea of airflow from San Francisco Bay as being a distinct character of the Stags Leap area. As I mentioned, there is a kind of box canyon, or funnel, that exists, made up of the Vaca Mountains and its Stags Leap palisades on one side and a series of small, round hills on the other. (Silverado Trail runs diagonally through these hills at one point.) While it was true that most of Silverado Vineyards' property lay outside that funnel, there was a preponderance of evidence that, as Jack had alluded to in his letter to Steltzner, it was historically thought of as part of the Stags Leap area and did share significant soil similarities and climate characteristics.

5. Letter in private archive of Stags Leap District papers and materials at Shafer Vineyards.

All of which is why on June 26, 1986, the Appellation Committee submitted their second amendment to the AVA petition, changing the western boundary to that of Napa River, rather than the series of peaks between the river and Silverado Trail. All other boundary lines remained fixed, including the ring of hills to the north, which were the northern boundary (the upper end of the funnel). This second amendment added another 350 acres to the proposed AVA, which included properties owned by Silverado Vineyards, as well as additional acreage owned by Mondavi. The AVA now totaled 2,550 acres altogether. When the BATF published notice of this latest amendment, in February 1987, they announced a period of sixty days in which they would accept written and oral comments.

On the final day of the comment period the BATF heard from Stanley Anderson of S. Anderson Vineyard, a sparkling wine producer, located on Yountville Cross Road, about a quarter of a mile down from Silverado Trail. Stan was a retired dentist from Pasadena, who, like my dad and a lot of others, had come under the spell of Napa Valley in the late '60s and early '70s. He and his wife, Carol, established their first vineyard, planted to Chardonnay, in 1971, and then built their winery in 1974. Like the rest of us they'd worked hard to make a success of things. Carol, in her forties, studied enology at U.C. Davis, and went on to become one of the Valley's first female winemakers. Stan continued to commute to Southern California for some time, maintaining his dental practice to ensure a steady income. By the late '80s, their winery was highly regarded and was a popular stop along Yountville Cross Road.

Stan sent to the BATF a counterpetition that at its core was pretty straightforward—he wanted to see the northern boundary moved five hundred yards further north to Yountville Cross Road, which would mean that his vineyard property would be included in the AVA along with a few other growers, including Richard Chambers. This would add another 150 acres to the AVA's overall size.

Anderson's proposal indicated real seriousness of intent, weighing in at almost fifty pages plus that many more in "exhibits," such as old property maps, photocopies of deeds, historical data, and so on. It was clearly a project that had been in the works for some time and certainly bore the professional flourish of a law firm's involvement. Yountville Cross Road, according to this proposal, had been the historic northern boundary of Rancho Yajome, when the Mexican land grant was given to the constitutional governor of the time, Juan B. Alvarado, in 1861. Rancho Yajome was essentially an overlay of Stags Leap District, according to the Anderson document. In the 1860s, an Act of Congress had granted this same land with this same northern boundary (Yountville Cross Road) to one Salvador Vallejo in a deed that was signed by the hand of none other than President Abraham Lincoln. It was as though Anderson was daring the BATF to go against the august wisdom of one of our greatest presidents.

Throughout Anderson's proposal he sprinkled the phrase a "logical, well recognized, and easily administered boundary" with respect to using the roadway as a line of demarcation. He must have assumed that "easily administered" would be catnip to bureaucrats in Washington. He illustrated his point thusly: "The northern boundary of the viticultural area as described in the original petition and subsequent amendments is difficult to describe and even more difficult to identify on land. The boundary, in fact, separates vineyards, cutting across rows of grapes in an arbitrary fashion, making it impossible to know which vines produce grapes within the Stags Leap District and which vines produce grapes of a supposedly different quality."[6]

Of course this sparked a lot of conversation within the Stags Leap Appellation Committee. Dad says he was inclined to cede to Anderson's request, given that it was only another 150 acres; however, he and everyone else on the committee worried about how far this would go. Apparently there was some neighborhood buzz about the idea of petitioning to get

6. Stanley Anderson, "Written Comments Submitted in Response to Petition to Establish the Viticultural Area of 'Stags Leap District' under Title 27 Code of Federal Regulations, Part 9," April 10, 1987, private archive at Shafer Vineyards.

the AVA extended *beyond* Yountville Cross Road. Any grower on the other side of that strip of asphalt would rightly ask, "What about me?"

But if the Appellation Committee gave in to everyone, they eventually would end up with a district with very little distinction or meaning. Somewhere in this process they were going to make someone feel unjustly excluded and angry. In the midst of all this, Richard Mendelson warned the committee that, as a government agency located in far-off Washington, D.C., the BATF was likely to be more comfortable with a road they could see on a map as a boundary than with a series of hilltops. But after weighing the various voices and possible outcomes Dad and the committee decided that the northern hills were quite literally where they would hold the line.

On May 28, Richard Mendelson FedEx'ed a counter to Stan's counterproposal. It said, essentially, that S. Anderson and the property of nearby growers, such as Richard Chambers, had always been considered part of the Yountville area, not Stags Leap. This contention was backed up by pages upon pages of exhibits, such as interviews with old-timers, clippings from newspaper in the 1800s, parcel maps, and more. (We had *never* been so enamored by the thoughts and opinions of Napa's Victorian-age vintners as we were when establishing AVAs.)

On June 29, Stan countered this counter to his counterproposal. This time he added a new twist, which would perhaps influence the direction of future disagreements, when he wrote, "in many ways, the proposed northern addition is more like the bulk of the appellation than the areas along the western edge and the southern end of the Stags Leap District."

On September 29, 1987—in the middle of harvest—the BATF announced that in the best interest of all sides on this, they had set a hearing for December 1 and 2, 1987, at the Yountville Veterans Home. Anyone interested in participating in the hearing would need to submit a written summary of the oral comments they wished to present by November 6.[7]

---

7. Department of the Treasury, Bureau of Alcohol, Tobacco, Firearms and Explosives, "Stags Leap District Viticultural Area; Public Hearing," 52 *Fed. Reg.* 199 (October 29, 1987).

For a process that had meandered on at a turtle's pace for two years, suddenly there was pressure to act.

Both sides begged for more time to prepare. In an overnighted letter dated October 12, Dad asked that the hearing be postponed at least three months. Stan Anderson shot a letter to Washington, D.C., a few days later asking for at least a twelve-month postponement. Both requests were denied.

The Appellation Committee knew that if they were to succeed they'd need to be organized and unified. Warren Winiarski headed the group's hearing subcommittee and worked vigorously to put together a list of speakers and to determine the strategy and substance of their presentation.

THIRTY-ONE

The Hearing

December 1 was rainy and overcast, typical weather for the holidays here. Inside the packed hearing room on day one, Dad opened with an overview of the process thus far and introduced the main tenants of their group's argument for maintaining the current boundary lines.

Each of the Appellation Committee's chosen speakers focused on specific areas of their contention with regard to the AVA's features. Winiarski spoke about the importance of maintaining their boundaries, saying, "The northern ring of hills is the key geographical link in the circle. Going beyond that ring to the Yountville Cross Road ... destroys the unity of the distinctive area."

It seems from the questions that followed, the BATF panel had its doubts. BATF's James Focaretta questioned Warren on this, asking, "How can we include the property between the river and the mountains [as outlined in the amendment to include Silverado] and not include the same—in other words, if we're going to say this is a natural barrier made by the mountains to the north, why not the mountains to the west?"

Later, after a meteorologist had testified on behalf of the Appellation Committee, making the point that wind flow was different on one side of the northern ring than the other, another hearing officer said, "I went up to those hills yesterday . . . and that wind came through pretty heavy. Is it even more heavy to the south and west of that?"

In a later question a third hearing panelist asked the meteorologist, "If you were basing it on the meteorological effects of the winds, the funnel effect, etc., then the boundary would not go to the river, is that correct?"

To which the climate expert replied, "If we were going to base the boundary strictly on meteorology the boundaries would be drawn differently than what we see here."[1]

Stan Anderson and the growers who were proponents of extending the northern boundary also had their say. The testimony of their long-time residents contradicted the memories of the old-timers the Appellation Committee had recruited. Their hired historian contradicted our hired historian. In some cases both sides used the same maps and the same ancient press articles to promote various parts of their causes. But in essence the speakers in both groups were delivering a live version of what they'd already stated in their petitions.

The surprise of the hearings came on the second day, when George Altamura took to the podium. Besides being a vintner George was a commercial property owner in the town of Napa. He was neither part of the Stags Leap Appellation Committee nor the group that wanted the Yountville Cross Road boundary. Instead he was challenging the validity of the southern boundary. He wanted the BATF to move the AVA's boundary two miles south to a point where Soda Creek enters the Napa River. This would have the effect of including his winery and vineyard (today the site of Darioush). Altamura contended that his property shared many of the same features found within the proposed Stags Leap District, including soils, vegetation, and the all-important wind pattern.

1. Karen I. Lillard and Doris Levine (hearing reporters with Lillard & Associates, Petaluma, CA), transcript of Stags Leap District Public Hearing, December 1–2, 1987, private archive, Stags Leap District.

We later learned that after the hearing, Ernie Weir, Altamura's neighbor to the south at Hagafen Cellars, had written to the BATF regarding the southern boundary question, saying if the boundary was moved those two miles to include Altamura, Weir would like his vineyards and winery to be included too. However, he noted, "perhaps a more appropriate and correct southern border will not include either of us."[2]

After four and a half years of petitions and proposals, the BATF's final ruling on this issue came on January 17, 1989. In a lengthy description of the nature of the various petitions, the written comments, and the oral comments at the hearings, the agency felt that all parties had successfully demonstrated that there was indeed a recognizable place called Stags Leap District, from a historical, geological, and climate perspective. In the end they sided with the concept of laying that northern boundary on Yountville Cross Road. The eastern boundary on the ridgeline of the Vaca Mountains had never been in dispute, so that stayed. The western boundary would be the Napa River and the southern boundary would stay as it was. The agency saw no historical merit in moving the line to Soda Creek as Altamura had suggested.

Basically the BATF fell in line with the terminology in Stan Anderson's counterpetition: "logical, well recognized, and easily administered." To its credit the agency kept the AVA small, just 2,700 acres, of which about 1,300 acres were planted to grapes.

When it comes to questions like this, I believe in the legitimacy of regional character. A Cabernet from Howell Mountain will typically have rich flavors and big tannins that settle down beautifully with age, while a Cab from Stags Leap District will be softer and a bit more enticing at a younger age. Cabernets from Rutherford and Oakville can be classics that tend to strike a balance somewhere between these two. I think the difficulty with defining the borders of an AVA comes down to a big contrast in the instruments used to draw the lines. Mapmakers and

2. Department of the Treasury, Bureau of Alcohol, Tobacco, Firearms and Explosives, "Stags Leap District Viticultural Area," 54 *Fed. Reg.* 17 (January 17, 1989).

government agencies work with fine-point instruments to draw their boundaries. They are mathematical and precise. Mother Nature's boundaries however are fat and circuitous. They overlap with other boundaries and regions. They're messy; the edges are fuzzy and defy definition.

A postscript of sorts happened during the early fall of 1989 when I was turning from Silverado Trail onto Yountville Cross Road and saw a picking crew at work in Richard Chamber's Cabernet vineyard. We had purchased all the fruit from Richard's site for a few years and our contract was set up so that we controlled a good deal of how the vines were cultivated and when the fruit would be harvested. In this case I'd told Richard we didn't want to pick anything for at least another two weeks. So discovering a team of guys picking Cab was surprising to say the least. I turned my car around and parked in front of the vineyard. When I found Richard I said, "What're you doing? We're not supposed to pick for another couple of weeks."

He explained without any signs of remorse that he was fulfilling an agreement with Stan Anderson. Since Richard hadn't had the cash to help cover the legal costs of participating in the haggling over the AVA, he said he'd make it up to Stan with five tons of Cabernet Sauvignon. And that was that. Five tons of grapes that were supposed to be ours went to help defend the northern boundary and gave Stan his first Stags Leap District Cabernet. And short of blowing my stack or some other useless gesture, there really wasn't much I could do about it. Once you pick a grape, you can't put it back on.

THIRTY-TWO

Chardonnay

I have to back up a bit now, because a couple of other significant stories were playing out while the Stags Leap Appellation drama was under way.

In addition to buying Cabernet from neighbors such as Richard Chambers, by the mid-1980s we were making more Chardonnay, augmenting our own fruit with tonnage purchased from Monticello Vineyards, located several miles south of us on Big Ranch Road, and Spicer Vineyard, situated across the road from us on Silverado Trail, as well as other nearby growers. (At that time you could buy Chardonnay from vineyards planted throughout the length of the Valley, unlike now, when nearly all of it is concentrated in the southernmost area of Carneros.) We had done pretty well with Chardonnay. Our 1980 became the first Shafer wine served at the White House, poured at a State Dinner during which President Ronald Reagan hosted visiting Indian Prime Minister Indira Gandhi.

The critical reviews for the wine were mostly positive, although *Wine Spectator* handed us a 67 for the 1985 vintage (our lowest score for white wine), which had prompted one of three attempts on my part to resign. I went to Dad in this particular case and said, "Look, this is not working out. I'm not cutting it."

Dad said, "Well, what'd you do?"

I gave him a long list of mistakes, including over-racking, using the wrong filters, and so on.

His response was simply to say don't make the same mistake twice. And get back to work.

To his everlasting credit he wouldn't let me quit. He knew that I was fully aware that we weren't doing the right thing with Chardonnay. We still hadn't figured out several key things. One was, we were still making Chardonnay like a red wine. We were crushing and destemming it and then letting it cold soak in a stainless steel tank for a few hours to give the juice contact with the skins. Then we pressed it.

We later realized that this was a terrible idea. To get pristine, lively, pure flavors, you wanted as *little* juice-to-skin contact as possible. The tannins in the skin of the grape detracted from all the beauty we hoped to find in the finished wine. Thus we had to completely reconfigure how we treated the grape on the crush pad and in the cellar—no more crushing, destemming, and cold soaking. We learned to put whole clusters of newly picked Chardonnay into a press, which gently cracks the skins open and pushes the juice out, leaving skins, seeds, and stems behind.

A second thing we hadn't sorted out yet was our cooperage, meaning our barrel usage: which kinds of wood to use, what level of toast, and for how long. At the time, we were still aging in sixty-gallon Limousin oak barrels. Limousin is the widest-grained of all French oak, and as such imparts a great deal of oak character to the wine. With white wine in particular it can overwhelm the fruit's aromas and flavors.

The third piece of the Chardonnay puzzle that hadn't snapped into place was the idea of where to cultivate the fruit.

Fortunately that began to change for us around 1986, when we made contact with a grower in Carneros named Larry Hyde.

Larry got his start in the wine industry in 1970 when he dropped out of U.C. Berkeley to work at Ridge Winery in the Santa Cruz Mountains. Later he moved up this way and worked at a vineyard leased by Mondavi; stints with Stag's Leap Wine Cellars and Joseph Phelps followed.

In 1979 his father wanted to invest in some vineyard land, and at Larry's urging, purchased 100 acres in Carneros. Here, Larry initially planted Chardonnay, Pinot Noir, and Sauvignon Blanc.

In some ways Carneros is a different world than the rest of the Valley. Sitting as it does next to the cold, salt water of San Pablo Bay, the climate has a distinct marine influence. Summers are markedly cooler, with near-constant breezes and soil that is predominantly heavy, gray clay with some remnants of seafloor, such as shells. The clay is very dense and viscous and holds a lot of soil moisture; however, it's so thick that root penetration is tough. Even though the moisture is out there in abundance, the vines can't get much of it—like the line in the poem, "Water, water everywhere but not a drop to drink." The difficulty accessing moisture, plus the low nutrient value of the clay, keeps the vines from fattening out with leaves and foliage as they tend to on the Valley floor.

The fruit from Larry's vineyards was fantastic, like nothing else I'd tasted locally. The acids were bright and lively, and the flavors were exotic and attractive. As an added plus, I liked Larry. His family had been farmers in California since the 1830s, and I appreciated his combination of wine-business savvy and being totally down-to-earth. He was constantly learning and was always trying to make improvements in his vineyards. Like Tony Soter, he paid attention to his vines, studied them, and got a sense for when they were being pushed too far with underwatering or overwatering.

After buying Larry's fruit for a couple of years, I started banging the drums that it was time to expand our property beyond the original ranch that Mom and Dad bought in the '70s. Buying Carneros land was no small thing. When Larry's dad had purchased their 100 acres in 1979, it came with a $400,000 price tag. Of course prices had simply continued to rise.[1]

---

1. Daniel Sogg, "The Wise Man of Carneros," *Wine Spectator*, October 15, 2007, accessed August 5, 2011, www.winespectator.com/magazine/show/id/12185.

After scouting the area, Dad and I zeroed in on a jewel of a site on Duhig Road that was owned by John Ahmann, an old cattle rancher. We ended up competing for the site with the Taittinger-owned sparkling wine house, Domaine Carneros, who had their eye on it too. In the end, Dad knew he couldn't outspend Taittinger, so he just sat down with the owner in his living room, and they had some coffee, talked for a long time, and got to know each other. Finally, Ahmann told Dad he'd rather sell the site to someone up the road, like us, than to a big, fancy French-owned company.

The purchase of the 68-acre site went through in 1988. The first thing to deal with was water. As I mentioned, there's usually a long dry season in Carneros, and we'd need a drip irrigation system to keep the vines healthy. We couldn't drill a well here, because we'd only get salt water thanks to our proximity to the bay. Given that, we opted instead to dig a rainwater collection pond. We studied the property, selected a spot on the east end of the site, dug our pond, and decided to wait for the winter rains to fill it, rather than trucking in water.

Then I dawdled on the whole project. If I'd hustled I could have placed an order at a nursery for 30- or 40-acres' worth of AXR-1 rootstock and planted that in the spring of 1989. Then we could have started grafting our Chardonnay canes onto the AXR-1 in the fall. But I had way too much going on to tackle a project of that scope.

As it turns out, my slowness to act in Carneros would come with a sizable payoff.

· · ·

The 1989 vintage was a disappointment no matter where you were growing grapes in the Valley. We didn't have a lot of fruit to begin with, and then we got pounded by rain during harvest. I remember talking with Larry Hyde about the fruit we were set to buy from him in Carneros. Larry was characteristically up front about what we were facing. "Look, we've had two or three storms," he said. "There's another one coming, the fruit can't take it." In other words, because of the cool, overcast weather, sugars weren't rising like they should, and we weren't getting ripeness. Due to the rain, the grapes were starting to rot and mold on the vine. Things were ugly and about to get uglier.

According to our contract I could back out if the ripeness wasn't there, which Larry was letting me know was in fact the case. I didn't want to see him take a financial hit—he was one of the hardest-working guys I knew, very meticulous about growing great grapes. None of this was his fault. Larry was as helpless in the face of this weather as the rest of us. So I proposed that he figure up his per-ton costs and I'd figure out how much I could sell the wine for on the bulk market. When we talked again, his numbers and my numbers worked out nicely. On the day we harvested I drove down to Carneros and as the guys were picking, in the pouring rain, I stood at the bin and pulled out sloppy, rotting clusters that shouldn't even end up in bulk wine. I think the pickers got a little annoyed with me because I was pulling out a lot of what they were dumping in.

Back at our cellar, I kept that batch of Chardonnay separate, made the wine, and sold it to the bulk market, and both Larry and I covered our costs.

The 1990 vintage was a different story. We had a fast harvest with an avalanche of fruit. (By fast I mean that all the grape varieties were ripening at the same time.) So many tons of fruit were being picked and crushed that we ran out of fermentation tanks. Every single tank in the winery was full, and tons more grapes were coming in. I called a local trucking company, and for a couple weeks I rented two tanker trucks in which I could simply store juice until we could get caught up. As it turns out Larry dropped by to see how things were going with the Chardonnay he'd sold us—which in this vintage was back to his usual gorgeous stuff.

I invited him in and walked through the winery and opened up the doors on the far side. There sat those two tanker trucks full of Chardonnay. Larry got this stricken look on this face and said to me, "You're not going to bulk this out too, are you?"

By this point, beyond digging our pond, I still hadn't jumped on prepping our Carneros site. And Larry, bless him, was always on me about it. Every time I'd bump into him he'd always ask if I'd gotten anything done out there. The fact is my plate was just too full.

THIRTY-THREE

Killer Bugs

By the spring of 1990, I was feeling a little guilty about not doing more with our new property. Then one morning I was up at 5:30 as usual and went down to a now-defunct coffee shop in St. Helena, where among the usual crowd I saw Bob Steinhauer, the longtime, highly respected vineyard manager for Beringer.

(As a quick aside, I have to say that I've learned more about what was happening in the wine industry at St. Helena coffee shops before 6 A.M. than I can possibly relate.)

Bob called me over and said to me, "You guys have some property down in Carneros, right?"

"Yeah."

"There's something you need to check out."

"What's that?"

"Phylloxera. You need to ask around down there."

I called Peter Nissen, a vineyard development consultant who we'd started working with to get things under way in Carneros. Peter worked with quite a number of clients in that part of the Valley, overseeing the planting or replanting of hundreds of acres. He was not aware of any phylloxera issues in the Carneros AVA, but he said he'd look into it. A few hours later he called me back—not happy. Turns out a winery with property in Carneros did have a phylloxera infestation, had known about it for a couple of years, and hadn't told anyone. Peter was livid. Had he known of this he would not have recommended that his clients plant more than 100 acres to AXR-1 rootstock that by that time was believed to have little resistance to phylloxera.

Phylloxera is a tiny, aphid-like insect that's the color of golden raisins. At one point in their overly complex life cycle, they congregate below the soil line on grapevine roots, where they seek sustenance by chomping into the wood and sucking out moisture. Their saliva is poisonous to the wood and doesn't allow the wound to heal, leaving the vine open to a host of fungal diseases, which slowly cut off the flow of water and nutrients within the vine's vascular system.

It'd be like wrapping a tourniquet around your throat and tightening it slowly over the course of a couple years. Not deadly at first, but ultimately very bad news.

Until that time it seemed that phylloxera was not something that would reappear on the Napa Valley scene in any serious way. For one thing we knew a lot more about the bug and how to control it than our forebearers did. The devastation in France and here in California in the 1800s was eventually stopped when something crucial was discovered, which joined the best of the Old and New Worlds.

The Eastern Seaboard of the United States and Canada has been home to wild grapevines for eons. When Viking explorer Leif Erikson landed somewhere in Newfoundland in about 1002 A.D., he and his men named this new continent "Vinland" for its abundance of grapevines. Over a great period of time the phylloxera insect, also native to this continent, and these North American grape species, with scientific names such as *Vitis labrusca* and *Vitis aestivalis*, had learned to live together in a sustainable balance.

However, the vines that were native to France, such as Cabernet Sauvignon, Merlot, Cabernet Franc, Malbec, and so on, were a species called *Vitis vinifera*, which had never seen this bug, and when phylloxera hitched a ride to France in about 1860, it laid waste to that country's grapevines. What the French eventually discovered is that they could graft their *Vitis vinifera* vines onto American grapevine roots and thereby put a halt to the bug's ravages.[1]

Over time French nurseries cultivated quite a number of rootstocks, including a very popular one called AXR-1, which they believed did the double duty of offering resistance to phylloxera and performing well in many different settings—varying soil types and climate conditions. As mentioned earlier, when Dad planted our hillside property, he used St. George, a rootstock preferred for decades by the old-timers in the Valley. Dad liked it because it performed better in shallow soils and proved more drought-tolerant.

In some of our newer plantings though, such as the Chardonnay planted on the flatter portions of the property, we had gone with AXR-1.

By 1985 a curious thing happened. About half an acre of vineyard upvalley, near St. Helena, developed an infestation of phylloxera. It was kept pretty quiet and in fact even its location was not widely known. What really threw researchers, who came in from U.C. Davis to study this, was that the bug was thriving on AXR-1, the very rootstock that the university had touted for its phylloxera resistance. This would be like discovering the smallpox virus snacking away happily on smallpox vaccine.

The spread of the infestation happened very slowly at first; in the *Wine Spectator* at one point James Laube likened it to watching crabgrass spread. This made it possible to ignore or to deny. For a few years U.C. Davis was still recommending the use of AXR-1, still unsure what they were facing.

The spread was aided in a couple of unexpected ways. In the winter of 1986 the Valley experienced some of the worst flooding on record. The center of the Valley floor was a wide, brown torrent passing through thousands of acres of vineyards, choking off roadways, flooding out

---

1. Jancis Robinson, *The Oxford Companion to Wine* (New York: Oxford University Press, 1994), 728.

houses and businesses, and causing millions of dollars of damage. And it is believed that those floodwaters, moving from north to south—in other words from St. Helena down through the center of the Valley to San Pablo Bay—spread that initial phylloxera population from one end to the other.

The other way the insect was spread was likely through the movement of farm equipment used by vineyard management companies. One morning you might be discing a vineyard in Rutherford, and in the afternoon you'd haul your tractor and its accompanying equipment up to the top of Howell Mountain and do the same kind of work there—and bring some phylloxera with you.

By about 1988 the researchers and the vintner community began to believe that this wasn't our great-grandfather's phylloxera. The bug had mutated, and we were dealing with a new version that was dubbed Biotype B.[2] Given that it was making a lunch out of the most widely planted rootstock in the Valley, the industry realized with growing concern that they needed a solution, some kind of counterattack, very quickly. But what?

In July 1990, Laube wrote in the *Wine Spectator*, that "[the infestation] continues to creep through the vineyards of Napa Valley....Just five years ago, when new mutations of Phylloxera were detected by scientists in California, most winegrowers were skeptical. Some vintners accused the media of sensationalism for merely reporting that Phylloxera was back."[3]

Laube reported that so far 300 acres showed signs of infestation. If that's accurate, then it represents just 1 percent of the Valley's planted acreage at the time (28,846 acres in 1990), which is why there still wasn't a full-blown panic under way. At first those seemed like pretty good odds, until it began to crop up everywhere, inescapably, at once. It was

2. Thinking has changed on this over time, and it's now more accepted that the emergence of Biotype B was less relevant than the fact that AXR-1 was simply not resistant to phylloxera.

3. James Laube, "Roots, Rhones and Resistance," *Wine Spectator*, July 15, 1990, 13.

like an old horror movie where someone's pursued by Frankenstein's monster—the creature moves slowly, clumsily, but relentlessly, and in the end it wins.

A phylloxera infestation created "a hole in your vineyard." The first year in the center of your property you'd find a cluster of vines that were dying. And each year, like ripples on a pond, the ring of infested and dying vines would grow.

In our Carneros vineyards, I realized, thanks to my year or two of delay, we had been spared from planting 30 or 40 acres of AXR-1, which we'd now have had to tear out and replant. We'd have lost our shirts in that scenario. Many of our neighbors were not so lucky.

Now we, like everyone else, were faced with the question of what rootstock to use in the new vineyard in Carneros. Somewhat more alarming is that by now we were seeing the first signs of phylloxera-induced damage on the Chardonnay we'd planted to AXR-1 back at the home ranch. We were more motivated than ever to tear out those vines, but the same question was staring at us there too—which rootstock to use?

Besides AXR-1 researchers had developed a whole host of rootstocks with names that sounded like bank accounts: 3309, 101-14, 5C, and 110R, to name a few. Elias and I debated back and forth which ones to go with next. We read the literature on the subject, asked around at the Wine Technical Group, checked in with various friends, and then we thought, why not talk to some old-timers who'd been working the land here since Prohibition?

We ended up finding a guy with a few acres of Zinfandel outside of Yountville—a sun-baked, old Italian grower who was as sweet as could be. He invited us in, but before we could get down to business he wanted to show us his vegetable garden, which was a wonder, bursting with beautiful stuff. Then he realized that, really, he had way more than he could eat so he insisted that we take some home. So now Elias and I are out in this guy's garden picking armloads of tomatoes and beans and squash. Then he wants us to try his Zinfandel. So we go inside and now we're sitting down drinking—not tasting—drinking his rustic homemade Zin at ten in the morning. And now we're laughing and telling jokes and having a good time. Finally, we get down to business. We tell him about our dilemma and he answers right away, doesn't skip a beat, "You boys gotta use St. George!" he said. "You can't kill that [blankety-blank] stuff even if you wanted to!"

Back at the winery we gave this some thought. St. George, turns out, was resistant to phylloxera, but at the same time it was a rootstock that had a reputation for producing lots of foliage and fairly small clusters. In spite of this reputation we were seeing different results on our hillsides because the scant amount of soil and moisture acted as a natural choke for St. George, giving us fewer leaves and shoots and at the same time giving us the small, loose clusters that produce rich flavors and extract. Ultimately we decided to stick mostly with St. George and to throw a few others into the mix.

While we got under way with our new planting, other growers and vintners faced a more daunting task. Once "the hole in their vineyard" got too big to ignore, then it was either time to sell and get out of the wine business or to replant. A lot of vineyard owners just swallowed the bitter pill and replanted, while others decided it was better to pack it in.

Replanting worked like this . . . first you had to hire a guy with a bulldozer to tear out your vines. At one point in the early '90s there was so much demand for this kind of work that construction guys, farmers, loggers, anyone with access to a bulldozer, got into the business of tearing out vineyards. Some of these sites had still been using the one hundred-year-old practice of head-pruned vines—individual vines were tied to a stake and then grew up and out, looking like row upon row of giant bouffant wigs in the middle of summer. Others were still using newer but outmoded trellis systems. The truly unfortunate were growers and vintners who'd planted vines in the past few years using all AXR-1 rootstock, new trellis systems, irrigation systems, and so on. Those men and women paid a terrible toll. At Opus One, half of one of the most expensive vineyards ever planted up to that time had to be torn out and replanted, delaying the official opening of the winery. The economic damage in Napa Valley at the end of all this totaled somewhere in the neighborhood of $3 billion.

The bulldozer-for-hire would rumble through your vineyard and rip out everything, forming large tangled piles within your property. You needed to line up a permit from the California Department of Forestry in order to burn these heaps of vines. If you'd torn out trellis wire and metal stakes you could pull them out of the ashes and sell those as scrap metal.

Once your vineyard site was cleared so that there was nothing but dirt, then you hired a guy with a tractor equipped with ripper shanks who drove up and down the rows tearing into the soil at a depth of one or two feet. Then another tractor came through, following the ripper's path, and injected methyl bromide into the soil, to sterilize it, meaning that every living organism, including the phylloxera, was wiped out. While doing this, the tractor simultaneously laid a long thin sheet of plastic across the surface of the soil, tarping it off. For a week or two it gave your property a pretty surreal look.

During this period you'd drive along Highway 29, say in the late afternoon, and the sunlight would catch these incredibly long narrow sheets, turning them silvery white. These shining rivers of smooth plastic were laid side by side for what seemed like miles, making half the Valley look like an eerie art installation.

There was, of course, a price to pay. In the years after the methyl bromide treatments growers and vintners noticed that they were having trouble with their rootstocks. Some would grow well and others wouldn't. It was spotty and unpredictable. Word was that since the methyl bromide killed everything in the soil, including the microbes, it caused anything newly planted to struggle and sometimes fail. It took a while for the soil to recover.

The incredibly high demand for rootstock material placed a big strain on the nursery system that supplied it. The Valley had entered the phylloxera era with a full-blown rootstock shortage already on its hands. In the late '80s the fine wine market had been very hot, and vintners were pouring their new profits into planting and/or replanting, which dried up the availability of rootstock. Some vintners were stuck waiting a year to get their orders filled. Now we faced a different problem as we entered the 1990s—the economy was going bust, everyone's profits were down, *and* our grapevines were being eaten alive by an invasion of tiny monsters.

Because the nurseries were scrambling to meet such a huge need, a lot of diseased and subpar plant material started making it out into the vineyards. This unhealthy rootstock gave us new problems in the vineyard, one nicknamed "young vine decline" and the other a fungal infection called "black goo," named for the ugly gunk that developed within the vine and blocked its vascular system, slowly killing it off, just as surely as phylloxera had.

With time, though, the soils regained their vitality, and the nurseries got a handle on the issue of high demand. The growing issue of fungal diseases sparked a new era of research that has helped keep these challenges under control and deepened our understanding of vine health.

·   ·   ·

The brutal scourge of phylloxera did not prove to be the death of the Valley but rather its transformation. The do-or-die replants brought about a large-scale change in a compressed space of time, which was a boon for wine quality. Viticultural practices such as head-pruned vines, which had hung around since the age of the telegraph, were largely gone, replaced by new approaches that resulted from decades of experimentation, research, and trial and error. Without the pressure of phylloxera, vintners and growers would have put off for another ten or twenty years replants that incorporated the best and latest understanding of grape growing. Instead, in the course of four or five years the Valley was now using new trellis systems and planting to a variety of rootstocks that were more fine-tuned to specific sites. Some rootstocks, for example, were better in clay, others were better in rocky soil; some were better for dry farming, others offered resistance to pests, such as nematodes. These new rootstocks were being budded to a wide range of clones—slightly different genetic versions of grape varieties—in sites that were believed to be better suited to a given grape. In other words we were acting on our new understanding to plant the right grape in the right place—like putting Chardonnay in Carneros instead of Stags Leap District. On top of that, we were moving forward with tighter vine spacing, forcing the vines to compete with each other for moisture and soil nutrients, which resulted in smaller berries and thus fruit of richer concentration and extract.

To picture the endless combinations, imagine a slot machine with five spinning wheels, one for rootstocks, one for clones, one for sites, one for trellises, and one for spacing. It was easy to geek out on this stuff, trying to sort out which went together best. It's also not hard to see that this changed our focus and our future for all time. Until phylloxera, the Valley had been focused on making wine in the cellar. Now winemakers were spending time planning their new vineyards, spending time doing what Tony Soter had encouraged Elias and me to do—paying attention to the vines, ensuring that the grapes had enough sunlight and air, and checking the balance between fruit and foliage. More than ever we woke to the idea that wine is made outside, under the blue canopy of the Napa Valley skies, rather than simply in a tank or barrel.

THIRTY-FOUR

Sustainability

One of the reasons I'd been too busy to head full-bore into our Carneros planting is that Dad had turned vineyard operations over to me in 1988. It was a lot to take on, first just to get all the details right regarding the annual processes that needed to happen, such as pruning, discing, and spraying. Of course none of this was made easier thanks to the industry-wide uncertainty inspired by phylloxera.

From the time Dad had planted our first vine, up through the late 1980s, a vineyard was supposed to looked as flat and clean as a pool table. Not a blade of grass, no hint of weeds. Not a single insect. Only knobby vines emerging out of bare soil. The way we achieved that look was by spraying powerful chemicals.

But change was in the air regarding how we, and others, should farm our land.

On one hand, rumors were circulating in local coffee shops that the government would soon start phasing out various chemical agents we had long relied on to make our land suitable for cultivation. On the other hand, some of us started looking into the future and wondering if there wasn't a healthier, more long-term approach to what we were doing.

Besides the obvious concern regarding responsible stewardship of the soil and local watershed, my children were playing in these vineyards,

Prior to sustainable farming, the vineyards at Shafer were kept insect- and weed-free through the heavy use of insecticides and herbicides.

our employees and other family members were working here, and our dogs were eating our grapes (when we weren't looking). Quite a number of compelling personal and professional reasons began moving me toward exploring a new approach.

John Williams of Frog's Leap Winery was a vintner in a similar frame of mind. He'd been moving toward organic farming and when we were on trips where groups of vintners would travel together to various cities to do Napa Valley Vintner tastings, he'd bend my ear about some of the things he was doing. John had heard that Fetzer was doing some interesting new things in relation to organic farming, and when he visited up there he met their consultant, a character named Amigo Bob.

Amigo Bob Cantisano had grown up a city kid in San Francisco, but in the 1970s had moved to the Sierra Foothills and started an organic farm. He also established an organic farm supply store out of his barn, which he called Peaceful Valley Farm Supply. Over the next few years he'd run several experimental farming programs with some success, and in 1981 was hired by a winery for his first consulting gig.[1]

When I met him, Amigo Bob was probably in his late thirties, with a long, thick ponytail, a whopping, Yosemite-Sam mustache, a tie-dyed T-shirt, shorts, and sandals, which I'm pretty sure is his idea of formal wear. At that first meeting, I can tell you he was not my idea of a consultant in a high-pressure business like Napa Valley grape growing.

At a meeting at neighboring winery Robert Sinskey Vineyards, Amigo Bob talked about how grape growers in the Central Valley had thrown tons of chemicals at an insect problem that hadn't gone away. He had introduced some growers there to more earth-friendly and cost-effective ways to deal with a variety of agricultural issues that did not involve using manufactured chemicals. And it sounded like he'd gotten good results.

What Amigo Bob proposed represented a big leap into the unknown. While at the Sinskey meeting I was looking at him thinking, "Here's this guy with long hair, shorts, and Birkenstocks in the middle of winter. He looks like a Deadhead—and I'm going to bank our future on him?"

But his ideas struck a chord, and I hired him as a consultant. (And yes, everyone calls him Amigo Bob. Not making this up. It's a nickname a high school girlfriend gave him and it fits.[2])

On his advice, we launched into sustainable farming by first planting cover crops between our vine rows at the end of harvest. Understand that this was a 180-degree turn from everything we'd done before. Rather

---

1. Robert F. Howe, "California's Eco-Oracle," *Wine Spectator*, November 30, 2005, accessed August 5, 2011, www.winespectator.com/magazine/show/id/11260.

2. Irene Reti, Director of Regional History Project, "Amigo Bob Cantisano: Organic Farming Advisor, Founder, Ecological Farming Conference," University of California Santa Cruz University Library Regional History Project, accessed August 5, 2011, http://library.ucsc.edu/reg-hist/cultiv/cantisano.

After the start of sustainable farming, with reliance on cover crops, the vineyards took on a much wilder, chaotic look, but created lively, beneficial habitats for insect life.

than spraying to wipe out weeds, we were now planting them—crops like oats, vetch, bell beans, and clover.

Amigo Bob said that the reason we had always been forced to spray to kill the vine-blighting bugs, such as leafhoppers and blue-green sharpshooters, is because our vineyards were all out of whack. We needed weeds. And we needed them for a number of good reasons. First, a thick tangle of plant life would create a habitat, which would attract a rich population of insects.

Wait, insects are bad, right? Not according to Amigo Bob.

If we created a habitat for all sorts of bugs, then vine enemies, such as leafhoppers and blue-green sharpshooters, would run up against their own natural enemies such as ladybugs, wasps, and spiders. One would cancel out the other without any need for spraying pesticides. The local

An owl box in the eastern portion of the Shafer property
serves as a safe, secure nesting site for barn owls to raise
their young—and consume lots of gophers.

environment had long ago created a healthy, beneficial balance and we
simply had to learn how to plug into it.

In addition, he said, cover crops would do more than create a big cage
match for insects; they would also prevent erosion. Add to that, throughout each spring and summer the cover crop competes with the vines for

water and nutrients, thus holding back the vigor of the vines and getting better balance between leaves and fruit. When the cover crops die off and decompose, they enrich the soil with nitrogen and other nutrients.

The benefits of cover crops go on and on, but in the beginning this method of farming took some getting used to.

By the middle of that first season of using cover crops, our vineyards had taken on an out-of-control wild and weedy look. We didn't have the right mowing equipment and through lack of experience missed our mowing window, so the cover crop just exploded. Alfonso approached me, full of concern. Apparently his friends who were vineyard managers in the area saw that Alfonso's vineyards were full of weeds. "They're giving me a hard time," he said. "They think I'm not doing my job!"

The next thing Amigo Bob got us started on was producing our own compost rather than purchasing chemical fertilizers. Until then, after harvest we had scattered the pomace—the skins and seeds—in the vineyards and had burned the stems.

Instead, he taught us how to pile all this up at the end of harvest and create great purple heaps of our harvest leftovers. During cold winter mornings I remember driving in and for the first time seeing great billows of steam rising up over the compost as the material in the center heated up past 100 degrees Fahrenheit, on its way to becoming a rich, natural source of fertilizer for our soils.

While we didn't always see it at first, everything Amigo Bob taught us to do worked out as planned, and we have stuck with sustainable farming. Over time he would make a considerable impact on farming here, consulting with quite a number of wineries throughout the Valley including Spottswoode, Honig, Chappellet, Araujo, Long Meadow, Storybook Mountain, Turley, Staglin Family, and others.

THIRTY-FIVE

Identity Crisis

In the early 1980s Napa Valley was already recognized as California's second most popular tourist destination, clocking in just behind Disneyland in annual numbers of visitors—somewhere around 2.5 million. Cars began to choke Highway 29's two lanes from Yountville to St. Helena on weekends. About the same time we started seeing circus-colored hot air balloons rising into the sky each morning, when conditions were clear, to give intrepid bands of tourists a bird's-eye view of the Valley's vineyards. (I remember a couple of times balloons got caught in our little box canyon where the winery sits, and the airflows sent the balloons in whirlpool-like circles, making it almost impossible for them to escape.)

More and more often we were seeing limousines and famous faces staying at the new Meadowood and Auberge du Soleil luxury resorts. The nighttime soap opera *Falcon Crest* starting filming throughout the Valley in 1981, introducing a whole new audience to our area. One of the opening shots of the show featured the Victorian grandeur of Spring Mountain Winery, and the sequences that came after focused on other local beauty spots—all of which was broadcast to millions of TV sets around the country and then around the world in syndication.

In the spring of 1983, not long after I'd started as winemaker here, Dad came up to me and said, "The *Falcon Crest* people are going to bury Lana Turner on our knoll."

"They're going to do *what* to *who*?" I asked, my mind fully occupied with decidedly non-Hollywood things like tanks and barrels.

"Lana. Turner," he repeated, as though extra enunciation would help.

"I don't know who that is," I said.

"She was the most famous of all the sweater girls in World War II," he said.

This was ringing no bells with me. I just shrugged. Dad walked away, shaking his head, kind of appalled. Apparently my education was incomplete without knowing something about pinup girls of the 1940s.

The *Falcon Crest* people had contacted Dad, it turns out, about using an unplanted knoll below his house to shoot a cemetery scene—it would be the opening shot for the first show of the 1983 season. Lana Turner's character had been killed off and was being "buried" in the "Tuscany Valley Cemetery."

It was quite a process. The production crew came out for a couple of days and essentially spray-painted the sun-fried knoll a grassy green and set up an impressive array of Styrofoam headstones. The shoot itself lasted a few hours, with Cliff Robertson, Jane Wyman, Lorenzo Lamas, and the rest of the cast looking suitably somber, while an actor playing a minister delivered an appropriately depressing, graveside service. A few years later when we planted that knoll we called it "La Vigna Lana" in honor of Dad's favorite sweater girl (whom I now knew all about).

Falcon Crest hung around a long time on the airwaves—its last season was in 1990 but by that time it had fallen way off the cultural radar, ranking something like sixty-third in the top one hundred shows that year. But the tourism the show helped bolster was here to stay.

By the mid-1980s there were wineries that wanted to open guest quarters or restaurants. One of our neighbors nearly won approval for a helicopter pad—something Dad fought. There was more talk of other

Planting an eastern knoll called La Vigna Lana, after the filming of an episode of a *Falcon Crest* funeral in which film/TV star Lana Turner's character was buried.

wineries, besides Mondavi, interested in becoming the site for concerts, weddings, and corporate events. *The New York Times* reported that one of the largest wineries in the Valley (they didn't identify whom) had been approached by a Florida marketing firm that wanted to create wine visits in which guests would tour the vineyard, "'perched high atop gigantic pachyderms,' each with plush seating for six, a wine-tasting bar, stereo headphones and a canopy in case of rain."[1]

This was a time when everything in the economy was ramping up, and there was a healthy profit to be made in the business of fine wine again. With so many people visiting the Valley's burgeoning wineries,

1. Jane Gross, "Shall Tourists or Grapes Rule the Valley?" *New York Times*, May 30, 1998, accessed August 15, 2011, www.nytimes.com/1988/05/30/us/shall-tourists-or-grapes-rule-in-the-napa-valley.html?pagewanted=all&src=pm.

there were countless ideas sprouting up as to how to make an extra buck. Wineries had started selling T-shirts, wine openers, logo glasses, sunglasses, posters, and picnic supplies. While the Valley's wine industry brought $150 million to the local economy in 1985, the tourism industry was growing at such a frantic pace it was now responsible for pouring an additional $139 million into local coffers.

All of this though—among soberer minds—started to create a worry that the Valley was headed down the wrong road. Some people pointed to San Francisco's Fisherman's Wharf, which had turned into a collection of tacky gift shops, candy stores, cheesy art galleries, and funnel cake vendors—none of it having to do with fish or fishermen or being a wharf. The worry was that Napa Valley could turn into that kind of plastic-y, noisy, strip-mall kind of destination.

These concerns were the latest in a long-running dialogue among Napa Valley residents. Issues of land use have loomed large in politics here since at least the mid-1960s, an era when this region was at another tipping point. Walnut and prune growers were seeing their profits decline, while the wine industry had not yet moved into a position of economic prominence. The Valley was only home to some twenty-five wineries then. There was a moment when it looked like local landowners might start making more profit selling to housing developers rather than maintaining their property's agricultural use. This very thing had happened in Los Angeles, Santa Clara Valley, and Livermore Valley, where within a generation vines had been replaced by development. But a group of local vintners and county officials created a first-of-its-kind proposal to protect much of the Valley from development: the 1968 Napa County Agricultural Preserve. The original county code protected 26,000 acres from development, which later grew to 38,000. One protection measure stipulated that landowners could only sell off their property in parcel sizes of 20 acres or larger. In the late '70s, when Dad was president of the Grape Growers Association, he worked to increase the minimum parcel size to 40 acres.

The debate taking place in the late '80s had shifted from property rights in relation to development to property rights in relation to the tourism industry. Both debates came down to a similar question—what kind of Valley would this be?

In the middle of all this came the Wine Train, a beautifully restored vintage passenger train, which probably seemed very innocent and fun and charming to outsiders, but which made locals completely flip out. Wine Train promoters were talking big numbers early on—with something like four trips per day, three hundred passengers per trip, we were looking at the potential for 400,000 additional visitors per year, which the Wine Train planners said they were going to deposit in St. Helena (a town of 5,000) and at winery stops in between. Those who paid an additional fee could be squired around our already choked local roadways to various wineries in London-style, double-decker buses.

Something about the scale and the visibility of this project, I think, was the straw that broke the camel's back. All the anger and anxiety about the tourism industry boom, related to the loss of a slower, more rural pace of life, could now be heaped on this one entity. Vineyard owners started posting large anti-Wine Train signs among their vines. Locals stuck waiting for the train to cross roadways would greet riders with the one-finger salute. The St. Helena City Council waged war on all efforts to allow the train to deposit its daily passenger load onto its streets.

This cumulative effect of the move toward a tourism economy prompted the wine industry and community leaders to take a look at where we'd come from, where we were now, and where we should be heading. At the center of the discussion that finally made it to the county supervisors was the question: What is a winery? Is it also a restaurant? A gift shop? A convention center? A resort? Or should it simply be a place where wine is produced? And should we define what a winery is and encode that into law?

The result of a three-year process was the Winery Definition Ordinance, passed in January 1990. Overall, the law said that a winery is a place that produces wine—not a resort, a venue for corporate events, or a wedding chapel. It further stated that wineries bonded after the passage could see visitors by appointment only, mandating how many visitors could be hosted in a given week, and had to use 75 percent Napa Valley grapes to produce its wine.

Guess which winery was the first to undergo the rigors of getting a use permit under this new law? Shafer Vineyards. Dad wanted a revised permit to do a couple of things, including get approval to increase our production. We eventually got approval to produce eighty thousand cases—a number we've never even approached. What we really wanted to do is get approval to go from twenty thousand to thirty thousand cases. But just in case we ever changed our minds, Dad wanted to shoot for that much higher number.

The approval process was like nothing the Valley had ever seen. During the first review we ended up with thirty to forty mitigating issues—items we had to change or tweak or promise to change and tweak. While I agreed with the new ordinance in the big picture, the nitty-gritty of it seemed like a triumph of bureaucratic hairsplitting. In any case, we survived and won approval.

THIRTY-SIX

Down and Up Again

The down economy of the early 1990s hurt the Valley more than I think a lot of people outside the industry realized. It was a perfect storm—big inventories were built up with the massive 1990 harvest, the bottom dropped out of the wine market, thanks to a recession sparked by the savings and loan crisis, and the phylloxera-mandated replants were break-the-bank expensive. A lot of people with high hopes who'd gotten into the wine business in the '70s and '80s got out, selling their wineries and land at the very moment prices were dropping. In 1989 the Eisele Vineyard had been sold to a new out-of-town owner who, within months, lost out in the junk bond collapse.[1] In early 1990 the vineyard was back on the market, listed for $3.5 million, purchased next by Bart Araujo. Mike Robbins's Spring Mountain Winery, which had been made famous as the *Falcon Crest* winery, was also on the market in 1990, for $18 million.[2]

---

1. Per-Henrik Mansson, "Eisele Vineyard for Sale Again," *Wine Spectator*, April 30, 1990, 12.

2. Terry Robards, "Selling the 'Falcon Crest' Life-Style," *Wine Spectator*, October 15, 1990, 20.

Nationally the consumption of table wine had been dropping since 1987, when it had peaked at 487 million gallons. By 1991 it had lost a lot of ground, to the tune of almost 100 million gallons.[3]

In the middle of all this gloom though we received a gift—again from the French. And its value ranked nearly as high as the last one they'd given us in the form of the Judgment of Paris.

On November 17, 1991, the news show *60 Minutes* ran a report examining "the French Paradox." The segment opened with correspondent Morley Safer sitting in a bistro in Lyon, France, reading some of the items off the menu—pig's head pâté, black pudding (basically congealed cholesterol), potatoes in oil, double-fat sliced tripe. His bemused dining companion was U.S. researcher Dr. Curt Ellison, Professor of Public Health at Boston University, who was conducting research on the eating habits of several countries, including France. Ellison noted that while the French consumed a higher-fat diet than Americans did (according to *60 Minutes* every man, woman, and child in France consumed an average of forty pounds of cheese per year), they suffered from far less heart disease than U.S. residents. "Something seems to be protecting them," Ellison said.

The magic ingredient? Safer spoke to a French researcher who laid the protection squarely on the fact that the French consumed twenty times more red wine than Americans.

Safer ended the report seated at a table with a glass of red wine. "The explanation to the paradox may lie in this inviting glass," he said with a smile, lifting the wine in the gesture of a toast.[4]

The report was only four minutes, sixteen seconds long, but it had a powerful, long-lasting effect. In the two months that followed, sales of red wine in the United States surged 44 percent.

3. Wine Institute, *Wine Consumption in the U.S.*, accessed August 1, 2011, www.wineinsti tute.org/resources/statistics/article86.

4. "The French Paradox," *60 Minutes* (CBS, November 17, 1991), accessed August 8, 2011, www.cbsnews.com/video/watch/?id=4750380n cbsnews.com.

Wine was no longer just a food (the idea Mondavi and many others in the industry had promoted), now it was good for you. It was medicine; a miracle elixir that could lengthen your very life span. The initial boost in red wine sales was of course a bubble; however, it started an upward trend. At the time, and even through the mid-1990s, bottles of white wine continued to outsell red wine, but that was changing. In 2004 red would finally edge out white in terms of sales and popularity.

THIRTY-SEVEN

Sangio-*what?*

A few years after the *Falcon Crest* people filmed Lana Turner's casket being lowered into the knoll below my parents' house, that whole little hilltop was still unplanted. We'd tried once before, but there was so little soil and so much bedrock we tipped over a tractor trying to prep the site for planting.

By 1988 Dad still hoped to plant the site to an as-yet-undetermined red grape as part of an idea of creating a new wine that would be a red proprietary blend. He felt that this could be a wine that would fill out our portfolio. We had two Cabernets, a Chardonnay, and a Merlot. A proprietary blend would give us the chance to do something new, and as he well knew, the wine marketplace is an ever-shifting landscape, which is constantly finding itself preoccupied by the next new thing.

Rather than create a proprietary red with roots in Bordeaux—which would involve some combination of Cabernet Sauvignon, Cabernet Franc, Merlot, Petite Verdot, Malbec, and/or Carménère—he'd become fascinated by a movement among vintners in Italy who were creating "Super Tuscans": rich, delicious blends of their traditional Chianti grape, Sangiovese, with Cabernet, Merlot, and occasionally Syrah. He'd been absolutely lovestruck by a bottle of Antinori's Tiganello at a restaurant in San Francisco. When he'd mentioned this to Peter Matt, one of the founders of Winebow (our New York distributor), Peter had said, "Any time you want to learn more about wines of Tuscany let me know."

In 1988 Dad was in London on winery business and called Peter, who was as good as his word. He got on a plane and met Dad in Milan. They spent the next week tootling around Tuscany, visiting one winery after another.

The day Dad got back he came into the lab, where Elias and I were busy with something, and he slapped his hand down on the counter.

"I've got our new wine," he said. "Sangiovese."

"Sangio-*what?*" I replied.

Dad rolled his eyes and looked over at Elias. "Four years of U.C. Davis viticulture and enology and he doesn't know what Sangiovese is."

Elias smirked and said, "Doug, straw baskets."

"Oh, right, Chianti," I said, thinking, *"Why would we want to make that stuff?"*

Dad shook his head, "No, no, no. Not straw baskets. Sangiovese—it's a beautiful wine and it's what we should plant on that knoll."

"That knoll" was the one we eventually called La Vigna Lana, giving it a little Italian twist.

Dad sent off for some vine cuttings, which for all I know may have been "suitcase clones," the name for cuttings that someone stuffs into their luggage and flies home with, a practice very much on the fringes of legality, but which happens on occasion.

We finally managed to plant La Vigna Lana by hiring a crew of guys armed with jackhammers, who pounded the earth open in each spot we wanted to plant rootstock. Once the rootstock took hold we grafted on the initial Sangiovese canes that Dad apparently got from Italy, and most of them promptly died.

We sourced the next round of canes from Robert Pepi, who was about a year and a half ahead of us in planting Sangiovese in Napa Valley. These took beautifully to the rootstock, and we were in business.

I thought I knew grape growing pretty well by that point, but Sangiovese was a whole new creature. Once it got going, this variety wanted to grow a fireworks show of shoots and foliage, grapes the size of plums, and clusters as big as my head. Keep in mind this was a hillside site, where the vine is supposed to struggle, putting out a few dark, loose clusters, not acting like an Italian opera diva.

In 1991 we harvested the first crop and crushed and fermented the fruit. Of course we'd cultivated it and then fermented it like we did our other red wines and the result was 800 gallons of juice that was reminiscent of pink Kool-Aid charmingly complemented with eat-your-face-off acidity. Dad came over to the cellar very excited to try the new wine, and I had to put him off.

I said, "You know, how about if you try it later. It's going through kind of a funky stage right now."

When Dad left, Elias and I looked at each other and said, "What're we going to do?"

In the end we blended in a whopping 40 percent Cabernet in that first vintage to give the wine color, mid-palate, structure, and just about everything else. Thank God it was a proprietary blend; out of the starting gate it made our lives a lot easier to have the kind of wide-open ability to blend as needed.

After the 1991 harvest, we learned that to give Sangiovese the richness we were looking for we had to really stay on top of its proclivity toward superabundance—pruning it back to what seemed like nothing in January and pulling off shoots, pulling off leaves, and green harvesting heavily throughout the spring and summer. We'd typically cut away 50 percent of the fruit in a given year so that the remaining grapes could achieve rich ripeness.

Among the Valley's vintners there were high hopes that Sangiovese would be "the next Merlot," meaning that consumers would flock to this one with the same kind of fervor. When we started making ours, Elias's U.C. Davis classmate Mia Klein was making it for Robert Pepi. Flora Springs and Swanson both jumped on Sangiovese. Atlas Peak—whose part-owner was none other than Piero Antinori of the Tuscan Antinori family who'd been making wine commercially for some six hundred years—had established themselves early on as the major player in the Napa Sangiovese game. By the mid-1990s, California had a total of 450 acres of the Chianti grape, and 120 of those belonged to Atlas Peak.

.   .   .

I don't know if jumping in with both feet into Sangiovese planting and production was the breaking point or not with my parents' marriage. But as it represented one more step toward expanded production, it may've played a role. In 1992 my mom moved out, eventually settling in Santa Rosa. For a long time she'd been disillusioned with the wine business. In her mind, the move to Napa Valley was supposed to represent a kind of semiretirement, in which Dad would spend a couple of days a week on his vines and the rest of the time they'd golf and live a quiet life among family and friends.

But for Dad, starting this business was fun and exciting; it was like being twenty-five years old again, and it proved impossible to back away from. By 1992 he'd been at this for twenty years and showed no signs of letting up.

One of the best examples I can give of the difference between them is that in the early days of the winery, when a visitor's car would appear in our driveway, more than once I'd see Mom turn off the lights in the office and hide. In the meantime Dad would show up out front, shake hands, ask where they were from, and invite them in for some wine. They were different people, whom I loved and admired as much as any son can. They divorced in 1994, and it was very hard to see them go their separate ways after so many years.

THIRTY-EIGHT

Identity Crisis (This Time It's Personal)

By 1994 the team of Elias, Dad, and me had been working together for ten years. In that time we'd started from a difficult place of inexperience and had, through a lot of effort, moved to an exciting new era, filled with experimentation and new confidence.

We'd learned a great deal in the cellar—a lot of which would bore you to death, because it has to do with filters, barrel types, adhesives for labels, cork quality, yeast types, pumps, and so forth. But in important ways the boring stuff makes a huge difference. (Whoever said "Don't sweat the small stuff" almost certainly never made wine.) The kind of filtration you use—or whether you filter at all—makes a difference in wine quality. We experimented with different types of oak for our barrels, eliminating the French oak Limousin, which is wide-grained wood, and moved toward the tighter-grained Nevers and Tronçais. To learn more about American oak, Elias visited an oak source in Missouri and observed how the trees were selected, cut, and processed there. At one point, in order to understand the world of corks, he flew to Portugal, where he toured cork forests, absorbing all he could on which parts of the cork-making process happened there. He then spent time with our cork supplier here in Napa, learning everything possible about every step a cork makes from the tree to the bottle.

We had learned a lot in the vineyard (and we still had some distance to go). A key concept was crop thinning, the technique of pruning away lesser-quality fruit and leaving the best on the vine. The idea is that you get the optimal results with uniform ripeness at harvest.

When it came to buying fruit (which at that time applied to each of our wines except Hillside Select) we had moved to a system whereby we established a price per acre with our grower partners instead of a price per ton. This removed the grower's traditional motivation to sell based on tonnage, and it freed us up to thin as much fruit as we thought necessary for better quality.

Elias and I were, of course, eager to see all that we'd learned show up in the bottle, only to be frustrated by the 1988 and 1989 vintages, which were difficult growing seasons—we simply were not able to get the level of ripeness for which we had hoped. As a result those wines from our hillsides, to this day, display a green character we are not fond of.

The 1990 vintage was good but still knocked us around a little. We had rains in May, which affected bloom, and later the fruit suffered somewhat from several one-hundred-plus-degree heat spikes in July and August. It was a huge harvest—the one in which we rented those two tanker trucks.

The 1991 vintage proved to be the one we'd waited for—it was long, long, long, and cool. No rain pressure, no humidity issues (which can give you mold and mildew within the clusters). The Cabernet was pristine. By this time we'd come to understand hangtime, leaving the fruit out on the vine until ideal ripeness. It's a tricky thing to master. Pick your fruit too soon and you miss the moment when sugar, acidity, and ripeness all come together in a delicious balance. However, if you leave the fruit on too long, then you end up with stewed or port-like flavors. The difference between too soon and too long is a moving target, and you often have only a window of one or two days. With harvest already such a hectic, seat-of-your-pants time of year, it makes nailing that perfect picking day a lot like threading a needle while riding a bull.

I remember there'd been a rocky spot in our transition to leaving fruit on the vine longer. One year in the late '80s Dad thought we should pick on a certain day, and Elias and I just shook our heads and said we should wait. And we waited another day. And another. And Dad got really concerned and took me aside and said, "What are you guys doing?" I said, "Do you want to make good wine or great wine?" He took a deep breath and let us do our thing.

Meanwhile, Dad's 1978 was still the benchmark at Shafer Vineyards. By the early 1990s it had matured into a gorgeous, enticing Cabernet, a real beauty that won every tasting we'd put it in, winning out over the top wines of California and Europe. Every now and then Dad would goad Elias and me, in a friendly way, by saying, "Hey when are you two going to make another '78?"

By 1994 we felt we'd finally produced that wine, one that embodied everything we'd learned; it was the 1991 Hillside Select. Elias and I held out a lot of hope for this one. It felt like our Ph.D. project.

In the spring of 1994 Elias and I surprised Dad by walking into his office one morning carrying a wooden magnum-sized box of 1991 Hillside Select. On the side of the box were the words "We Think We Did It." He saw that inscription and got a big smile. After uncorking the wine, Dad was very pleased to agree with our assessment. What a great moment, the sweetest victory imaginable, to have slugged it out that long and finally to have achieved something we felt was first-rate.

Dad's goal from the start—the very rocky start—was to create a winery that was world-class. And with the 1991 Hillside Select, that idea no longer seemed like a mirage.

Robert Parker said the 1991 Hillside Select was a "knock-out Cabernet Sauvignon...layered, multi-dimensional, complete feel in the mouth...juicy, succulent...A terrific 1991!"[1]

1. Robert M. Parker, "1991 Shafer Vineyards Cabernet Sauvignon Hillside Select," *Wine Advocate* 99 (June 1995), accessed August 3, 2011, www.erobertparker.com/newSearch /th.aspx?th=34850&id=1&___z=4xf2%2fhSSkX1iFr2zG1b3kg%3d%3d.

In *Wine Spectator*, James Laube called it, "Sleek and elegant...tempting now for its elegance and finesse, but it has the stuffing to age through another decade."[2]

The wild ups and downs of the early to mid-1980s were a thing of the past. Critics and consumers alike were, I think, getting the sense that we'd paid our dues, we'd hung in there, and we were in this for the long haul.

Others in the Valley took notice as well, which pushed us into a new era in a way I hadn't seen coming. Elias started to get job offers—a lot of them. And several were very attractive.

One morning I was at the winery and noticed that Elias was acting funny. When you've worked that closely, been through that much together, and become good friends you know when something's up. Neither of us are very good at dancing around stuff like this.

"What's going on?" I asked.

He had such a hangdog look I actually thought someone had died. Then he told me about an outstanding job offer he'd gotten—the kind of thing you can't say no to—and that it looked like he was going to take it.

A lot of important things came into focus in that moment. Elias wasn't the kid just out of U.C. Davis I'd hired back in 1984. He was married and had three young boys and a house payment. He'd blown his knee out the previous year and had undergone surgery, his first inkling of the changes that come with age.

Add to that, he was turning into a remarkable winemaker. At some point in the late 1980s I'd changed our titles to co-winemakers. Now it was clear that he was thinking in a bigger-picture way. And I realized it was time for Shafer Vineyards to do the same.

We weren't the same place we'd been just ten years ago. It was time to take stock of where we'd come from, where we were today, and where we wanted to head.

2. James Laube, "Shafer Cabernet Sauvignon Stags Leap District Hillside Select 1991," *Wine Spectator*, November 15, 1995, 176.

Mid-1990s (left to right): John Shafer, Elias Fernandez, and Doug Shafer during harvest.

When I sat down and discussed this with Dad, he completely agreed and indicated that he was ready for a change as well. By 1994 Dad was seventy years old and had run the show for just over twenty years, nearly as long as the time he'd spent at Scott Foresman.

Increasingly, Dad was involved in projects close to his heart, such as raising money and awareness for Clinic Olé, a local medical facility that offers health care for the uninsured. He was also deeply involved with the Napa Valley Wine Auction's grants review committee, which considered and evaluated the increasing number of requests for Wine Auction support. He wanted to stay involved in the winery but also wanted to allocate more time to some of his philanthropic ventures, to travel, and to pursue new interests. By this time Dad had also started spending time with a lovely woman named Barbara Howell, who would eventually introduce Dad to new interests in travel (for fun rather than business), dance, and art. For a guy who'd been working at one thing or another full-bore since the 1940s, it seemed like a change of pace was more than deserved.

My own situation had changed too. I'd been in charge of the cellar and winemaking initially, then I took over vineyard operations in the late '80s, and beyond that I was now spending more time than ever on the road. I know I've mentioned travel throughout this story, but I really can't overemphasize the importance of meeting your distributors and their reps over and over again, if nothing else because the turnover among representatives can be so high. You constantly have new people who are out there representing your wines, and they need to get to know you—they know your wines, of course, but they need to know where you've come from and what your brand represents and to learn some of your stories.

It's also of paramount importance to connect with wine buyers at top restaurants and hotels and with the owners of retail shops. I use the word "connect" for good reason. Wine is a very personal business, I think, because it's something you don't just look at and admire, like art; you actually consume it, you take it into your body, it becomes part of you. People at every point of the chain from distribution to that final purchase want to connect with something more than just the liquid in the bottle.

Briefly, this is how the wine business works for us. We make the wine and hold some of it to sell through our mailing list or to winery guests. But the majority of it goes into distribution channels. This simply means that each wine distributor in the states where we are represented orders a certain number of cases, which they then turn around and sell to restaurants and retailers, who in turn sell the wine to local customers. This is the basic structure of what is called the three-tier system.

You may recall Dad's great saying adapted from his days at Scott Foresman: "A great wine seldom mentioned is soon forgotten." That's precisely what happens if you're complacent.

By 1994 I was away a lot, meeting with key accounts and our distributor partners in Indianapolis, Denver, New York City, Boston, Miami, Dallas, Seattle, Los Angeles, and so forth. As our export business grew I was also making trips to Japan, the United Kingdom, Singapore, the Netherlands, Germany, and other faraway destinations. Early on I'd learned a great deal from Dad about meeting with people and representing Shafer on the road. I took to it well, though I always hated being away from my family.

The upshot of all this is that my situation had changed in ways that had me focused more and more on the administrative side of things than on winemaking. So we were all in a state of flux, which hadn't yet been recognized or reconciled.

A day or two later Elias and I had a chat about next steps. I told him that I'd like the chance to put together a new offer for him as the start of a new era at the winery.

"If you take this other job, you're going to have a whole new experience and you'll do good things. You'll be fine. And we'll hire someone else, we'll keeping working hard. And we'll be fine," I said. "Everything will be okay. But if we stick together, I think we could do something great."

Elias nodded in agreement, and that kicked off a two-week conversation. Dad and I talked, Elias and I talked, Dad and Elias talked . . . we were doing something we probably should have done at least a couple of years earlier—mapping out what could come next, who wanted to do what, how we should configure things, articulating our goals.

All in all, it was a healthy process to go through for the winery, and it was a lesson I've never forgotten. Periodically since that time we have done this on a business-wide level—we'll meet and talk about the next five or ten years, put everything on the table for discussion, set goals, and alter course as needed. This way we're getting ahead of any changes, rather than simply reacting to things as they happen.

At the end of that process in the mid-1990s, Elias was named winemaker, I was named president, and Dad was named chairman.

Elias was certainly ready to take over the winemaking side of things, and I was capable of taking over the president spot. But desk work was the thing, you may remember, that I'd hoped to avoid all those years ago when I'd admired the life my dad and his buddies lived in their worn jeans and pickups. Frankly, my heart will always be with vineyards and wine cellars far more than dealing with taxes, employee hires, marketing, and administration. Fortunately, the position I have straddles both the worlds of business management and vineyards.

In their own ways Elias and Dad helped this transition. For Dad's part he made a point of being gone a lot, which forced me to make certain important calls without his input. It was nerve-wracking at times, but a trial by fire that was beneficial. It took me a while to realize that his being gone during these first months of my new position was by design. If I was going to run the winery there were some things I could only learn by doing. One day I went into his office and said, "You son of a gun, I'm running this place." My tone wasn't declarative or chest-pounding, it was more like incredulity. He just smiled and nodded. As far as he was concerned it had all gone according to plan.

It was very much the opposite of what my uncle Bill had experienced when he'd stepped into the president's spot, following his father at the *Tucson Citizen* newspaper. My dad wasn't looking over my shoulder, wasn't calling me at night questioning my every move. He was in on a lot of key decisions, of course; he was still part of the team, but ultimately he put the business and our relationship first. It was a wise and loving thing to do.

I'd also learned something valuable from him in terms of managing people. Anytime I'd come to him to confess some mistake or shortcoming, he didn't focus on the error; he was more interested in the solution and in my next steps. He knew I cared about what I was doing and that I was going to be harder on myself than anyone else—including him. I didn't forget that.

Years later, a great guy was working for us, a young man named Jesus, whom everyone called Chuy. He came into my office, terribly remorseful. I already knew from Elias what had happened but I wanted to hear it from Chuy.

He said, "Mr. Shafer, I'm sorry."

He was 100 percent certain that I was going to tear him up one side and down the other and then send him packing.

"What'd you do?" I asked.

Poor guy, he was sweaty and nervous as he explained that he'd walked away from a pump that he was using while washing out a fermentation tank. He'd gotten preoccupied with another task, and the pump had run dry. When this happens a plastic part of the pump called the impeller heats up and disintegrates, scattering bits of black plastic everywhere. The cost to replace the part was about $250. The reason I knew all of this is that I'd done precisely the same thing during my cellar rat days at Lakespring Winery.

"What'd you learn?" I asked him.

He still thought he was going to be fired at this point. But he told me he'd learned never to leave a pump.

I nodded and said, "Okay, don't do it again."

I'll never forget his look—stunned. He started to stand up to go, and I asked him to stay.

And I told him the story about my doing the very same thing.

I'm happy to say that fifteen years later Chuy is still working here and is a master at what he does in the cellar. You couldn't ask for a nicer, smarter, harder-working guy on your side. If I'd fired him for that one mistake I would have missed out on having a great member of our team.

Elias also did his part to help with the transition. Even though he didn't have to, he still came to me with almost everything—showing me lab numbers on the wines as they matured, discussing when to rack, going over the bottling schedule, every little, tiny detail. He kept this up for at least a year until I couldn't take it anymore. He was bombarding me with all these decisions, which he was 100 percent capable of making on his own, until I told him to stop it.

And then I realized he'd done it on purpose to help make my break from cellar life easier. It was thoughtful. It worked, and I've always appreciated that.

THIRTY-NINE

Nonstop Nineties

The 1990s were an incredible time of change for Napa Valley and for us. In 1991 we dug a wine cave, needing more space for barrels to keep up with expanding production and the increasing amount of time we were letting the wine mature in oak.

In 1992 we finally tore down the old adobe house that we inherited with the property. In its place we built a winery structure that would house the administrative area, as well as a guest reception area in the front.

By 1996 Napa Valley was enjoying a string of great vintages, and interest in our wine continued to grow. Perhaps as a result of this we got the biggest attention from the media we'd ever known. It started with a phone call in October from a producer of *The Today Show* in New York. In six weeks they were going to film for a few days in the Valley, and they wanted to know if their host Bryant Gumbel could come to the winery and experience harvest.

This put me on the spot, because I knew full well that by the time they'd arrive here with lights, cameras, and crew, harvest would have been over by at least three weeks. However, before my factual, sensible, logical side had a chance to ruin a great opportunity, my president-of-the-winery side said, "No problem!" The producer was thrilled and said we'd talk details again soon.

I walked over to the crush pad and told Elias what I'd done.

"All the grapes are going to be gone," he said.

"Yeah, I know."

He laughed. "What're we going to do?"

"I don't know."

Dad, Elias, and I tossed around a few ideas and ultimately decided to hold on to a two-ton block of Cabernet grapes, just leave them on the vine, and hope that these New Yorkers wouldn't realize, or perhaps care, that we were going to be picking some really overripe fruit.

When the trucks with all the cameras and equipment showed up in late November, we brought in a crew of pickers to harvest fruit that was as black and wrinkly as Greek olives.

The crew filmed all aspects of the harvesting and crushing process. Then they were trying to figure out what they could have host Bryant Gumbel do on camera. I talked them into the idea of shooting Gumbel shoveling out a tank.

This is one of the toughest, stickiest, dirtiest jobs during harvest. After a tank of red wine has finished fermentation we drain off what's call the free run, which then goes to barrel. What's left inside the tank is a purple, heavy gloop of skins, seeds, and pulp. If a person of average size is standing inside the tank, the load of skins comes to about shoulder height. And indeed someone has to climb inside the tank and shovel all of this out so that we can dump it into the press and squeeze out just a bit more juice.

Once the producers got the idea of what the job would look like, they loved it. Gumbel, however, was a bit reluctant. For one thing he was dressed in what was surely an expensive shirt and pair of pants. They were under tremendous time constraints and no one would be able to run back to the hotel for something more suited to tank shoveling. Gumbel thought he was going to get out of it.

Dad, however, offered to grab a pair of jeans from the house, which the producers said was a great idea. Seeing there was no way of avoiding it, Gumbel agreed and taped the segment, slogging through purple muck and wearing Dad's pants.

·   ·   ·

Of course life is never all good or all bad; it's a blend of bitter and sweet. In the middle of 1996, one of the best years at the winery, my marriage faltered. The divorce that followed was as difficult as anything I'd ever been through. I tried, as Dad had tried, to keep my personal challenges from affecting things at the winery. But at such a small business, where it's an outgrowth of who Dad and I are, everything seems tied together in one way or another. It was a tough time, one of my darkest hours, and my friendships with several people here, including Elias and Mary Kay Schatz, our longtime marketing and administration manager, proved a tremendous support.

FORTY

Syrah

No matter what you're going through, life in the vineyards continues, a constant process of change and maturity. As harvest-related work ramped up, Elias and I started grabbing a bite to eat after work more frequently as a way to unwind. A lot of times we'd end up over in Yountville at Mustards or the (much missed) Diner. I found that I was hungry for something new wine-wise and started searching restaurant lists for a varietal with which I wasn't as familiar. This led to the wines of France's Rhone Valley, and specifically Syrah.

When we had moved here in 1973, there was little or no Syrah.[1] It doesn't show up in the Napa County Ag Commissioner's annual crop reports until a mention of 25 acres in 1980.[2] By 1996 the Valley's Syrah plantings in production had a little more than doubled to 54 acres,

1. Aldo Delfino, Agricultural Commissioner, *1973 Napa County Agricultural Crop Report*, Napa County Department of Agriculture, Napa, CA, 1974, accessed June 28, 2011, www.countyofnapa.org/AgCommissioner/CropReport.

2. Stephen J. Bardessono, Agricultural Commissioner, *1980 Napa County Agricultural Crop Report*, Napa County Department of Agriculture, Napa, CA, 1981, accessed June 28, 2011, www.countyofnapa.org/AgCommissioner/CropReport.

qualifying it as still very much a novelty.[3] (Today, by contrast, there are about 1,000 acres.)[4]

This is a grape, however, that has a long, celebrated history in France, finding perhaps its finest expression in the tiny appellation of Hermitage, where it was a favorite even in the time of the Caesars. In the early 1800s, vine cuttings were taken to Australia, where the Aussies started calling it Shiraz. They planted it in places such as the Barossa Valley, where the grape delivers rich, beautiful reds, such as the great Penfolds Grange.

Elias and I tried as many Syrahs as we could find and began to understand the possibilities inherent in this grape—it could be made successfully in such a divergent number of styles, from light and fruity to rich and meaty.

The more we tried this wine, the more we found ourselves talking about an 18-acre piece of property Dad had purchased in the early 1980s. It lay about two miles south of the winery just beyond the Stags Leap District border in the rugged foothills of the Vaca Mountains. We'd known for a long time that with its sharp southeastern slope it'd make a perfect site for a red grape, such as Cabernet Sauvignon or Merlot. Now, though, we were thinking about what an ideal site it would make for Syrah.

Beyond that, we wanted to give this wine our own twist. The idea of a blend was appealing, although we didn't simply want to parrot the style of a Côte-Rôtie or a Châteauneuf-du-Pape. The more we thought about it, the more we liked the idea of blending Syrah, a noble variety, with its more rustic cousin, Petite Sirah—a rough and ready grape that had been part of Valley plantings going way back. In fact a lot of the

3. David R. Whitmer, Agricultural Commissioner, *1996 Napa County Agricultural Crop Report*, Napa County Department of Agriculture, Napa, CA, 1997, accessed July 11, 2011, www.countyofnapa.org/AgCommissioner/CropReport.

4. David R. Whitmer, Agricultural Commissioner, *2010 Napa County Agricultural Crop Report*, Napa County Department of Agriculture, Napa, CA, 2011, accessed July 11, 2011, www.countyofnapa.org/AgCommissioner/CropReport.

older Italian growers we knew made their own homemade wines from Petite Sirah, so in a sense this would be like bringing together France and Napa Valley in a single bottle. The final piece to this was that we wanted to put our new understanding of the role of the vineyard to work in an exciting way—we wanted to plant the blend. In other words, we wanted to plant the site to about 80 percent Syrah and 20 percent Petite Sirah. We'd grow these two varieties side by side and pick, crush, and ferment them as one.

We drove out to the remote site a number of times and mapped out how we'd situate the vines.

Finally, Elias and I felt like we'd worked out the major details of this thing, and we approached Dad with this idea. We sat in his office and talked about what a great grape Syrah was, how we thought it could be the next big thing, how much we wanted to plant some on that 18-acre site, and so forth.

Dad absorbed all of this and then said, "Boys, in the corporate world, you'd need a business plan and you'd want to test the market. Make a little bit, get it out in front of consumers, and see how it flies."

Elias and I sat back, pretty disheartened by this. There was a moment of defeated silence. Neither Elias nor I wanted to do a business plan. The plan was we'd make a really killer wine, and bottle it and sell it. Done. However, this was an actual business, not a hobby, so—

"But," Dad continued, "you two have been ringing the bell lately with everything else you've been doing, so I'd say you should just go ahead and do it."

That was more like it.

We prepped the site and planted our rootstock the following spring. By 1999 we had our first harvest. The resulting wine was opaque, liquid-midnight, a flavor wave of meat and spice and smoke and blueberry. It just washed all the way through your mouth. We were extremely pleased.

The problem now was, we didn't have a name for the wine. On my own I went into Dad's office, shut the door, and broached the idea of naming this wine in honor of Elias.

"You want to call it Elias?" Dad asked, a little puzzled.

"No, that'd sound weird, but I want to figure out a way to name it for him," I said.

"Maybe a characteristic."

"Yes, something like that."

This resulted in a couple of months of Dad and I trading secret notes back and forth to each other like schoolkids. We tried out hundreds of names until we regrouped and asked ourselves, what is Elias known for?

Among the vendors we worked with he was known for being uncompromising when it came to quality. When new barrels were delivered to the winery he personally smelled each and if the aroma was wrong, he sent it back. If the labels weren't sticking properly on the bottling line he got on the phone with the vendor to fix the problem right away. With our cork vendor, he's re-engineered every step a cork takes on its journey from Portugal to the winery. Our contact at Portacork just rolls his eyes on the subject of Elias and says that if all his clients were like our winemaker he'd be out of business.

When I asked our vendors at one point how they would describe him, they used words such as demanding, a perfectionist, and a pain in the neck.

"We can't call our wine Pain in the Neck," Dad laughed, when I told him this.

We finally hit on Relentless, which Dad and I both loved, because it honored Elias's relentless pursuit of quality. It also captured the character of the wine.

We finally had to submit the label for BATF approval and couldn't keep it from Elias any longer. Dad and I sat him down and let him know the name and the reason we'd selected it. He leaped out of his chair and screamed and pumped his fists and shouted for joy...just kidding. Actually he was surprised and honored in his quiet, unassuming way. To this day, when discussing the wine with guests or members of the wine trade, he never tells that part of the Relentless story. He's a pretty nonflashy person and blowing his own horn like that runs completely contrary to his nature. Which is a great reason to like the guy.

As a final move in his honor, we released the first vintage of Relentless on Elias's birthday in January 2001.

FORTY-ONE

Cults

By the mid- to late 1990s the Napa Valley I knew was in the middle of another transition. The tech bubble was in full effervescence. Billions of dollars in venture capital were flooding Silicon Valley and San Francisco. Twenty-somethings in the Bay Area were, it seems, being awoken every morning by the thud of bales of cash falling all around them. The birth of the Internet was under way, and it had all the hallmarks of another gold rush. Overnight, computer programmers with a PC and a dream were finding themselves behind the wheel of a new Italian sports car. Nerds were the new rock stars. Housing prices were rising every month; credit was easy and getting easier. If you weren't a millionaire by age twenty-five you were probably defective in some way.

The Internet was going to change our lives. You could have pet food delivered to your door. You could meet the next love of your life online. *Encyclopedia Britannica*, *The New York Times*, and the *Oxford English Dictionary* were as close as your keyboard. New websites were attracting customers by giving away free stuff left and right. Making a profit was a hopelessly antiquated business model. All you needed was to be incredibly awesome, and your stock price would hit $500 a share (as I saw Yahoo's do one day in this era).

Napa Valley wine was rather suddenly yanked out of its early '90s list-lessness. In 1995 Caymus got some attention for breaking the $100-a-bottle barrier with the release of its 1991 Special Selection (less remembered is that Far Niente actually got there first with its half-bottle of delicious Dolce dessert wine). Bryant Family, Diamond Creek, Grace Family, Harlan Estate, Opus One, and Screaming Eagle all crossed the $100-per-bottle line with their releases in 1998. Araujo, Colgin, Dalla Valle, and our 1996 Hillside Select joined this Benjamin Franklin club in 1999.

Then there came a day, also in 1999, when I got a call on my cell phone from Dan Sogg, a writer at *Wine Spectator*. I was in San Diego, and my reception wasn't very good, so I pulled off the road and found a pay phone and called him back. He had a bunch of questions about Hillside Select and about our winery, which I answered and hung up and forgot about.

A few months later, I realized what the interview had been about when the latest *Wine Spectator* landed on my desk. On the cover in large type were the words "Cult Wine" and a photo of Jean Phillips, who owned Screaming Eagle. We've known Jean for a long time, going back to when she was a real estate broker in St. Helena. In the early 1990s she'd gotten into the wine business, purchased a nice vineyard site on Silverado Trail near Dalla Valle, and started making a Cabernet Sauvignon, working with winemaker Heidi Barrett (who's married to Bo Barrett of Chateau Montelena and is the daughter of longtime winemaker Richard Peterson). Jean's first vintage, a 1992 Cab released in 1995, received rave reviews from Robert Parker, who gave that first release a score of 99. The *Wine Spectator* awarded it a 96. She only made 175 cases. This meant the wine was exceptionally good and impossible to get. And thanks to the tech boom there were suddenly more and more people out there whose stock portfolios were bursting with value, who wanted the wine at any price.

Screaming Eagle's 1997 vintage received a perfect 100 score from Parker in January 2000, which sent the already high-intensity interest in the wine into berserk mode. Lots of collectors on both coasts, people with an enormous amount of disposable income, wanted that wine, and the prices spiraled upward.

I suppose the term "cult wine" had been around for a while, but it was this April 30, 2000, *Wine Spectator* cover story that really brought it into clear focus for me. According to the *Spectator* this list included Araujo, Bryant Family, Colgin, Dalla Valle, Grace Family, Harlan Estate, Marcassin, Screaming Eagle, and Shafer Vineyards Hillside Select.[1]

As it turns out, though, various critics and collectors had their own lists. While the *Spectator,* for example, included Hillside Select on the cult list, *The New York Times* said that we, Marcassin, and Ridge *might* be on this list.[2]

No matter who you talked to, the wineries being identified with the cult wine phenomenon fell more or less into two camps. One group was made up of the hot newcomers. These brands hadn't existed ten years previously. Harlan's first vintage was 1990, Araujo's first Eisele Vineyard Cabernet was 1991, and Bryant Family's and Screaming Eagle's first vintages were 1992.

In the older group was our Hillside Select, which debuted in 1983, the same year as Grace Family's first Cabernet. Dalla Valle's first vintage was in 1986.

The core group was largely, in my mind, identified by very small production—Harlan at that time made 500 cases, Bryant Family produced 600 cases, and Grace Family just 150. Our production level of 2,200 placed us on the outer ring of the cult wine phenomenon.

The term "cult wine" always made Dad and me a little uneasy, given that it indicated a certain kind of mass hysteria, like the tulip craze in seventeenth-century Holland. It was also equated, largely, with a kind of

1. James Laube, "California's Cult Wines," *Wine Spectator.* April 30, 2000, accessed August 16, 2011, www.winespectator.com/magazine/show/id/8606.

2. Frank J. Prial, "Reality Check, Please, for Cult Wines," *New York Times,* October 17, 2001, accessed August 16, 2011, www.nytimes.com/2001/10/17/dining/wine-talk-reality-check-please-for-cult-wines.html?pagewanted=all.

instant success, which didn't exactly mesh with our history. By this point the first Shafer Cabernet was some twenty years old, a near-archeological relic by New World standards. Our prices had risen as the result of growing more and more meticulous about the way we cultivated and made the wine. By the late 1990s we were spending a tidy sum to produce Hillside Select. French oak barrels, which we only used once, cost a fortune, the kind of man-hours that hillside cultivation required were costly, and we put a lot into the overall package.

Dad, Elias, and I had a pretty steady-as-she-goes approach to our entire business. We believed in taking a long-term view and saw the potential for this kind of meteoric rise to come with some negatives.

In that *Wine Spectator* cover story on the cult wine phenomenon, James Laube reminded readers that while prices for Napa Valley's hottest wines might seem high, they paled in comparison to those of "Chateau Margaux, Chateau d'Yquem or Domaine de la Romanee-Conti."

It was a good distinction to make but I'm not sure it had a lot of impact. I'm pretty certain that one of the reasons that there was such a dust-up about California prices at that time was the underlying sense—especially among more traditional connoisseurs—that we simply didn't deserve it. No one in California had a three-hundred- or four-hundred-year history. None of us could stroll down a sunlit hallway filled with aged oil paintings of our ancestors adorned in white-powdered wigs. None of us dwelt in chateaus built before the age of Napoleon. In short, we still weren't France, so where did we get the hubris to charge one-tenth of what some of France's first growths were charging? Yes, while Napa Valley was being accused of price gouging, Burgundy's Domaine de la Romanee-Conti was releasing its 1996 Romanee-Conti for $1,022 per bottle. Slightly less startling was Chateau Lafite Rothschild Pauillac 1996, released for $196, and Chateau Margaux 1996, released for $282. Double what the newly coronated Napa cults were charging.

Even so, it represented something new. And I began to realize that two wine industries were emerging. One was the real wine business, in which a couple of hundred Napa Valley brands were slugging it out in the $20 to $50 market, and then there was the new fantasy wine business, which was the domain of the cults and the near-cults. And frankly, which world would you rather live in? The one in the trenches or the one with all the buzz? The one where you worked your tail off figuring out your marketing and advertising strategy, spending nearly your entire year on the road working with distributors and reps, riding from retailer to retailer and restaurant to restaurant to pour your wines and spread your message, crafting another letter to your wine club … or … having your door pounded on constantly, your fax machine run out of toner for all the requests for your wine, your employees bribed with cars and vacations to sell a few bottles out the back door, and vaults of cash hurled at you, while simultaneously being praised for your vision and overall marvelousness?

Our winery was in a unique position in that we straddled both of these worlds. With Hillside Select we were regularly listed as one of the cults, whereas with our other wines we were fully engaged in the more traditional marketplace alongside a number of other vintners.

On one hand, the real wine market is a tough place to do business, but we understood it and we could see how to make it work long term. On the other hand, Dad and I worried that the cult side of things was a flash in the pan that could ultimately swing back on us in a damaging way. We tried to be careful with our pricing for all the wines but especially for Hillside Select. We didn't want to be seen as gouging anyone, yet at the same time it's a wine that's distinguished itself. We felt like we were doing the right thing when we were hearing that the wine was a virtual bargain at $150 per bottle, given that the "flippers"—people who were buying the wine solely for the purchase of flipping it, that is, reselling it—could still turn around and make a handsome profit on it within days of its release.

•   •   •

The biggest difference of opinion Dad and I had over the years occurred during this era. With some success under our belts and dot-com money washing into wine country, Dad started making noise about the idea that the winery should be growing—in fact doubling its production to fifty thousand or sixty thousand cases. For me this was a nonstarter.

"I want to keep it at thirty thousand," I told him. "At thirty we can have a small staff and can stay on top of everything. I know that I can guarantee what thirty thousand cases will taste like."

To grow much beyond thirty thousand cases would mean that Elias and I would have to start delegating significant parts of our operation— we'd need a sales team, more people in hospitality and administration, and a bigger cellar crew. Elias might need a couple of assistant wine-makers. I might need an administrative assistant (which I've long re-sisted). It was a risk that I thought had more potential for headaches than payoff. We had been in this business long enough to know that it is a long series of ups and down. No matter how well we were doing today, at some point, things were going to get tough again. I didn't want to double our production and then get stuck with a lot of unsold cases once the market-place slowed down again.

He heard me out and said, "Okay, it's your call."

Inwardly I couldn't believe this turnabout—Dad and I had traded roles. I was thinking to myself, "Who's the child of the Depression here? Who's supposed to be the conservative one?"

I reasoned with Dad that there are other ways to grow. Instead of bumping up our output, I suggested that our current profits go toward ensuring the quality of our future wines. With every upswing in the Valley's fortunes had come a hard smackdown on the other side, and I wanted to be ready.

One thing we'd learned over twenty years is that the smartest thing you can do in regard to quality is to ensure your grape source, and there is no better way to do that than owning your own vineyards. Consumers understand this, and it's the reason the words "estate grown" on your label is such an important distinction.

Since 1983 we'd been producing two Cabernets. One was Hillside Se-lect and the other we'd simply called our Stags Leap District Cabernet

Sauvignon. Inevitably people referred to this as our second Cab or our "regular" Cab, which I always felt did the wine a disservice. It automatically achieved a secondary status next to Hillside Select. This was further exacerbated when we lost our ability to purchase fruit from growers within Stags Leap District in the mid-1990s. As the financial picture for the country and for Napa Valley grew brighter, growers who'd been fine with cultivating and selling grapes for years started making their own wine and creating their own brands.

As a result, Elias and I decided that we'd make a Cabernet that would represent a snapshot of the entire Valley in a given growing season. Our debut vintage for this approach was the 1996. We sourced fruit from Calistoga to just outside the town of Napa. Long term, though, our hearts were with Stags Leap District and in 1999, we were finally able to purchase a 25-acre hay field located at the southern end of the District, just south of where the old Chimney Rock Golf course had been located.

It was the largest unplanted piece of property within the District, and we'd spoken with the owner on and off for more than ten years. He'd cannily held off selling it until it reached a sky-high value—the whole parcel would cost us $100,000 per acre for land that we would then have to prep as a vineyard site.

We'd been careful with our funds for years and were able to buy the site without taking out a loan. Once we made the purchase, I wanted to be sure that we could grow hillside-quality fruit in this broad, fertile, Valley-floor property. A key thing we'd learned with our home ranch fruit is to never let the vines sit in a lot of moisture. When the rains hit, the water drains off the hillside very quickly.

To equate that phenomenon on this new site, the first thing we did was spend another $100,000 or so on an extensive subsoil drainage system. When it rained, I wanted water out of that soil quickly, as if it were on a sharp hillside incline. Even in late spring, long after the winter rains, there's often still water trickling out of the drainage system.

We planted the vines very close together in rows that are only six feet apart, so that the vines would be forced to compete with each other for moisture and soil nutrients. We also established a thick cover crop to further stress the vines.

We got the entire site planted and ready to go by 2001 and started calling it "Borderline," as it sits on the southern border of Stags Leap District.

A second step toward growing in terms of quality was an evolution in our approach to barrels. Elias and I felt that all the wines could gain more richness and complexity if they spent more time maturing in oak barrels. Over the years we'd been slowly increasing the amount of time the wines were in the barrel, and particularly in the case of Hillside Select and Relentless, the wines exhibited such concentration and extract that they continued to respond well to more time in oak.

To pull this off we'd need more physical space to store additional barrels—about 2,200 is the number at which we were aiming. At that point we had the original barrel room off the cellar, where we were already barrel-fermenting and aging our Chardonnay, and the wine cave we'd dug in 1991, dedicated to storing all our red wines. We checked on prices for digging another cave and discovered that in the decade since we'd established our first cave in the hillside, the cost for such a project had risen tenfold. Talk about sticker shock.

Rather than bore a new hole in our hillside, we began to talk about building a new barrel room. The more we discussed this, the more exciting it became. We could design something purely to our specifications. A chief goal would be to create a space as unfriendly as possible to cork taint, a chemical compound called 2,4,6-trichloroanisole (TCA). It's volatile and likes to live in wood, paper, and cardboard. Toward this end we would use laboratory-grade flooring and a ceiling made of Alaskan cedar, whose natural oils would prove highly resistant to TCA and mold. Next we designed a large stainless steel rack structure to hold those additional 2,200 barrels. We designed racks that served the dual

Shafer built its new barrel room in 2001.

purpose of offering no surface that could harbor TCA and that would give the guys on our crew a better ergonomic environment than in a traditional wine cave.

These were the two main ways we spent our Internet bubble profit: on things that will last. The land will be here eons after we're gone, and those stainless steel barrel racks have about a five-hundred-year life span. I just couldn't see doubling or tripling our output. I don't wake up in the morning with fire in my veins to expand this business. I'm not an empire builder. After having worked here for more than three decades I still believe there are things to learn and still ways we can do a better job with the tasks already in front of us.

·   ·   ·

The boom of the late 1990s was reflected in the success of the Napa Valley Wine Auction. By this period we were raising more money than our original model at Hospices de Beaune. Just when you thought the annual total could go no higher, we were surprised by the following year's results. The original vision to help support our two local hospitals had expanded with the auction's ballooning totals. It had started to fund a wide variety of nonprofit organizations in the areas of health care, affordable housing, and youth development.

Dad was named chairman of the 1999 Napa Valley Wine Auction, a job he thoroughly enjoyed. In an event attended by comedian Robin Williams and basketball legend Michael Jordan, auction bidders broke all previous records with a total of $5.5 million—officially making the Napa Valley Wine Auction the most successful charity wine event in the world fewer than twenty years after its inception.

The following year, the dollar figures rose even higher. My collaborator on this book, Andy Demsky, was a public relations assistant at the Napa Vintners office in St. Helena. Late on the Friday afternoon before the 2000 auction he was the only one in the office and picked up the phone when it rang. On the other end was a first-time auction-goer named Chase Bailey wondering if he could still get an auction catalogue for the next day's big event. As a matter of fact they were all spoken for, but Andy said he'd cut Chase some slack and managed to get this latecomer a catalogue anyway. Turns out, during the live auction the following day, Chase Bailey, a new dot-com retiree, made wine history by purchasing a single bottle of wine for $500,000—a six-liter of Screaming Eagle. The cheers and the music nearly sent the roof of the auction tent into orbit. Less than an hour later, another bidder won a six-bottle vertical of Harlan for $750,000.

．　　　．　　　．

In January 1999, Dad sent Elias and me a memo—this was not uncommon. When your Dad is John Shafer, you get used to all kinds of ideas flying your way. This time, though, he was very much in long-term planning mode. He was struck by the change in our competition. We were essentially two wineries now—we were in the "real wine business" with our Merlot, Chardonnay, Cabernet, and Sangiovese, and we were also a member of the new "fantasy wine market" with Hillside Select. More than anything he wanted to take some time to define, once again, our sense of who we were and who we wanted to become.

Part of that definition would, of course, depend on our business goals. But to an even greater extent it meant defining ourselves in terms of our mission. Now we were wading into the murky waters of philosophy, not an area that we Midwesterners were comfortable traveling through. Once again, though, we got good consultant help. In this case, Dad called Danny Meyer, who'd already made a name for himself in the cutthroat restaurant world by being the sweetest guy around and understanding the importance of core values to the long-term vitality of a business.

We first met Danny in 1985 with the launch of his restaurant, Union Square Café, in Manhattan. With his opening just four years after the release of our first wine, Dad always felt a kinship with Danny. Not only did Union Square Café gain a reputation for its great food, it went further and earned a reputation for its beloved world-class hospitality. Dad and I would visit the restaurant on trips to New York, and right off the bat there was something different going on at Danny's place. It was easy to see why it consistently scored so high on Zagat ratings. Danny Meyer has a genius for making customers feel valued and welcomed. His restaurants are popular for good reason. You always leave them feeling better than when you went in.

We more or less knew our Shafer core values, but we'd never discussed or defined them, and we'd never written them down. So we had Danny come out in February 1999, and we picked his brain and asked him to challenge our thinking. It was a wonderful, defining moment for us.

After meeting with Danny, we had a staff retreat at Bodega Bay (about an hour from the winery on the Sonoma coast). We found it helpful to get away from the workaday world in order to focus on bigger issues.

Ultimately, we crafted a mission statement and a set of core values that would determine our course as a business.

What we came up with was simple and straightforward, but has helped guide our planning and decision making on every level ever since:

Our Purpose:
·   To provide an unforgettable experience

Our Core Values:
·   Respect and care for each other, our customers, our suppliers, our environment
·   Integrity and authenticity in all aspects of our work and interactions
·   Service to our community
·   Excellence in everything we do

Working from this outline we pushed further, developing a detailed road map for becoming the winery we wanted to be by the year 2010. The plan defined what we wanted a visit to Shafer to look and feel like, how our wines should be packaged, how our promotional material should look and feel, and, of course, how we wanted to continue improving our vineyard and cellar operations. We believed that the surest way to being the kind of winery that people found engaging would be to make sure our employees felt encouraged and supported and to recognize and reward the good work of the many vendors who'd helped our success. (Every year we throw a vendor party, inviting everyone from the FedEx driver, to our plumber, to the people we buy case boxes from, in order to say "thank you" for helping us achieve our goals.)

The 2010 plan that emerged from all this process defined nearly everything we did over the course of the next decade.

FORTY-TWO

El Niño

I can imagine that from the outside looking in, the roaring tech boom of the 1990s must have looked like a nonstop party. But in fact there was plenty going on to keep us anchored to planet Earth.

If nothing else, every growing season delivers a whole new lineup of challenges. Amigo Bob has said before, "Mother Nature bats first and last." Any time you're tempted to feel like a Master of the Universe, the natural world is always more than happy to pound your ego like a cheap piñata.

The 1990s had delivered a string of outstanding vintages, including the justly celebrated 1997 vintage. The year that followed was a reminder of how rough things can get.

For us it happened to be the year we hired a new director of vineyard operations, David Ilsley. David grew up on the other side of the hill from us, just north on the Silverado Trail, where his grandfather Ernie had purchased vineyard property in the 1950s. David was thus the third generation of a grower family, whom we had known as friends and neighbors for a long time. He attended local schools and played football at the University of Washington, going to the Rose Bowl three times with his team.

He started college in 1988 at the beginning of the phylloxera era here and when he came back, he says, everything vineyard-wise had changed. For example, summer had always been a pretty easy season for growers. You just sort of sat back and let the vines grow. By 1998, however, summer was an incredibly busy season. There was a greater understanding now of the role that exposure to sunlight played in fruit development. Also, canopy[1] management had become a big deal. We wanted to remove a certain percentage of leaves to give the fruit the right amount of solar exposure.

During summer, besides leafing, we were now tucking and hedging—in other words, keeping vine growth within the trellis structure and trimming back any wild growth. We were also now doing micro-irrigation. This meant that instead of watering all the vines at once, we'd created complex systems that allowed us to deliver small amounts of water to just one vineyard block, to one row, or to a single vine, if that's what was required.

Once the vines reach *veraison*—the point in the season when grapes such as Merlot and Cabernet turn from green to purple and Chardonnay turns from green to yellow—we want to start gearing up for harvest by removing all but the best fruit. This "green harvesting," as it is called, might entail culling all or part of a cluster or even snipping off individual grapes.

We were now going cluster by cluster throughout the vineyards in the weeks leading up to harvest to do everything possible to ensure uniform ripeness for the fruit being crushed and going into our fermentation tanks. Getting an unprecedented level of uniform ripeness now guided everything we did in the vineyard, beginning with pruning in January through the entirety of the growing season.

1. The term "canopy" refers to the vine's foliage, mainly its leaves. Canopy management includes tucking and hedging to keep shoots and foliage within the trellis system, while leafing refers to pulling off a number of leaves to ensure the grapes receive the right balance of sunlight and shade for the best possible development.

As if that wasn't a baptism by fire in itself for David, the 1998 season was one of the most difficult we'd seen in at least ten years. It was an El Niño year, a weather pattern that recurs every few years and gives us more rain than normal. This was a particularly wet version of that phenomenon. In fact August was the only month that year we didn't get rain. By contrast, in the year that followed, which was considered an outstanding vintage, we got no rain in June, July, and August, and only a trace in September.

The 1998 vintage began with a massive rainfall in February, almost twenty-five inches. Rains continued into May, in which we got a very unusual four inches. This affected bloom, in that we got smaller clusters with far fewer grapes. The summer that followed was relatively hot. Near the end of June, the day after we'd spread sulfur dust on the crop (to prevent mildew), temperatures unexpectedly spiked over 100 degrees, and the combination of heat and sulfur badly burned much of our fruit. David felt terrible, of course, and the only thing that made him feel a percent or two better is that a lot of other very experienced vineyard managers throughout the Valley had done the same. In the weeks that followed, we got more heat. The first of August saw temperatures up over 100 degrees again, which succeeded in scorching our already dwindling crop.

It was the first year in which we seriously considered not producing a Hillside Select. However, before making that call, David, Elias, and crew cut away a lot of mediocre and sunburnt fruit, and at harvest we only picked grapes that were looking and tasting up to a high standard.

If you ask Elias which vintage he's most proud of in his entire career, he'll tell you it's 1998 Hillside Select, because it was a year that called on everything we'd learned about working the vineyard. And in spite of all the knuckleballs Mother Nature threw at us, we believed that we produced a wine that was a real gem.

·   ·   ·

There was another reason to celebrate the 1998 vintage—at a small ceremony that took place on September 26 of that year on the lawn in front of the winery, Dad and Barbara got married. It's no small thing to find love when you're in your twenties or thirties, but it seems a very special thing to find it later in life. Since their marriage, they've started collecting art together, Dad's taken up sculpture and drawing, and they've even traveled to Argentina for tango lessons. They've had a great time together.

A new adventure had begun in my own life as well. In the summer of 1997, when I was single again, I ran into Annette Williams on a gorgeous morning at the St. Helena Farmers Market. She was smart, fun to talk with, and loved wine. She had come to the Valley in the mid-1990s after working in marketing for two California governors. Her first love was the culinary world (she's a graduate of the Culinary Institute of America, Hyde Park, New York), and she'd been happy to leave Sacramento politics to accept a position as director of operations for the newly opened Culinary Institute of America, Greystone, in St. Helena. We spent as much time together as we could, which was tough, because we were both busy. One of Annette's projects was her book *The Wine Sense Diet*. In it she profiled me (among other winery owners) as a single, vintner dad. But the timing was such that by the time the book was going to press, the publisher had to change her last name on the dust jacket to Shafer.

On the first day of October 1999, after crushing sixty tons of hillside Cabernet, I took a shower and put on a pair of jeans, cowboy boots, and a sport coat, and Annette and I exchanged vows on the hillside. It was a beautiful sunset ceremony at the edge of a vineyard block we have since named "Hitching Post."

Annette and I have been incredibly fortunate. We have a boy and a girl now, Tate and Remington, and have often joked that ours is a great pairing of food and wine—interests that have inspired many of our new adventures together.

FORTY-THREE

A New Millennium

Following the stellar conditions of the 1999 vintage, our hopes were that another string of great growing seasons was on its way. However, the 2000 vintage turned out to be another wet one, in which we had to work harder than usual to get the best possible fruit. After that, though, we did get back into a great stride with ideal conditions in 2001 and 2002. There's little point in reviewing the details of those growing seasons, because in the best vintages very little happens. The vines simply experience day after day of beautiful weather. As a result the best growing seasons are often the ones you can't remember.

In 2001 we released the first vintage of Relentless to a great deal of enthusiasm from consumers and critics alike. We'd managed to get in early on a new wave of California and Australian Rhone varietals, which were proving popular in the marketplace.

By this time Elias was being recognized in other ways. In October 2002, the prestigious magazine *Wine & Spirits* honored him as "Winemaker of the Year" at an event in San Francisco, and twenty-four hours later he was recognized at a White House ceremony for leadership in the Latino community. Elias took his wife and his mother (a former seasonal farmworker) with him to meet President George W. Bush and other dignitaries at this private event. It's the *only* time that Elias has been lured away from the winery during harvest.

•   •   •

By 2003 it was clear that Sangiovese was not going to become the next Merlot. I think a lot of wine consumers ended up saying some version of "Sangio-*what?*" and simply passed the wine by. We always liked the wine and got very nice critical and consumer attention for it. But the thought that persisted with Elias and me is that those Sangiovese vines were sitting in some of the best Cabernet Sauvignon soil known to human-kind. The idea of having that land planted to that grape—which was a difficult creature to begin with—ate at us vintage after vintage.

Following the 2003 harvest, after a lot of discussion, we took out all the Sangiovese from La Vigna Lana and replanted to Cabernet. When we released that final Sangiovese, we had some fun with it. First of all we called it Last Chance Firebreak, which harkened back to our 1983 Zin-fandel, which we called Last Chance Zinfandel. In addition, we wrapped our last bottle of Firebreak Sangiovese in a white flag and sent it to Piero Antinori, saying, "We surrender." We thought they had a better handle on the grape. Sangiovese has been cultivated in the soils of Tuscany for thousands of years. It has history there, it's planted in the right places, and Tignanello is a wine we still admire. We never believed our Sangio-vese reached those heights, so we refocused on our area of strength, which was Cabernet.

As such, the next big thing on the horizon for us was the introduc-tion, or reintroduction really, of our Stags Leap District Cabernet. The vines in our new Borderline Vineyard were coming along nicely, and it was clear that we would be harvesting our first fruit the following year, in 2004.

By this time, we were clear that we no longer wanted a wine that would be called our "Regular Cab." It deserved a name that would dif-ferentiate it from the shadow cast by its sibling, Hillside Select.

Our sales manager at the time was coming back from consumer tastings around the country and reporting that wine enthusiasts in their mid- to late twenties were asking if there were still any Shafers at Shafer Vineyards. At first it seemed like an odd question but on further reflection, we realized that this was a perfectly legitimate thing for a new generation of wine drinkers to ask—young people who'd grown up in a world where more and more of the wineries that we saw started in the '60s and '70s were now brands in corporate-owned portfolios.

We'd never made any noise on our labels about being family owned, because twenty years ago nearly everyone in the Valley was family owned. It was a non-story. But we took a look around and realized that was less often the case, at least with the wineries of our age.

It was time to make sure people knew we were still a family winery, and putting that on a label would be a good way to do it. We made lists of ideas—every permutation we could think of that had to do with "family" and "fathers and sons." The first thing we crossed off the list was anything that used the word "generations." That had been done before. We worked our way through hundreds of names. At one point, feeling a little punchy, I joked that we should just call it "Brad" after my younger brother. We got a lot of comedic mileage out of wondering aloud how it would sound for people in a restaurant to order a bottle of "Brad."

After going through more ideas, I started to think about the many times writers had asked Dad and me about our "second-generation story"—that classic narrative in which a parent starts a business and twenty years later, once it is successful, hands it off to a son or daughter, the story that mirrored my uncle Bill's experience at the Tucson newspaper. But things had happened differently here. Dad had started later in life, I joined him early on, and we worked together for such a long time that in many ways we'd learned the business together. We finally started answering that question by saying ours was a "generation-and-a-half" story.

That's a lot to put on a wine label. We noodled this concept around for a while and one morning at the winery before anyone else got here, when the place was quiet, an idea hit me, which I wrote on the back of a legal pad—the words "One Point Five," which played off the generation-and-a-half idea. I called some of our distributor partners and ran the name by them. Everyone seemed to think it'd be fine. We'd already been through the process of releasing a wine with a semi-inscrutable name when we'd come up with Red Shoulder Ranch Chardonnay. We had gotten a lot of quizzical looks and questions like "What's the name of that wine—Burnt Shoulder? Big Shoulder?"

In that case, too, we'd gone with a name that helped tell something important about the winery. By the time we'd planted Red Shoulder Ranch in Carneros we were fully in sustainable farming mode and raptors such as the red-shouldered hawk were helping us keep the vineyard free of gophers. So we named the wine in honor of our feathered partners, and the name gave consumers an idea about our approach to caring for the land.

After being on the market, everyone got used to the Red Shoulder Ranch name, and away we went. In the case of One Point Five I knew we'd have a three- or four-year phase of answering the question "What does 'One Point Five' mean?" Answering that—as we did hundreds of times—created an opportunity to talk about who we are as a family winery.

The first vintage of One Point Five was greeted with a lot of excitement from consumers and positive reviews by critics. And it was great to once again be fully in the business of Stags Leap District Cabernet. Since we now owned the fruit source, we'd never get aced out of it again.

FORTY-FOUR

Going Solar

At about the age of eighty my dad took up sculpture, making a lovingly lifelike bust of his yellow Labrador, Tucker. He did an impressive job, and the sculpture lived for a couple of years at the bottom of our stairway up to the winery visitor area. Next, he produced a life-sized model in clay of Tucker and had it cast in bronze; today it welcomes guests as they enter the winery. People love to rub the sculpture's head and pose for photos with it. Dad also stayed busy with a variety of charitable causes. In 2000 he'd helped conceptualize and raise the funds for a health center in Napa that housed four local health-related nonprofits. He continued his work with Clinic Olé and later started working closely with a nonprofit called VOICES that supports youth who've aged out of the foster care system. Once a month or so he continued to enjoy spending time with a group called "Men Who Cook," a collection of friends, including Mike Martini from Martini Winery and Peter McCrea from Stony Hill. They like to get together and cook up some pretty lavish meals.

My point in saying all this is that he wasn't exactly kicking back in an easy chair and watching the world go by. Since his long-term-planning days at Scott Foresman, he's been a lot more oriented toward what's happening in the next five or ten years than anything else.

In early 2004 Dad showed up in my office with a binder of materials and a stack of newspaper and magazine clippings. He plunked it all down in front of me with the look he gets when he's about to make a case for something.

"We should do this," he said.

"Do what?"

"We should look into converting to solar power."

I was up to my eyeballs in all kinds of other tasks and projects related to the business. I couldn't take this on too.

"I like it," I said to him, shoving the pile of documents back toward him. "You do the research and come back to me with a proposal."

"Okay," he said, gathering up his materials. "That's what I'll do."

In another month or so he was back, relentless in his own way, with potential costs and the names of three top companies we should talk to, Northern California vendors who were building big commercial solar arrays. The solar power business, he said, was hot at that point, because you could lock in a credit from the state that could pay for half your array. In our case the proposal was for about 750 panels that would produce power equal to our needs in the cellar and winery.

The price was just shy of $1 million but with the credits, the size of the check we'd write came down to around $450,000. If the projections were right, we looked to recoup our costs in eight or nine years.

Even so, it was a big project with lots of zeros attached, credit or no credit. Dad was intent on going 100 percent solar. To our knowledge no other winery in the country had done that yet.

After studying the proposal and absorbing all the facts and figures, it became clear how much sense solar power made here. The reason we're in a superb region for wine grapes is the same reason we're in a prime location to take advantage of solar energy—we're awash in sunlight throughout much of the year. Typically, from May through late October we don't get much, if any, rain. It's day after day of sun.

The construction of the array began in the fall of 2004, just after harvest, and by late November we flipped the switch. It was a tremendous

In 2004 Shafer constructed its first of two large solar arrays. The roof-mounted array seen here was part of the first, which totaled more than seven hundred panels. A second array of one hundred panels was constructed in 2008.

feeling to watch our electric meter run backward on sunny days and to eventually get those statements from Pacific Gas & Electric that credited us for the excess energy that we were producing and pumping into the regional electrical grid.

Beyond the financial advantages, the smart-energy side of this was exciting too. We were producing clean kilowatts. No oil, coal, or natural gas was being burned—and then polluting the atmosphere—on our behalf. Over the lifetime of our array, the amount of carbon *not* spewing into the skies on our behalf was equal to the carbon-absorbing ability of seventeen thousand adult trees. The more I learned about solar, the happier I was that we were a part of it.

After we installed our system, I got calls from lots of vintner friends who were kicking the tires on the solar power idea as well. It's been heartening to see this technology take hold in a big way in the wine business. Not long after we went 100 percent solar so did John Williams at Frog's Leap, joined by many others who were building arrays of varying sizes. Far Niente constructed a great system that floats on their pond—a smart use of space—which they dubbed their "floatovoltaic" array. If science can raise the efficiency of solar panels, in terms of converting a higher percentage of sunlight to electricity, it will make huge strides toward a clean energy future.

Some of our early enthusiasm was dampened a bit in the spring and summer of 2005, when we began to notice that our array was not generating as much power as it should. As the days went by we were disappointed to see a continuing decline. We called the company that did the installation and after some investigation, we discovered the problem— dust. We kicked up more dust around here than we realized, thanks to driving pickups on our gravel roadways through different vineyard blocks, driving tractors through vine rows, and so forth. It's a farm after all.

We discovered that more often than most other businesses we needed to wash the panels to keep them at peak efficiency. If you visit us and see guys up on the cellar roof with water hoses and squeegees, you'll know what we're up to.

A few years later, in 2008, we built a second array of another one hundred panels to produce power equal to what our irrigation system uses to pump water throughout our 50 acres of vines.

FORTY-FIVE

Hospitality

While we continued to explore new ways to run our winery in earth-friendly ways, we also worked toward the goals we'd outlined in our 2010 plan. That end date was looming faster than we'd expected. An important part of the plan was to create an unforgettable experience for those who visited the winery. And we knew we hadn't adequately tackled that one. Until about 2003, if you entered our winery's hospitality area, you'd be greeted by one of our staff members at the front desk, who would pour a taste or two of whatever bottle happened to be open at the time.

It was informal, relaxed, and free. However, customers began to let us know that they wanted a lot more than we were offering. The thing we heard again and again is that they wanted to taste our entire portfolio of wines, including Hillside Select.

As a group, here at the winery, we started tossing around ideas for what a more structured Shafer tasting would look like. In twos and threes I sent some of our office and hospitality employees to other wineries to get a sense for what Napa visitors were experiencing at the hospitality rooms of our neighbors.

What struck us is how times had changed and what a myriad of experiences were out there. At one place you might sit with the owner and crack open just about any bottles you wanted and hang out for a couple hours with a view of the Valley; at another you might walk through a cave, tasting barrel sample after barrel sample. Some places, such as our neighbor Robert Sinskey Vineyards, offer little nibbles designed to pair nicely with their wines. Another neighbor, Cliff Lede, is into classic rock, so their tasting room plays a lot of my favorite music. Some wineries offer the chance to create your own blend.

All the successful tastings had an authenticity to them. It felt like the soul of the owners or winemakers put its stamp on the visitor experience.

Less successful, we thought, were some of the traditional belly up to the tasting bars, where you paid ten dollars for a taste of four or five wines. The host behind the bar gave you the same sales patter they gave the next couple who walked in the door just behind you. This sales-driven approach wasn't the way we wanted to go.

Other tastings, in which a group of fifteen to twenty people, by appointment, would be taken by a tour guide through the winery's grounds and production area before guests could try the wine, seemed more personal. One thing we noticed is that a lot of people mentioned that they'd seen crush pads and fermentation tanks before and just wanted to get to the wine-tasting portion.

As a group, we discussed a lot of this in light of what we wanted to create here. Primarily we all agreed on one thing—when people visited here we wanted them to feel as if they'd joined a wine tasting in our home. By our very nature we didn't wish to become a destination for tour buses and bachelorette parties. We wanted to operate on a more personal scale. Out of these conversations we created a plan to offer two by-appointment tastings per day, one at 10 A.M. and one at 2 P.M., and we initially capped the group size at twelve guests. However, once we started, we discovered that at that number people didn't ask questions, talk much, or participate. Everyone was really quiet. We were left to deliver a lecture about the wines, which wasn't much fun for us or for our

Shafer Vineyards as it looks today.

visitors. After some experimentation we found that in groups of ten there was much more interaction—the whole thing felt like a conversation. We don't know what law of group dynamics is responsible for this, but that's where we set the guest count.

As much as we've worked on our tasting visit, it still isn't a perfect situation. On one hand, guests who book four to six weeks ahead are able to secure a spot and have an enjoyable time. But a number of people call a lot later than that or drop by at the last minute, and we have to turn them away. We hate saying no. Those who work in this business do so because we like to be welcoming and help people enjoy themselves. Among those customers who get the word that we don't have an opening, I know there are those who feel we're simply being elitist, which stings a bit. Fortunately, I think the intent behind the system has become better known and understood over time.

In our staff meetings we are constantly asking ourselves how we could have handled this or that situation with a customer differently. Is there a better way to deal with the situation when the answer is no? Is there a way to restructure our tastings that will allow us to say yes more frequently?

This is a part of the winery that will always be a work in progress—like nearly everything else we do.

FORTY-SIX

Television Gets Real

As our world was changing in terms of how we met people in our visitor area, we also began to sense other rapid changes in the larger world of wine. A whole new generation of wine and food enthusiasts was emerging who didn't know much about us. This is a phenomenon that never goes away, and we've experimented with many different marketing tactics over the years and are open to new ideas that enhance the brand and have the potential to introduce our wines to new consumers.

In the first part of the 2000s one such new concept landed in our laps when we were approached by a company in Los Angeles that specialized in product placement. For a fee they would work on our behalf to get our wines to show up on TV and movie screens. This is a practice going all the way back to the early days of the entertainment industry. Everything from cars to sunglasses to cigarettes has been strategically placed on TV and film screens.

The product placement company contacted us several times over a period of months. And we debated it back and forth internally. Our chief concern was that our wines would appear in a way that would hurt us rather than help us—show up in some negative light, such as being chugged at a frat party with underage drinkers or used in some ugly bludgeoning scene. Who knew? It seemed risky. I don't believe that any publicity is good publicity. However, the company assured us that we would have final say when it came to this kind of thing.

We finally signed on the dotted line and tried it for a year. The results were pretty unspectacular. One of the bottles showed up in a popular show on HBO, but in a way that was so fleeting you'd have to go frame-by-frame to really tell whose label it was. In one movie, which I never saw, the wine apparently appeared briefly being glugged from a bottle by a thief. In another instance a bottle showed up on a cable show that I'm not sure anyone watched. It was an interesting experiment, but nothing we wanted to continue.

About this time we got a call from a production company that was creating a reality show called *Hell's Kitchen* with British chef Gordon Ramsay. We'd known of Ramsay for a long time, as our wines were carried by a couple of his outstanding restaurants in London. The producers asked for a couple hundred bottles, which for us was a massive amount. They said we'd be the only wine used on the show, which would be seen nationally on Fox.

We were hesitant to do it, because television—other than *The Today Show* back in the '90s—had not been much of a boon for us. But on the strength of our relationship with Ramsay we decided to go forward with it. In fact several of us attended the taping of one of the shows, an episode in which the crew of competing chefs sweat it out under Ramsay's severe eye (and tongue), serving guests in the Hell's Kitchen restaurant for the first time. Before the taping started we all signed pretty lock-tight nondisclosures, so I can't detail much about how things went, but I will say we left the taping extremely hungry. If you've seen the episode you'll know why. Not a lot of food made it to the table.

Hell's Kitchen premiered in the United States on May 30, 2005, and it was a great success in many ways. It certainly made a name for Gordon Ramsay here in the United States. However, it was pretty quiet on the

Shafer Vineyards side of things. I saw one or two episodes and did notice a quick flash of a label here or there, but I was watching with my Shafer eyes, not those of a regular viewer, for whom, I suspect, one bottle of wine on the TV screen looks very much like another.

So that was that. We'd had some fun. We'd seen interesting behind-the-scenes stuff in reality television, but ultimately it was time to turn our backs on Hollywood.

That's when Tom Colicchio called and starting telling me about a new reality show he was involved with called *Top Chef,* on a cable channel I'd never heard of, called Bravo. I'm listening to this thinking, "Here we go again…" He was wondering if the production could have a few bottles of Hillside Select for something related to the show, an episode having to do with Napa.

I could not say no to Tom. Even if he'd asked for five times that number of bottles, I could not have turned him away, because years ago Tom and I got stuck together on a weeklong boondoggle on a cruise ship in the Baltic Sea. He was the guest chef and I was the featured vintner (aka "meet the geek") on this ship that was built for one hundred passengers, which on this trip was carrying a grand total of twenty-eight. With next to nothing to do—other than play cards, eat cheeseburgers, and drink champagne—we got to know each other pretty well.

We shipped the bottles of Hillside Select, and I assumed that's the last we'd hear of it. It was the most painless participation in a TV show to date, and that alone made it worthwhile.

To my surprise, in May 2005 *Top Chef* became a big hit. It tapped into a huge and growing interest in the United States in restaurants, chefs, and foodie culture. In the next-to-last episode of the season, called "Napa's Finest," the challenge to the competing chefs was to pair a truffle dish with Hillside Select. When they introduced the wine, one of the TV hosts held the bottle up for the camera and then thrust it toward the lens, so that no one watching could miss the label. It nearly filled the screen. The hits on our website quadrupled overnight.

With numerous repeat airings on Bravo, Shafer was indeed introduced to a whole new audience.

I've been very happy to see Tom's success with the show. Before long he was profiled in *The New York Times Magazine* and did a Diet Coke commercial—that's when you know you're big.

FORTY-SEVEN

The Internet

While we explored the possibilities in television, we also began to wrap our heads around another medium that made TV feel almost antiquated—the Internet. In the late 1990s I hadn't really seen where the Internet was going. But everyone said you had to do something with it, so we did. Our first website was an electronic version of one of our brochures. "There," I thought, "pictures, words, done." But the Internet would not let go.

Since the mid-1980s we've worked with a designer and marketing consultant named Michael Kavish. I first befriended Michael when we were both students at U.C. Davis, and we stayed in touch long afterward. We brought him on board to design our wine labels in the early days, and we've worked with him ever since. By the first of the 2000s Michael was always after me that we needed to redesign and update our website. Consumers, he said, were increasingly getting their information online rather than in print or broadcast media, and to remain competitive we needed to keep up with this trend. And he was right. What I began to see is that our visitor experience no longer began when people drove up to our winery. It began when they visited our website, and we needed to start creating that memorable experience on their computer screen days or even weeks before their arrival.

As the Internet has continued to explode into our culture, it's been a scramble to keep up. One thing we realized is that more and more of the writers and editors on our media list were getting cut from their jobs as print media was pushed into a tumultuous, unknown future. It was heart-wrenching to see people we liked and admired suddenly thrown into such upheaval. Wine coverage in newspapers was being scaled back to simple laundry lists of "here's what to buy this week" or was being cut altogether. Magazines that had been around for decades began to disappear. It made me wonder if the golden age of wine writing had come and gone.

While the jobs in print media were drying up we encountered a sudden proliferation of people who called themselves "bloggers."

I remember getting a phone call from a staff member letting me know there was someone with this title on the line who wanted to speak to me.

"A what?" I asked.

"A blogger."

"What's that?"

"A person who writes a blog."

"What's a blog?"

It started to sound like the old "Who's on first?" sketch.

In 2004 there was one wine blog that I knew of, Vinography.com, written by a guy in San Francisco named Alder Yarrow. Within a few years there were hundreds. There were bloggers who were newly unemployed writers and critics. There were bloggers who were writers and critics who still had employment but, figuring they'd get pink-slipped soon enough, thought it best to build an online following sooner rather than later. There were bloggers who were wine retailers and sommeliers. And there were bloggers who were people who simply loved wine and owned a laptop.

When it came to this new classification of media—bloggers—the numbers kept mushrooming, as did the requests for information, photos, interviews, sample bottles, or media visits. Several times a week we were hearing from online writers/critics we'd never met, who were running blogs we'd never heard of. Fortunately, in almost every case it has been a pleasure getting to know the personalities behind these new ventures. Most of the online writers and critics we've met are passionate and diligent and do what they do for love, because so far, unfortunately, there isn't a lot of financial reward involved.

The other key phenomenon born of the Internet has been forums or chat rooms. Both Robert Parker's and *Wine Spectator*'s sites, among others, host very active online forums in which wine aficionados, collectors, newbies—anyone—can start conversation threads on every topic imaginable.

Some of the forum contributors would get together with friends for a special dinner, get home at midnight, and instead of going to bed, they'd stay up until 2 A.M. writing their tasting notes regarding that evening's wine. These were true diehards.

There were dynamics that emerged, though, in some discussions that at times left me utterly baffled. I remember a friend forwarded a link in which a discussion on the Parker site had to do with Shafer wine. The conversation went back and forth between those who supported us and loved our approach to winemaking and those who thought our wines were terrible for various reasons. One guy said he was through with Shafer, detested our style, we were too this and too that, and he hadn't purchased from us in years and wouldn't dream of buying our wines again. Of course his name was right there on the computer screen, and it looked familiar, so we punched it into our records and found this guy's order history. He'd purchased from us for years and in fact had just ordered three bottles the week before.

Besides this kind of thing (which has happened a few times now), some of the information is shockingly inaccurate. I remember seeing one contributor who wagged a finger at us (electronically) for not posting tasting notes of Hillside Select on our website. It was an appalling oversight on our part, he wrote. As it turns out we've posted tasting notes for Hillside Select on our website for years, and it's consistently one of the top five pages people visit. Thousands of people a year visit that page.

At the winery we've been torn as to how to respond to this kind of thing. Good customer service might say that one of us should wade into these conversations and try to provide some useful information. But at the same time the chat rooms seem geared toward wine enthusiasts talking among themselves and our response could be read as an intrusion. For now the group vote here is that it's probably best to let the forum commenters do their thing without our involvement.

In spite of occasional misgivings, however, the Internet has clearly made some huge and historic positive contributions to the wine community—first, it has given customers a much greater ability to access wines that they couldn't in the past. Second, it offers wine lovers the chance to talk to each other about the wines that get them excited. Facebook, Twitter, CellarTracker, forums, and other online media offer consumers an unprecedented opportunity to simply chat with one another, compare notes, discuss trends, and make recommendations.

It feels something akin to the fall of the western Roman Empire (allow me a big overstatement to make a point)—once the traditional political structure was dismantled, Europe broke into innumerable tiny kingdoms, which over time reformed into new and growing nations.

In similar fashion the Internet came along in the 2000s and upended the traditional way wine writing, criticism, and reporting had worked. And we're seeing a period in which anyone with a blog or a social media account can become the leader of a micro-kingdom. Some of these new voices will almost certainly develop larger and larger followings.

Simultaneously, it's been fascinating to watch some of the traditional wine and food media outlets work to stay ahead of the curve and grow increasingly savvy in terms of social media, apps, online videos, and consumer interaction. Where this takes us, I'm not sure. With any luck it will wind up helping more people feel engaged in the world of wine and encourage a healthy give-and-take between wineries and consumers.

FORTY-EIGHT

Points

On September 1 of each year we release a small allocation of our new release of Hillside Select to anyone who visits the winery. This is a limited production wine, which is difficult to acquire, but we want to make it as accessible as possible. This is one way of accomplishing that. We limit it to two bottles per purchaser for the length of this particular allocation. We specifically use the word "purchaser," because one year an overzealous attorney challenged us on the previous wording, which was simply "two bottles per person." He showed up with his wife and two young children and would not let go of the idea that his children were persons; therefore, he was entitled to purchase two bottles per child.

On September 1, 2006, we were in the middle of a major winery renovation. Our walkways were torn up and our parking lot was a mud pit. There were orange safety cones everywhere, and the air was filled with the sound of construction workers, the *beep-beep-beep* of trucks backing up, and the chink of hammers on our stone walls. We were a mess.

This was the day that we released 2002 Hillside Select, which we suspected would be a little busier than most September 1 releases, since Robert Parker had awarded that vintage his highest rating of 100 points. Even so, we were surprised to see a line out the front door and across the parking lot by opening time. That's the difference one point can make.

We'd received a 99 for the 2001 Hillside Select and had never seen this many people all at once. At its peak that morning we had more than seventy people waiting to purchase their two bottles.

We saw all kinds of shenanigans too. One guy showed up in the morning, purchased two bottles, and then came back an hour later, wearing a pair of sunglasses and a ball cap on backward, and tried to purchase two more. Another guy arrived in the morning sporting a thick mustache, bought his two bottles, and returned in the afternoon after shaving off all traces of facial hair—hoping to buy two more.

Later in the day we had people showing up, looking around the winery, and seeming a little lost. They had the exact dollar amount in cash for two bottles of Hillside Select—down to the penny—and told us they wanted to "buy the wine." Even with the gentlest of questioning regarding which of our wines they had in mind, these individuals had no idea what they were there for—couldn't even come up with the name Hillside Select. What had happened is they'd met a flipper at a restaurant in Yountville, who'd given them the cash to come up to the winery, buy the two bottles, bring them back, and presumably receive some kind of financial reward.

From a business standpoint these are good problems. But I have enough of my Midwestern roots in me to be a little mixed on this kind of thing. Frankly, I'd rather be selling our wine to people who will one day actually uncork a bottle and enjoy it, rather than flippers. I know I shouldn't care, but I do. My hope is all those who "invest" in our wine are in fact, at some point, enjoying a glass or two of their liquid portfolios.

FORTY-NINE

The Downside

By the end of 2007 and the start of 2008, we had much bigger headaches to deal with than the wiles of flippers. Since the '70s we'd seen plenty of ups and downs in the national economy and in the fortunes of fine wine. But this was something new—the biggest, deepest recession we'd ever seen was under way and it was a rock-solid reminder that this business is all about investing in the highs in order to survive the lows.

Guests were still reserving spaces in our tasting visits, but they were buying fewer bottles on their way out the door. Restaurants, which always take the worst hit in an economic downturn, were still ordering wine; however, now they were waiting until their inventory was nearly gone, and then purchasing more. This meant instead of ordering once a month, as in the past, they were buying wines once every six months or once a year.

Our wines were still moving, but at a slower pace. Our Merlot, for example, usually took eight or nine months to sell through a vintage, but was now taking a year or more. But by comparison, at Shafer, we were feeling lucky. Some of our competitors, especially those who had doubled or tripled their production levels in the dot-com era, now found themselves with thousands of cases of unsold wines sitting in warehouses.

A recent photo of John Shafer with his canine companion and sculpture muse, Tucker.

During a meeting in which we were looking at sobering sales numbers, we got to talking about how glad we were to only be selling some thirty thousand cases, rather than one hundred thousand or more. Dad turned to me and said, "Thank God you didn't take my advice." He was referring to the decision to grow in quality instead of quantity in the late '90s.

Everyone in the wine business was hearing stories of doom. Industry watchers were making guesses about how many wineries would close or have to sell, and some of those predictions came true. Hardest to take was the snarky delight a handful of writers and online commenters seemed to derive in California wineries taking this kind of hit. I know the impact such things have on hardworking men and women and their families. It's hard to imagine being gleeful about that sort of thing.

At one point in 2009 I spoke to the whole staff to ease jitters, saying, "We'll get through this. We've taken the cautious route for a long time and don't owe any money to the banks. We're going to be fine. It'll take a little longer to sell through these vintages and we'll just keep going."

One thing that helped us through this period is an interesting facet of human nature: when times are tight, consumers turn to brands that are familiar. They lose their taste for experimentation and don't roll the dice on unknown wines or lesser known regions; they go with those that have a track record. After thirty-plus years the Shafer brand had become one of those that wine lovers believed they could count on.

The recession that began in 2008 demonstrated to me, like nothing else could, the strength of what my dad had done from early on. He had tried to work with our neighbors in positive, mutually beneficial ways, had worked to build up our local community, he'd avoided outsourcing our marketing (even though it meant an exhausting workload), and he'd planted or replanted carefully—one vineyard block at a time. He hadn't borrowed money from anyone and hadn't spent money we didn't have. His vision had always been on long-term success versus short-term gain, such as when we didn't release a 1981 Cabernet. He had set a tone of high standards for all of us but had also been quick to forgive errors.

Of course he and I have worked together on this for decades, but everything has been built on the foundation he laid.

The fact that our winery passed through the worst economic downturn since his boyhood, nearly eighty years prior, with such little damage said that we'd gotten it right more often than we'd gotten it wrong.

There have been many events and incidents that slapped us around and made us feel we were headed nowhere. I was going through some notes recently and found an old file of records kept by my sister, Libby, when she was working for us in sales in the early 1980s. There are letters back and forth with a restaurant owner in Los Angeles setting up a special, private event to taste Shafer wines. The invitations to media are in this collection, as are invitations to wine enthusiasts in the area. There are RSVPs and a guest list written in Libby's neat handwriting. She and the restaurant owner were expecting a good crowd, something like thirty consumers, as well as some wine media. The event took weeks to set up. The wines had to be shipped, the menu had to be selected, and scores of details required attention. The very last item in this file is a note on a small card, again in Libby's hand, which is a summary of how things went: "No one showed up."

I've been asked many times by men and women just coming into this business what our secret is. And I don't want to burst anyone's bubble, but there is no one secret, no silver bullet.

The key thing is to live through your disappointments. Don't quit. Avoid making the same mistake twice. Don't get blinded by scores—high or low. And remember that every time you feel like you're the king of the mountain, Mother Nature or the economy or a bug you've never heard of will obligingly step in to keep you humble.

Postscript

Stags Leap at Last

If you stand on our oval lawn in front of the winery looking south, you can see the heart of Stags Leap District—formed by the huge, rocky palisades and dry Vaca Mountains on your left and a line of thickly wooded hills to the right. The width of this little valley within Napa Valley may be a quarter of a mile across.

If you let your eye move along the base of the palisades, you'll see a thick cluster of trees with a couple of palms sticking out. Obscured by that foliage is where Horace Chase's imposing stone manor house still stands. It remains the soul of Stags' Leap Winery and is rumored by past winemakers to be full of ghosts. In 1997 Carl Doumani sold it, and today it's owned by Beringer Estates and its parent company, Foster's Group.

Let your eye move across this little valley and on the right, at the top of the farthest of the ridgelines forming the hills, you can see the rooftop of Warren Winiarski's house emerging from the trees. Before this was his place it belonged to the Heid family, who lived there for much of the first half of the twentieth century. They hired German POWs to work their vines and fruit trees at the end of World War II. The property and winery that came under Warren's ownership in the 1970s is today owned as a partnership of Italy's Antinori wine family and by Chateau Ste. Michelle in Washington State.

A bit farther south, in the center of this little valley, is the property where Nathan Fay planted Stags Leap's first Cabernet Sauvignon during the Kennedy years. Beyond that, hugging the eastern hills, still stands the old stone Occidental winery built by Terrill Grigsby in the 1880s, which is now Regusci Winery.

On a clear day you can see Chimney Rock and past that is Clos du Val, started in the 1970s by our old friend Bernard Portet. Where their property ends you'll find our Borderline Vineyard, which is about one-third of the original 75 acres of vines owned by Horace Chase's neighbor, W. H. Staggs.

Having lived here this long I can look down this corridor of land and see one time period melting onto another. I like to think that if our property's 1880s owners, a grape grower and winemaker named Jacob Ohl and his wife, Lena, were standing here with me, the view would be as recognizable and as important to them as it has been to our family. Very little has changed in Stags Leap District over the past 130-plus years. A few new houses are here now, and different varieties are planted within the same vineyard footprints. But on a warm summer day it is still a picture of serenity. There is the rustle of the breeze from San Pablo Bay, the rattle of a distant tractor, and the trill of songbirds. That's it and that's all I hope it ever will be.

•   •   •

One final story to end on... the last time I saw Nathan Fay was in the later part of the 1990s. He was in a wheelchair, because late in life he was struck by Parkinson's disease. We were both at the Napa Valley Symphony fund-raiser, which was being held at Robert Mondavi Winery. I'm not always terribly comfortable at events like these, as my orientation is more along the lines of vineyards and cellars than the world of classical music and cocktail chat. I was looking around to find

A recent photo of John Shafer (left) and Doug Shafer (right) taken in the upper portion of the Sunspot vineyard block.

someone to talk to when I spotted Nate. I sat down next to him, and he was the same as always—insatiably curious about the vintage.

"How're the grapes? How's the weather? How're things shaping up?" he'd always ask. And this time was no exception. We'd had this kind of conversation countless times. In this instance, for some reason, I took things in a more personal direction, though. "Nate," I said, "I envy you, you're so lucky."

"Why?" he asked, kind of surprised.

"Because you were here in the early days. You got to see the start of all this."

He shook his head, growing serious, touching my shoulder with his index finger, and said, "No, I'm jealous of you, because you get to see what comes next."

It's easy to assume that things were better "back then" or more authentic or easier. They weren't. Each day, no matter the era, we wake up

A recent image of Shafer Vineyards, looking from the Sunspot vineyard block toward the west, with La Vigna Lana wrapping around the far side.

and do what we need to do, and eventually those days become history. But when you're in the middle of it all—the people, the phone calls, the issues of pulse-pounding importance—none of it has a feeling of quaintness or the glow that remembrance gives. Moment to moment, day to day, we really have no good idea how any of this will turn out, which is why the future has such a hold on us.

It's been a joy to have seen and lived through Napa Valley's latest chapters. In forty years I've seen the Valley transform from a backwater to one of the finest wine regions in the world. It's unprecedented, and it's been an honor to be part of it. As always, I look forward to the next year, the next decade, and beyond to see how all this will turn out.

For the moment, we've managed to outlast the latest economic downturn. Things are beginning to improve. The wines are selling through at a nice clip again, and for our last harvest we started using an insanely cool new mechanism on the crush pad called an optical grape sorter, which doesn't replace people but adds a whole new means to control the quality of grapes that we crush and transform into wine. Now that harvest is over, things have calmed down a bit, which allows Dad, Elias, and me to start refining our next long-term plan. This time we're taking aim at 2020.

INDEX